Dual-use Objects under International Humanitarian Law: Towards a Paradigm Shift

Francesca Capone

Dual-use Objects under International Humanitarian Law: Towards a Paradigm Shift

ASSER PRESS

Springer

Francesca Capone
DIRPOLIS Institute
Sant' Anna School of Advanced Studies
Pisa, Italy

ISBN 978-94-6265-678-9 ISBN 978-94-6265-679-6 (eBook)
https://doi.org/10.1007/978-94-6265-679-6

Published by T.M.C. ASSER PRESS, The Hague, The Netherlands www.asserpress.nl
Produced and distributed for T.M.C. ASSER PRESS by Springer-Verlag Berlin Heidelberg

This T.M.C. ASSER PRESS imprint is published by the registered company Springer-Verlag GmbH, DE, part of Springer Nature.
The registered company address is: Heidelberger Platz 3, 14197 Berlin, Germany

To my mentor, Prof. Andrea de Guttry.
I am immensely grateful for the guidance, the patience and the rewarding work that we did together.
I hope to have learnt as much as possible from the "smartest guy in the room".

Preface

The book examines a crucial and yet under-explored topic that has increasingly gained momentum during modern armed conflicts, i.e. dual-use objects under international humanitarian law (IHL). Dual-use objects, e.g. energy infrastructures, water installations and civilian means of transportation and communication *which could be used also* for military purposes, is a term that has entered the IHL jargon but has not attained the status of a legal concept. Dual-use objects are easily identifiable and yet remain difficult to pin down, in particular when it comes to separating them from military objectives and determining the applicable rules to enhance their protection. Therefore, this book pursues a twofold aim.

The book's first goal is to fill a significant gap in the IHL scholarship, whilst the second one is to introduce and promote a paradigm shift to make the approach to dual-use objects coherent with the IHL framework. Concerning the first goal, so far, the topic of dual-use objects has attracted scant attention, and it has been marginally considered by academics and practitioners. Through an exhaustive and multilayered study, the present work will shed light on some crucial aspects that have significant theoretical and practical implications. The starting point is the "mainstream approach" to dual-use objects, according to which those objects represent legitimate military targets, that this book openly challenges, and its genesis, which is grounded in well-known military theories. The most widely shared view on dual-use objects under IHL merely portrays them as military objectives and only occasionally evokes the fact that, more often than not, they mainly fulfil civilian functions. As the examples discussed in this book will show, the targeting of dual-use objects—including bridges, electrical power stations, oil refineries and radio and television stations—does not represent an exception in armed conflicts, but rather a common strategy of warfare. Regardless of its diffusion and extensive practice, resorting to this tactic has triggered widespread criticism and strong reactions from different commentators. The armed conflicts in Iraq, the Former Yugoslavia, Ethiopia/Eritrea, the Occupied Palestinian Territory (OPT), Yemen, Ukraine etc… have all been, and in some cases unfortunately still are, characterised by widespread attacks against dual-use objects that have an important, if not crucial, role in ensuring the survival of the civilian population. The ubiquitous condemnation, however, has never resulted in a thorough examination of the issues at stake, which range from understanding "why" and "how" the mainstream approach has emerged to "who" is responsible and "what" can be done to reverse this tendency and start looking at dual-use objects from a different perspective.

With regard to the second goal of the book, which is promoting a much-needed paradigm shift, the rationale for this lies in the necessity to reconcile the notion of dual-use objects with the legal framework in force. To affirm that a concept is not legally defined does not mean that it can be erased, nor ignored. The reality is that attacks against dual-use objects have proved to be lethal and irreversible, in the short- and even more so in the long-term. It would be interesting to point out the shortcomings of the existing set of norms and suggest amendments and changes that are unlikely to take place, but it would also be pointless. The only way to provide a, hopefully, useful contribution is to offer a reading of the applicable *corpus juris* that is in line with the key tenets of IHL and that places enough emphasis on the civilian function of dual-use objects and the role that individual actors, i.e. those who plan, order and execute attacks against dual-use objects, ultimately play in each and every armed conflict. This is the essence of the paradigm shift.

The book is composed of six chapters, leading up to a new paradigm to deal with dual-use objects. The analysis carried out first covers the identification of the relevant concepts and definitions, which are introduced in Chap. 1 alongside the key elements of the paradigm shift. This introductory chapter also provides an overview of the existing scholarship, explaining the limitations of the state of the art and of the previous attempts to strengthen the protection of dual-use objects in armed conflicts. Chapter 2 retraces how the predominant approach to dual-use objects has come to light, what are the theoretical foundations, and the underlying reasons. Chapter 3 discusses the definition of military objectives and its shortcomings, which obviously have severe repercussions also in its application. To set apart dual-use objects from military objectives, the inquiry first reflects on the two-pronged test that lies at the heart of the definition and then it focuses on two important notions, that of military advantage and of "attack as a whole", which are increasingly subject to interpretations that are at odds with the principle of distinction and should be consistently rebutted. On the purpose of drawing a neater line between dual-use objects and military objectives and of filling a conceptual gap, the chapter ends with the drafting of a "working definition" of the former.

Chapter 4 delves into the paradigm shift by outlining the civilian function of dual-use objects, rendering this characteristic no longer just an "ex-post concern", but a prism through which to reconsider several relevant IHL rules and the key IHL principles. Chapter 5 places the role of individual actors under the spotlight and it does so by focussing on the notion of "reasonableness", which doubles as a theoretical concept and as a legal standard that can be applied in practical contexts, including situations of armed conflict. The central argument advanced is that targeting decisions, including those that concern attacks against dual-use objects, are taken by individual actors that must act in accordance with certain rules and standards. The standard of the "reasonable military commander" serves as the touchstone for determining the appropriate application of specific targeting rules and for assessing the lawfulness of action after the fact. Although the standard has been mainly applied to proportionality assessments, and only sporadically to other settings, the present work claims that it should be regarded as transversally applicable to all the IHL principles, i.e. distinction, precautions, proportionality, military necessity and humanity. Furthermore, the analysis provides a "sliding scale" of reasonableness, reconstructing what is the threshold that must be met for each principle. Affirming in general terms that the "reasonable military commander" shall be able to anticipate the expected consequences of an attack carried out against water installations, and/or to stop an attack against a bridge because it violates the principle of proportionality or the prohibition on indiscriminate attacks, is not enough. It is necessary to identify how the standard unfolds in each specific circumstance and what is required of the actor(s) called to implement it. Finally, Chap. 6 contains some concluding observations that aim both at summarising the main findings of the book and at pointing to the ramifications of this inquiry, by introducing the new paradigm's application to new weapons and technologies.

Whereas the rationale, the goal, the methodology and the structure of the book are outlined in the introductory chapter, I believe that it is important also to dwell on the personal motivations behind this work. As an academic who spends a lot of her time explaining to talented and motivated students the nuts and bolts of IHL, over the years I started to notice that there is a widespread and profound sense of uneasiness towards certain topics. I understand that and I deeply share the frustration. For this reason, I started to be more and more drawn to researching topics that are not only stimulating from an intellectual perspective, but that could also trigger concrete changes in the society in which we live and interact with one another. The thought of the Ukrainian population dealing with yet another freezing winter because of Russia's claim that it is "usual business in warfare" to destroy the power infrastructures of its enemy is unbearable. The same goes for the civilians affected by the many, and often forgotten, armed conflicts fought in other regions of the world. It is not acceptable to worry about the consequences of attacks against critical infrastructures only after the event has taken place or in the aftermath of the conflict. Civilians and civilian objects must be protected, this is the bottom line of IHL, this is the first sentence that comes out of my mouth when I welcome the students to my IHL course. This is an imperative rule and a moral obligation, this is the reason why this book was written.

Although all errors and mistakes in the book remain mine, this work has seen the light thanks to the support and friendship of many people. It is simply impossible to name everyone, but I would like to start by thanking my colleagues at Sant'Anna School of Advanced Studies, in particular Andrea de Guttry, Emanuele Sommario and Lorenzo Gasbarri for the many inspiring exchanges of views and ideas. I wish to express my gratitude to my "younger" colleagues Alessandro Mario Amoroso, Marta Stroppa, Francesco Paolo Levantino and Matteo Colorio, and to my student, Matilde Bufano, who assisted me with the editing of this book. A heartfelt "thank you" obviously goes to Frank Bakker and the amazing T.M.C. Asser Press team, in particular the irreplaceable Kiki van Gurp, who has a very keen eye and the kindest heart. Working with you all is a privilege and I cannot wait for our next project!

I am grateful to my amazing family, and to all my friends, near and far, academics or not, for their guidance in life and endless affection. Last, but not least, I am indebted to my two favourite persons in the whole world, Daniele and Filippo, who are funny, loud and very opinionated. I love you more than words can express, thank you for making every day special (and messy) despite my clumsy attempts to keep everything under control!

Pisa, Italy Francesca Capone

Contents

About the Author

Prof. Dr. Francesca Capone is Associate Professor of International Law at Sant'Anna School of Advanced Studies and Co-Director of the Master's Degree in International Security Studies (MISS). Prior to being appointed as Associate Professor in 2021, she served as Assistant Professor (tenure track), Senior Research Fellow and Coordinator of the Master in Human Rights and Conflict Management at the same academic institution (2014–2021). In 2012–2013, she worked as Research Fellow in public international law at the British Institute of International and Comparative Law in London, UK. She holds a joint Ph.D. in international law from Sant'Anna School of Advanced Studies and Tilburg University, earned in 2013. She has been a visiting fellow and a guest lecturer at several academic institutions across Europe, including Leiden University, Tilburg University and the Max Planck Institute for Comparative Public Law and International Law and beyond Europe. She has undertaken research on a wide range of topics, focusing in particular on international humanitarian law and counterterrorism. She co-edited, together with Dr. Christophe Paulussen and Prof. Andrea de Guttry, the volume Foreign Fighters under International Law and Beyond (T.M.C. Asser Press/Springer 2016); as well as the follow up volume Returning Foreign Fighters: Responses, Legal Challenges and Ways Forward (T.M.C. Asser Press/Springer 2023), co-edited with Dr. Christophe Paulussen and Dr Rebecca Mignot-Mahdavi. Both volumes have been well received, becoming pivotal academic contributions in the field. Prof. Capone's book Reparations for Child Victims of Armed Conflict: State of the Field and Current Challenges (Intersentia 2017) won the 2018 Ciardi Prize for the best book in the field of international humanitarian law.

Abbreviations

ABiH	Army of Bosnia Herzegovina
AI	Artificial Intelligence
AOAV	Action on Armed Violence
API	Additional Protocol I
APII	Additional Protocol II
AWS	Autonomous Weapons Systems
C2	Command and Control
CCC	Command, Control, and Communication Sites
CCW	Convention on Certain Conventional Weapon
CENTCOM	US Central Command
CHMR-AP	Civilian Harm Mitigation and Response Action Plan
DIB	Defense Industrial Base
DSS	Decision Support Systems
EECC	Eritrea-Ethiopia Claims Commission
ELN	Ejército de Liberación Nacional
ELSI	Concerning Elettronica Sicula S.p.A
ERW	Explosive Remnants of War
FRY	Federal Republic of Yugoslavia
GCIII	Third Geneva Convention
GGE	Group of Governmental Experts
HPCR Manual	Harvard Air and Missile Warfare Manual issued by the Program on Humanitarian Policy and Conflict Research at Harvard University
HPS	Hirgigo Power Station
HRW	Human Rights Watch
HVO	(Hrvatsko vijeće obrane) Croatian Defence Council
IAC	International Armed Conflict
ICC	International Criminal Court
ICJ	International Court of Justice
ICRC	International Committee of the Red Cross
ICTY	International Criminal Tribunal for the Former Yugoslavia
IDF	Israeli Defense Forces

IHL	International Humanitarian Law
IIAs	International Investment Agreements
ILA	International Law Association
ILA-SG	International Law Association Study Group
ILC	International Law Commission
INEW	International Network on Explosive Weapons
ISR	Surveillance and Renaissance
ITLOS	International Tribunal for the Law of the Sea
JAG	Judge Advocate General's Corps, also called JAG Corps
JFACC	Joint Forces Air Component Commander
KTO	Kuwaiti Theatre of Operations
LAWS	Lethal Autonomous Weapons Systems
LOAC	Law of Armed Conflict
MHC	Meaningful Human Control
MS	Military support, production, and research facility
N	Naval ports and facilities
NATO	North Atlantic Treaty Organisation
NBC	Nuclear, Biological, and Chemical
NIAC	Non-International Armed Conflict
OAU	Organisation of African Unity
PCIJ	Permanent Court of International Justice
PGM	Precision Guided Munitions
PI	Positive Identification
POL	Petroleum, Oil, and Lubricants
POW	Prisoner of War
PTSD	Post Traumatic Stress Disorder
R&D	Research and Development
RAF	Royal Air Force
RG	Republican Guards
RMA	Revolution in Military Affairs
RoE	Rules of Engagement
RR	Railroads and Bridges
RTS	Radio Television of Serbia
SAD	Strategic Air Defenses
SC	Scud missile facilities/sites
UAV	Unmanned Aerial Vehicle
UCAV	Unmanned Combat Air Vehicle
UNCLOS	United Nations Convention on the Law of the Sea
US DOD	United States Department of Defense
VCLT	Vienna Convention on the Law of Treaties
WFP	United Nations World Food Programme
WSO	Weapon System Officer
WWI	World War I
WWII	World War II

Chapter 1
Introduction: "Dual-Use Objects" as an Undefined and Controversial Notion

Contents

Abstract "Dual-use" objects under international humanitarian law (IHL) is not a term of art, despite being effectively part of the IHL lexicon. The vagueness associated with the lack of a stricter legal terminology is not surprising. Because dual-use objects do not represent a legal category, it is almost natural to associate the notion with certain items, but not with specific rules. Yet, traditionally dual-use objects have been described as military objectives that play a relevant civilian function. The idea itself is confusing as it brings together the two elements that the principle of distinction, i.e. the cornerstone of IHL, strives to keep separate. It is exactly from this feeling of discomfort that the idea of this book comes from. How can something that plays a civilian function be lawfully attacked during an armed conflict? Is it possible to stir the discussion in a different direction and single out the uniqueness of dual-use objects in a way that takes, first and foremost, into consideration their inherent relevance before an attack is launched in addition to the impact of their destruction or damage ex post? The present book starts from these questions and articulates a new paradigm to enhance the protection of dual-use objects and promote a reconsideration of their status under IHL.

Keywords Military objectives · Civilian objects · Attack · Principle of distinction · Targeting · Principle of proportionality · Civilian function

F. Capone, *Dual-use Objects under International Humanitarian Law: Towards a Paradigm Shift*, https://doi.org/10.1007/978-94-6265-679-6_1

1.1 Setting the Scene

Dual-use objects under international humanitarian law (IHL) or the law of armed conflict (LOAC) is not a term of art, despite being effectively part of the IHL lexicon. The vagueness associated with the lack of a proper legal terminology is not surprising. Because dual-use objects do not represent a legal category, it is almost natural to associate the notion with certain items, but not with specific rules. Yet, traditionally dual-use objects—including electrical power systems, industrial plants, oil refining, distribution and storage facilities, broadcasting stations, traffic infrastructures, water systems and installations—are described as "military objectives that play a relevant civilian function".[1] The idea itself is confusing as it brings together the two elements that the principle of distinction, i.e. one of the cornerstones of IHL,[2] strives to keep separate. It is exactly from this feeling of discomfort that the idea of this book comes from. How can something that plays a civilian function be lawfully attacked during an armed conflict? In this author's view it is possible to stir the discussion in a different direction and single out the uniqueness of dual-use objects in a way that takes, first and foremost, into consideration their inherent relevance before an attack is launched rather than the impact of their destruction or damage *ex post*. The present book moves from these questions, challenging the consistency of dual-use objects' status against the backdrop of the key IHL principles. To this end, it articulates a new paradigm to enhance the protection of dual-use objects under the international humanitarian legal framework. This work considers all the relevant factors that shape the current developments of warfare, including the changes in the means and methods used by belligerent parties in the conduct of hostilities, the disappearance of the battlefield in lieu of an ever-expanding "battle place" that spans across populated areas and even refugee camps and the asymmetries between the actors involved in armed conflicts.

The world has undoubtedly witnessed an impressive military and technological progress since WWII, to the point where, for example, a US stealth fighter with a single, laser-guided bomb can now destroy a target that in WWII required 4500 B-17 sorties dropping 9000 bombs.[3] Although military forces have relied on the increasing use of so-called "smart" bombs, bombing campaigns that took place well after WWII in countries like Iraq, Afghanistan and Serbia, have resulted in what some experts consider to be an intolerably high level of civilian casualties, especially when compared with the low level of combatant casualties in the attacking force.[4] This trend has not been reversed over time, as the number of recorded civilian deaths due to armed conflicts has risen dramatically and it is constantly associated with attacks against dual-use objects.

In 2023, the United Nations (UN) recorded at least 33,000 civilians killed in armed conflicts, a number that went up by 72% from 2022.[5] The proportion of women

[1] Gillard 2018, p. 34.

[2] Kalshoven 1977, p. 116; Henckaerts and Doswald-Beck 2005, pp. 3–5.

[3] Rizer 2001, p. 1.

[4] Byron 2011, p. 176.

[5] UN Secretary-General 2024, para 6.

and children killed doubled and tripled, respectively, as compared with 2022.[6] The intensity of conflict has also risen year on year in the reporting period of The Armed Conflict Survey 2023 (1 May 2022–30 June 2023), with the number of fatalities and events escalating by 14% and 21% respectively.[7] The 2021 UN Security Council Resolution (UNSC) 2573 notes with concern "the threats posed to civilian infrastructure, *including that which supports essential services to the civilian population*, by the use of any means or methods of warfare in violation of international humanitarian law, and the potentially devastating humanitarian impact of such use in situations of armed conflict".[8] The Resolution also condemns indiscriminate or disproportionate attacks, which result in the deprivation of the civilian population of objects indispensable to their survival, "as flagrant violations of international humanitarian law", and furthermore it deplores "the long-term humanitarian consequences of such attacks for the civilian population and demands that all parties to armed conflict immediately put an end to such practices".[9]

The latest report of the UN Secretary-General on the protection of civilians in armed conflict paints a grim picture, that indeed confirms the tendency emphasised by UN SC Resolution 2573. Consistent with the warnings enshrined in Resolution 2573 (2021), the Report stresses that, in the armed conflicts taking place in 2023, critical infrastructures, including for the provision of electricity, health care, water, and sanitation, were damaged, and access to these services disrupted.[10] In the Ukrainian territory, fighting—including multiple strikes on water systems, electrical plants, and substations—interrupted power, heating, health care, drinking water supply and sewage facilities, as well as mobile and Internet communications.[11] Cyber-operations also affected electricity, Internet, and transportation services. Similarly, in the Syrian Arab Republic—a country notably plagued by armed conflicts since 2011—water infrastructure suffered extensive damage in attacks or was forced to shut down owing to loss of power, affecting access to water for millions of people.[12]

In Burkina Faso, 48 types of water infrastructure were destroyed, hindering access to water for more than 149,000 people. In Myanmar, essential infrastructures, such as bridges, key transport routes, telecommunication towers, schools, hospitals and power plants, were targeted. During the armed conflict in Sudan, extensive damage to water, sanitation and electricity networks, as well as hospitals and clinics, was reported across the country.[13] In the first month of the current Israeli military campaign in the Gaza strip, over 25,000 tons of incendiary munitions have been

---

[6] Ibid.

[7] IIIS, The Armed Conflict Survey 2023, p. 5, available at https://www.iiss.org/publications/armed-conflict-survey/2023/editors-introduction/ (accessed 2 February 2024).

[8] UN Security Council 2021, Preamble (emphasis added).

[9] Ibid., para 1.

[10] UN Secretary-General 2024, para 10.

[11] Ibid., paras 10–11.

[12] Ibid.

[13] Ibid.

fired. The Israeli military struck over 12,000 targets with extensive human consequences.[14] In 2024, hostilities in Gaza left 23 hospitals and 56 health-care centres out of service, as well as widespread damage to agricultural infrastructure, including wells, farms and warehouses.[15] The growing attention towards the destruction and long-term damages caused by attacks against civilian infrastructures, including dual-use objects, and the blatant inconsistency of this military strategy with the key tenets of IHL, has prompted some shy efforts to strengthen the protection of the population in situations of armed conflict. One example of such efforts is represented by the 2022 Political Declaration on the Use of Explosive Weapons in Populated Areas signed by 83 States.[16] The initiative has been promoted by the UN, the International Committee of the Red Cross (ICRC) and civil society organisations, appearing under the umbrella International Network on Explosive Weapons (INEW). In a nutshell, the Political Declaration enshrines new international standards for protecting civilians from the use of bombs, rockets, artillery and other explosive weapons in populated areas during situations of armed conflict.[17] According to Action on Armed Violence (AOAV), between 2011 and 2020, 238,892 civilians were killed or injured by the use of explosive weapons in populated areas, i.e. areas likely to contain high concentrations of civilians.[18] As alarming as these numbers are, it is worth recognising that the impact of such weapons is not limited to deaths and injuries caused at the time they are deployed. Notably, the use of explosive weapons is associated "with a widespread pattern of long-term harm resulting from damage to or destruction of essential civilian infrastructure, such as hospitals and water and electricity supply systems".[19] It has been widely acknowledged that the damage to and destruction of such essential infrastructure has important "reverberating" (or "knock-on") effects.[20]

Their negative consequences are hardly confined in both time and space, and they affect the provision of health care, water, and electricity to a far broader proportion of the population than those within the vicinity of a specific attack.[21] In commenting on the adoption of the Political Declaration, the ICRC noted the devastating effects of the use of explosive weapons in urban or densely populated areas, and it stressed how much of this harm depends on human decisions: "choice of weapon, choice of tactic, choice of fighting ground, choice of applicable policy, procedures and

---

[14] Asi et al. 2024, p. 3.

[15] UN Secretary-General 2024, para 10.

[16] Political Declaration on Strengthening the Protection of Civilians from the Humanitarian Consequences Arising from the Use of Explosive Weapons in Populated Areas, 18 November 2022 (Political Declaration), available at: www.dfa.ie/our-role-policies/international-priorities/peace-and-security/ewipa-consultations/ (accessed 2 February 2024). The list of endorsing States as of 5 February 2024 is available at www.dfa.ie/media/dfa/ourrolepolicies/peaceandsecurity/ewipa/List-of-endorsing-states-18-November-2022.pdf.

[17] Bagshaw 2023, p. 1294.

[18] AOAV 2021, p. 3.

[19] Bagshaw 2023, p. 1297.

[20] Zeitoun and Talhami 2016; Wille and Malaret Baldo 2021.

[21] INEW 2016; Boer and Zwijnenburg 2020; Bagshaw 2023, p. 1298.

regulations".[22] Although the ICRC encouraged States to reflect in the Declaration a political commitment to ban altogether the use of heavy explosive weapons in urban and other populated areas, the text ultimately falls short of that, making instead a strong, but still insufficient, statement that States need to "change the way they plan and conduct hostilities in populated areas to protect civilians and civilian objects from harm".[23]

The States that have endorsed the Declaration, in para 3.1 confirm their resolution to implement, and, where necessary, review, develop or improve national policy and practice regarding the protection of civilians during armed conflict involving the use of explosive weapons in populated areas. Notably, endorser States have also committed to ensuring that their armed forces consider "the direct and indirect effects on civilians and civilian objects which can reasonably be foreseen in the planning of military operations and the execution of attacks in populated areas".[24] Additional waypoints to enhance the full protection of civilians are emerging at the global, regional and national levels in the form of policies and commitments,[25] whereas from the legal perspective developments are less tangible.

The doctrine, for example, still disagrees on whether customary international law requires the use of Precision Guided Munitions (PGMs) in bombing campaigns over urban areas.[26] Some authors claim that an obligation to deploy PGMs in context where there is a high concentration of civilians has emerged,[27] but the majority view, as expressed by the Harvard Air and Missile Warfare Manual issued by the Program on Humanitarian Policy and Conflict Research at Harvard University (Harvard Air and Missile Warfare Manual), still holds that "[f]irst, there exists no obligation in the law of international armed conflict for States to acquire particular types of weapons. Second, operational concerns may limit the use of precision guided weapons".[28] Yet, the Harvard Air and Missile Warfare Manual goes on explaining that the "recourse to precision guided weapons (if available) is called for in circumstances when an attack is undertaken and resorting to such weapons is necessary to prevent indiscriminate attacks" and "to avoid – or, in any event, minimise – expected excessive collateral damage to civilians or civilian objects as compared to the anticipated military advantage".[29] In other words, although the obligation to use PGMs is not an absolute one

[22] Statement by the International Committee of the Red Cross delivered by Laurent Gisel, Head of the Arms and Conduct of Hostilities Unit at the Legal Division on Friday, 17 June 2022 (ICRC Statement), available at https://www.icrc.org/en/document/political-declaration-on-explosive-weapons (accessed 5 February 2024).

[23] Political Declaration, para 3.3.

[24] Ibid., Preamble.

[25] UN Secretary-General 2024, paras 65–68.

[26] Byron 2011, p. 197.

[27] Belt 2000.

[28] Harvard Air and Missile Warfare Manual 2013, Rule 8.

[29] Ibid.

and could be perhaps described as a "*prima facie* duty",[30] it can be inferred that whenever States have the possibility (and capability) to resort to PGMs they are expected to do so. As Ross suggests, the term "conditional duty" is an alternative to the term "*prima facie* duty", therefore the obligation is subject to some sort of condition,[31] which, in the case under scrutiny, are attached to the availability of PGMs,[32] and to the risk of breaching either the prohibition of indiscriminate attacks and/or the rule on proportionality.

There is a widespread and undeniable awareness of the devastating impact of armed conflicts on the civilian population. Nonetheless the overall failure to undertake significant steps to minimise said impact becomes even more striking when one realises that there is so much room for improvement. By explaining that "when critical civilian infrastructure, such as energy, food, water and sanitation systems, are damaged or destroyed, the provision of basic needs and essential services, such as healthcare and education, are disrupted";[33] the Political Declaration is implicitly condemning the calamitous effects of attacking dual-use objects. Similarly, by affirming that there is a need to "improve the commander's ability to *distinguish non-adversarial aspects of the operational environment* and to provide guidance to the forces under his or her command", the Civilian Harm Mitigation and Response Action Plan (CHMR-AP) issued by the United States Department of Defense is stressing the centrality of individual actors and the importance of prioritising the protection and restoration of the civilian environment as a critical factor in the planning and conduct of military operations.[34]

The present work moves from the premise that none of the efforts towards enhancing the protection of civilians, mitigating civilian harm and protecting and restoring the civilian environment, can be successfully achieved without reverting the current approach towards dual-use objects. Put it simply, in this author's view, none of the above-mentioned progress will really make a difference in the battlefield if attacks against power infrastructures, water installations, transportation and communication services, airports and so on, are not outlawed or at least limited to the maximum extent possible. The former would be the most welcome option, although both impracticable and unattainable. The latter instead can be pursued by arguing in favour of a paradigm shift, which places at the centre of the analysis the civilian function of dual-use objects and the role of the "reasonable military commander" standard, thus promoting a novel approach that reconciles this controversial notion

[30] Ross 1930, p. 19.

[31] Zimmerman 1996, p. 143.

[32] According to the Harvard Air and Missile Warfare Manual, "availability" refers to both the question of the potential general availability of these weapons (in the sense that such weapons can be acquired by a Belligerent Party) and the question of actual availability to a specific commander in specific circumstances. Harvard Air and Missile Warfare Manual 2013, Rule 8, p. 83.

[33] Political Declaration, para 1.4.

[34] U.S. Department of Defense, Civilian Harm Mitigation and Response Action Plan (CHMR-AP), 25 August 2022, p. 9, available at https://media.defense.gov/2022/Aug/25/2003064740/-1/-1/1/CIVILIAN-HARM-MITIGATION-AND-RESPONSE-ACTION-PLAN.PDF (accessed 5 February 2024).

with the key tenets of IHL. The following sections will delve more into the main arguments of this work, by presenting the state of the art, discussing the key terminology, and providing an overview of the book's goal and structure.

1.2 Aim of the Study: Challenging the *Status Quo*

Before diving into the essential task of defining the key terminology, it is important to better frame the aim of the present study, also in light of the existing literature. As discussed in the previous section, the notion of dual-use objects, as it is interpreted and applied nowadays, mainly refers to a sub-category of military objectives, i.e. lawful targets under IHL, whose destruction or damage has a severe impact on the civilian population.[35] The mainstream approach to the issue so far has been to consider the civilian function of dual-use objects only when applying the principle of proportionality. In a nutshell, the principle recognises that, in the conduct of hostilities, causing incidental harm to civilians and civilian objects while attacking military objectives is often unavoidable, especially given the peculiarities of contemporary armed conflicts. However, the proportionality rule places a limit on the extent of incidental civilian harm that is permissible by spelling out how military necessity and considerations of humanity must be balanced in such situations.[36] The goal is thus to factor the civilian function of dual-use objects into the application of the proportionality principle. There are two different, but parallel, options that have been considered to this end.

The first one, which expresses the prevailing and less controversial view, focuses on the assessment of the collateral damage (or incidental harm, or civilian losses, etc...), by enlarging the scope of this crucial notion to also include the so-called "reverberating effects" that can result from an attack to a dual-use object.[37] The second, less popular but bolder, option to make the application of the proportionality rule more effective in case of attacks against dual-use objects is the one developed by Shue and Wippman.[38] According to these authors, the proportionality assessment, as traditionally understood, is unlikely to exercise much of a constraining influence on targeting decisions in case of attacks against dual-use objects, whenever it is difficult to appraise the extent of the military advantage and the extent of the civilian harm at issue.[39] Therefore, they propose two readings that can contribute to overcoming what they define as the "limited application" of the proportionality principle, in which considerations of the civilian function of dual-use objects tend to disappear or in any case are not sufficiently taken into account. The first reading essentially advocates for the inclusion of long term and cumulative effects in the reverberating effects

[35] Geiß and Lahmann 2012, p. 383.

[36] Capone 2023, p. 751.

[37] Gillard 2018, pp. 18–19.

[38] Shue and Wippman 2002.

[39] Ibid., pp. 570–572.

category and thus is in line with the first trend. The second reading instead promotes a new approach, which the authors call "protective proportionality" and that places the emphasis on the indispensable nature of certain dual-use objects. In their view "one way to render the proportionality standard more stringent would be to insist that attacks against indispensable objects [...] be treated *as impermissible unless the expected incidental civilian harm would not be excessive in relation to an anticipated military advantage that was compelling, not simply concrete and direct*".[40] The goal of promoting the adoption of a "compelling military advantage" standard is to strike a better balance between a level of protection that military planners would perceive as "unacceptably high" (i.e. the removal of dual-use objects from target lists) and what amounts to very little protection of civilians from harms caused by attacks on infrastructure (i.e. the current interpretation of the norms in force).[41]

In addition to focusing on proportionality, a few authors have joined the discussion on dual-use objects, by putting forward alternative proposals to overcome the shortcomings of the current approach to the matter. Schmitt, for example, suggests a different interpretation of the notion of "military objective", claiming that the term "object" in the provision of Article 52(2) of the 1977 Additional Protocol I (API)[42] to the 1949 Geneva Conventions can be understood to refer to a distinct, tangible entity.[43] More in detail, he claims that the mere fact that distinct entities are physically connected does not preclude treating them as separate. Schmitt's argument entails that the aspect of a structure currently used by the enemy would qualify as a military objective, but its separate and distinct components, i.e. those that are not being used for military purposes, shall retain their civilian character. This reading of the norm would allow, in Schmitt's view, to treat the same building as both a military objective and a civilian object if it is feasible for the attacker to distinguish between the two and strike only the part constituting a military objective. There are two main problems with this proposal. The first one has to do with the complete lack of support by States. As Schmitt himself notes, this approach has not been endorsed by any State so far, confirming that the restrictions on attacks against dual-use objects have only been implemented as a matter of practice and policy.[44] Second, this interpretation of Article 52(2) infuses IHL with relativity because some armed forces can conduct surgical attacks on structures while others cannot. So, the "feasibility" will be constraining only the former's operations, while if the attacker cannot strike surgically, the interpretation preserves the option of striking the entire military objective, as long as other IHL rules are satisfied. Furthermore, this reading of the existing legal framework would have no bearing in cyberspace, where the entire cyber infrastructure, e.g. computers, servers and cables etc...., is a dual-use

[40] Ibid., p. 574 (emphasis added).

[41] Capone 2023, p. 753.

[42] Article 52(2) of Protocol Additional to the Geneva Conventions of 12 August 1949, and relating to the Protection of Victims of International Armed Conflicts (API), opened for signature 8 June 1977, 1125 UNTS 609 (entered into force 7 December 1978).

[43] Schmitt 2021.

[44] Ibid.

object and could be qualified as a legitimate military objective in times of armed conflict.[45] In other words, since the interconnectedness of civilian and military cyber infrastructure makes it largely impossible to distinguish between civilian objects and military objectives, in the artificial, yet hugely important, domain of cyberspace the application of Schmitt's approach would be impossible.

The Harvard Air and Missile Warfare Manual also grapples with the issue of dual-use objects. It does so when reflecting on whether objects which may qualify as military objectives by nature, as enshrined in Rule 22 of the Manual, include also dual-use objects such as factories, lines and means of communications (e.g. airfields, railway lines, roads, bridges, and tunnels), energy producing facilities, oil storage depots, transmission facilities and equipment.[46] The majority of the Group of Experts who drafted the Harvard Manual endorses the compromise solution by which military objectives by nature were to be divided into two subsets. The first, reflected in Rule 22 (a), consists of "military objectives by nature at all times", like "military aircraft (including military UAV/UCAVs); military vehicles (other than medical transport); missiles and other weapons; military equipment; military fortifications, facilities and depots; warships; ministries of defence and armaments factories".[47] By contrast, the second subset consists of (dual-use) objects which "become military objectives by nature only in light of the circumstances ruling at the time".[48] As will be discussed in Chap. 3 of this book,[49] this reading of the provision contained in Article 52(2) of API is not correct as it does not take into due consideration all the essential elements of the definition of military objectives, which is undoubtedly unsatisfactory but still represents the customary law in force.

Another solution aims to exclude from the ambit of legitimate military targets, either *per se* or under certain conditions (that is, for instance, in cases of minimal use for military purposes), specific infrastructures.[50] The promoters of this approach propose an extension of the list of objects contained in Article 56(1) of Additional Protocol I, which exempts certain objects from attack, even where these objects qualify as military objectives, because of the severe humanitarian consequences that attacking these objects might have.[51] As is well known, Article 56(1) lists dual-use objects whose destruction could release dangerous forces, thereby significantly affecting the civilian population.[52] Therefore, the proposal of the enlargement of the list contained in this provision would have a very limited impact as additional objects shall be able to satisfy the entry criterion of Article 56 of Additional Protocol I, which requires "emissions that are dangerous in and of themselves".

[45] Geiß and Lahmann 2012, p. 383. See also Schmitt 2019, p. 347.
[46] Harvard Air and Missile Warfare Manual 2013, Rule 23, p. 120.
[47] Ibid., Rule 22, p. 116.
[48] Ibid., Rule 23, p. 120.
[49] See Chap. 3, Sect. 3.2 in this book.
[50] Geiß and Lahmann 2012, p. 391.
[51] Ibid., pp. 390–391.
[52] Ibid.

Kalshoven and Zegveld frame the problem of dual-use objects' status in different terms as they affirm that, between the two categories of military objectives by nature and civilian objects that are normally dedicated to civilian purposes, such as a place of worship, a house or other dwelling or a school ex Article 52(3) of API, "remain all sorts of objects that fall under neither presumption".[53] They go on to identify those objects "such as a road, bridge or railway line, (parts of) a sea port, a power-generating facility, any industrial plant, or a means of transport", which "may or may not come within the terms of a military objective"; further arguing that "they will do so when they meet the dual criterion that they not only (normally by their location or use) make an effective contribution to military action", but that their "total or partial destruction, capture or neutralisation, in the circumstances ruling at the time, offers a definite military advantage".[54] Unfortunately, Kalshoven and Zegveld failed to develop any argument from this taxonomy, thus opening the doors for further, and much-needed, research and analysis in this complex area.

The short overview presented above clearly shows that there is widespread awareness of the problems attached to attacks against dual-use objects and some attempts have already been made to enhance the protection of civilians by either putting forward alternative interpretations of existing norms or urging for a more stringent application of the proportionality rule. The present work aims at bridging the gap between these two different approaches by looking at dual-use objects from all possible angles and thus proposing a paradigm shift. The first step of this process must focus on the analysis of the existing legal framework, shedding light on its shortcomings and incongruencies and starting with the definition of the key terms.

In addition to the IHL framework in force and the relevant doctrine, the analysis will rely on State practice by referring to past as well as ongoing armed conflicts, in order to assess whether the suggestion that "governments are uncomfortable with the notion that the civilian function of a dual-use facility can be ignored"[55] has already triggered or is about to trigger any noteworthy legal development.

1.3 Definition of the Key Terms

Before undertaking the effort to define the key terms used in this work, it is important to shed light on the central role played by the principle of distinction. The International Court of Justice (ICJ) famously described the principle of the distinction between combatants and non-combatants as the first of "the cardinal principles [...] constituting the fabric of humanitarian law".[56] According to the ICJ, this principle

[53] Kalshoven and Zegveld 2011, p. 105.

[54] Ibid.

[55] Shue and Wippman 2002, p. 565.

[56] Ibid.

> is aimed at the protection of the civilian population and civilian objects and establishes the distinction between combatants and non-combatants; States must never make civilians the object of attack and must consequently never use weapons that are incapable of distinguishing between civilian and military targets.[57]

To use Chetail's words, the principle of distinction is grounded on the basic axiom underlying IHL that only the weakening of the military potential of the enemy is acceptable in times of armed conflict.[58] The principle was originally laid down in the Saint Petersburg Declaration of 29 November/11 December 1868. Since then, it has been restated in numerous multilateral instruments under various forms. Kalshoven authoritatively reports that this key tenet of the law of warfare was not doubted by the delegates at the Diplomatic Conference which led to the adoption of Additional Protocol 1.[59] Indeed, it was only in 1977, with the adoption of the two Additional Protocols of the Geneva Conventions, that this customary rule obtained a fully-fledged conventional expression at the universal level. Notably, Protocol I in its Article 48, significantly titled "basic rule", affirms that

> [i]n order to ensure respect for and protection of the civilian population and civilian objects, the Parties to the conflict shall at all times distinguish between the civilian population and combatants and between civilian objects and military objectives and accordingly shall direct their operations only against military objectives.

It is possible to infer, already from the formulation of the "basic rule" that it is specifically prohibited to launch attacks directed deliberately at civilian objects, attacks with the purpose of terrorising the population, reprisals against civilians, and indiscriminate attacks.[60] The principle, as noted by many authors[61] and as crystallised in the ICRC study on customary international humanitarian law (hereinafter ICRC study),[62] is undoubtedly well established in customary international law, with the consequence that it is considered binding also on States that are not parties to API. The corollary to the principle of distinction, and the precondition to apply it, is that under IHL it is necessary to distinguish between the categories of civilian population and combatants as well as civilian objects and military objectives. As Spaight eloquently noted more than a century ago "the separation of armies and peaceful inhabitants into two distinct classes is perhaps the greatest triumph of International Law. Its effect in mitigating the evils of war has been incalculable".[63] Despite this crucial achievement, the intermediate (and non-legal) category of dual-use objects blurs the lines between legitimate targets and unlawful ones, thus challenging the effectiveness of the principle and its scope of application. Bearing in mind those premises, the next

---

[57] ICJ, *Legality of the Threat or Use of Nuclear Weapons*, ICJ Advisory Opinion (8 July 1996), ICJ Rep 226, p. 257, para 78. See also Chetail 2003.

[58] Chetail 2002, p. 201; Doswald-Beck 1997, p. 37.

[59] Kalshoven 1977, p. 116.

[60] Chetail 2002, p. 202.

[61] Greenwood 1993, p. 70.

[62] Henckaerts and Doswald-Beck 2005, pp. 3–5.

[63] Spaight 1911, p. 37.

sub-sections will analyse the notions at the heart of the principle of distinction and will introduce the contested stance of dual-use objects as a *tertium non datur* that inevitably jeopardises the attempts to correctly differentiate between civilian objects and military objectives.

1.3.1 Civilian Population and Civilian Objects

The essence of IHL is to protect persons who are not, or are no longer, directly, or actively participating in hostilities, and imposes limits on the means and methods of warfare. At its core the normative framework guarantees that civilians and civilian objects enjoy key legal protections from attacks.[64] The term "attack" is defined in Article 49(1) of API as an "act[s] of violence against the adversary, whether in offence or in defence". Notably, any act of violence "fits this matrix";[65] not only massive air attacks or artillery barrages, but also small-scale attacks, like a sniper firing a single bullet. As explained in the 1987 ICRC Commentary this definition essentially equates the word "attack" with "combat action", and therefore "combat action" against civilians, not taking a direct part in hostilities, is prohibited at all times under API.[66] Several authors support the position that the concept of "attack" must be modernised. To this end, Schmitt affirms that

> "attack" is a term of prescriptive shorthand intended to address specific consequences. It is clear that what the relevant provisions hope to accomplish is shielding protected individuals from injury or death and protected objects from damage or destruction […] Significant human physical or mental suffering is logically included in the concept of injury.[67]

Schmitt has substantially contributed to the development of a novel approach that considers the far-reaching effects of an attack, rather than just the act in itself. Nowadays, it is possible to claim that his view is widely shared within the IHL academic community and beyond.[68] Consistently, the Tallinn Manual states that "the crux of the notion [of attacks] *lies in the effects that are caused*",[69] and therefore in the consequences of an operation. Also endorsing this view, the International Criminal Court (ICC) held that "in characterizing certain conducts as an *attack what matters was the consequences* of the act",[70] and particularly whether injury, death of civilians and damage or destruction of civilian objects are intended or foreseeable consequences thereof. This "consequence-based" interpretation of the notion of attack acknowledges that the continuing evolution of civilian protection, covering

---

[64] Drew 2017, p. 96.

[65] Dinstein 2002, p. 141.

[66] Sandoz et al. 1987, p. 603.

[67] Schmitt 2002, p. 377.

[68] Dörmann 2002, p. 4.

[69] Schmitt 2013, pp. 92–94 (emphasis added).

[70] ICC, *Prosecutor v Bosco Ntaganda*, Decision, (Pre-Trial Chamber II) 9 June 2014, ICC-01/04-02/06, para 46 (emphasis added).

both individuals and objects, calls for a broader and more expansive interpretation of the term than has traditionally been the case.[71] Attacks against dual-use targets usually have a devastating impact on the civilian population. Therefore, applying the "consequence-based" approach to the notion of attack is perfectly in line with the main arguments advanced by this study. In fact, the foundation of the paradigm shift is placing a stronger focus on the foreseeable short- and long-term effects that stem from targeting objects that have a civilian function and are, thus, important or even essential for the survival of the civilian population.

As is well known, the provision in Article 50(1) of API defines "civilians" negatively, by excluding those labelled as combatants based on the Geneva Conventions and Protocols. In the commentaries to API it has been emphasised that the definition of civilians also includes individuals linked to the armed forces without being members thereof, such as civilians accompanying, serving and transporting the military or employed in munitions work, as well as civilians who have previously taken part in hostilities without combatant status.[72] Furthermore, API contains a definition of the term "civilian population", clarifying that the category comprises all those who are civilians.[73] The provision also specifies that "t]he presence within the civilian population of individuals who do not come within the definition of civilians does not deprive the population of its civilian character."[74] This entails, for instance, that combatants coming home on leave from the front line during an armed conflict would not deprive their village population of its civilian character.[75]

A civilian, hence, is any individual who neither takes direct part in any military action or hostilities nor belongs to armed forces. It follows that a civilian is not a member of a militia, paramilitary police, or even a resistance movement. Civilians lose their status only if, and for the time during which, they take direct part in the hostilities.[76] In particular, civilians taking a direct part in hostilities may be attacked, do not factor into proportionality calculations, and need not be considered when trying to minimise harm to civilians.[77] Clearly, it would have been easier if international humanitarian law had provided a positive definition of civilian. The key reason for refraining from giving one was to avoid narrowing down the concept too much. To this end, the drafters of the Geneva Conventions and the Protocols wished to limit the risk of leaving out exceptions or specific cases.[78] Notably, under IHL there may be no category of "quasi-combatants", i.e. civilians contributing so

---

[71] Drew 2017, p. 97.

[72] Sandoz et al. 1987, p. 603; Bothe 2013.

[73] API, Article 50(2), above n 42.

[74] API, Article 50(3), above n 42. See Byron 2022, p. 178.

[75] Ibid.

[76] API, Article 51(3), above n 42, clearly states that: "[c]ivilians shall enjoy the protection afforded by this Section unless and for such time as they take a direct part in hostilities." On the definition of direct participation in hostilities, see ICRC 2008, pp. 1013–1014; Akande 2010; Byron 2022, pp. 287–290.

[77] Schmitt 2010, p. 702.

[78] Van Engeland 2011, pp. 30–31.

fundamentally to the military effort or the war effort, for example workers in factories producing ammunitions,[79] that they lose their civilian status although not directly participating in hostilities. If the civilian population shall be protected, only one distinction shall be considered admissible, namely the one between those who directly participate in hostilities, on the one hand, and all others, on the other hand, who "do not, may not, and cannot hinder the enemy militarily […] regardless of whatever their contribution to the war effort may be".[80]

As far as civilian objects are concerned, the notion is once again negatively defined since Article 52(2) of API describes them as "objects which are not military objectives", and therefore shall not be the object of attack. At the Diplomatic Conference leading to the adoption of the Additional Protocols, it was remarked that Article 52 was so essential that it "cannot be the subject of any reservations whatsoever since these would be inconsistent with the aim and purpose of Protocol I and undermine its basis".[81] Despite the lack of an explicit definition an/or of a list of civilian objects, as noted in the ICRC IHL database State practice considers

> civilian areas, towns, cities, villages, residential areas, dwellings, buildings and houses and schools, civilian means of transportation, hospitals, medical establishments and medical units, historic monuments, places of worship and cultural property, and the natural environment as *prima facie* civilian objects, provided, in the final analysis, they have not become military objectives.[82]

Also worth noting, is that the doctrine excludes from the notion of objects "intangible things", such as computer data, because "the correct interpretation" of the term "object" in API refers only to "a material, tangible thing".[83] Several IHL norms serve the purpose of enhancing the protection of civilian objects and will be briefly described here to show that there is a strong, albeit not always coherent and effective, commitment to guarantee the protection of civilian objects under IHL. For instance, indiscriminate attacks are prohibited under IHL rules, as they "are of a nature to strike military objectives and civilians or civilian objects without distinction".[84] Moreover, certain rules under IHL, including customary rules, protect civilian objects by establishing the obligation that precautions must be taken in an attack. Thus, for example, an attacker must "do everything feasible to verify that the objectives to be attacked are neither civilians nor civilian objects and are not subject to special protection" and "take all feasible precautions in the choice of means and methods of attack with a view to avoiding, and in any event to minimizing, incidental […] damage to civilian objects".[85]

---

[79] Schmitt 2010, p. 710.

[80] Sassòli 2003, p. 9.

[81] Mexico, Statement at the Diplomatic Conference leading to the adoption of the Additional Protocols, cited in Henckaerts and Doswald-Beck 2005, para 679.

[82] Ibid.

[83] Pompson 2023, pp. 357–358; Dinstein 2002, p. 142.

[84] API, Article 51(4)–(5)(a), above n 42.

[85] API, Article 57, above n 42. Sivakumaran 2012, pp. 351–357; Neuman 2018, pp. 29–32.

Furthermore, Article 52(3) of API affirms that the intrinsic nature of an object is not totally irrelevant when assessing whether it is a legitimate military objective. In fact, according to this provision "[i]n case of doubt whether an object which is *normally dedicated to civilian purposes*, such as a place of worship, a house or other dwelling or a school, is being used to make an effective contribution to military action, it shall be presumed not to be so used". The goal of the norm is to impose a higher standard of verification based on the intrinsically civilian nature of a given object. As stressed by Sassòli, the presumption was meant by the drafters as a partial replacement of a definition of civilian objects, but already at the Diplomatic Conference it met some objections and even those favouring the presumption admitted that it did not reflect customary law, but constituted a progressive development.[86] Indeed, besides the general difficulty of considering presumptions as customary, this particular one simply did not enjoy sufficient State support to be customary, at least when the Protocols were drafted. The lack of widespread support, which anyhow did not result in any reservation been made to this provision,[87] was allegedly motivated by the fear that a defender may be tempted to conceal its military forces in civilian installations. Despite the initial reticence, States practice has significantly evolved over time, with the US even reversing its stance that the rule is not customary.[88] In fact, the US Department of Defense (DoD) has recently rectified its previous claim that "under customary international law, no legal presumption of civilian status exists for persons or objects".[89] Consistently with this important development, the revised version of its Law of War Manual now incorporates an obligation whereby those responsible for targeting must "presume that persons or objects are protected from being made the object of attack unless the information available at the time indicates that those persons or objects are military objectives."[90]

The provision that crystallises the presumption of civilian status is unquestionably crucial. As a result of it, where nothing indicates that an object contributes to military action, it may clearly not be attacked. This entails that when a "reasonable military commander" is confronted with the choice to strike civilian objects *such as* a place of worship, a house or a school, only very strong clues that they effectively contribute to military action may raise doubts about their civilian character. In this sense, such objects benefit from what Sassòli and Cameron call "a factual presumption that they are civilian".[91] Equally important, is the consequence that, in cases of genuine doubt, there is no room for "opposite presumption" that the object is a military objective. The attacker must, rather, as always when he or she lacks information, do everything feasible to obtain such information.[92] This is not only enshrined in Article 57(2)(a)(i) of Protocol I, but corresponds to general international law, flowing as a

[86] Sassòli and Cameron 2006, p. 41.

[87] Henckaerts and Doswald-Beck 2005, Rule 10, pp. 35–36.

[88] US DoD 1992, para 752.

[89] Ibid. See Goodman 2022.

[90] US DoD 2023, para 5.4.3.4. See van Coller 2023; Lawless 2023.

[91] Sassòli and Cameron 2006, p. 41.

[92] On the "reasonable military commander" standard, see Chap. 5 in this book.

kind of procedural obligation from the customary obligation to distinguish civilian objects from military objectives. The decision-maker who gives the order to launch an attack without knowing what she/he is attacking and without verifying the nature of the target, despite her/his own doubts and the fact that she/he could verify the target, launches a deliberately indiscriminate attack.[93]

Finally, as far as the scope of the protection granted to civilians and civilian objects is concerned, Article 49(3) of API clarifies that the relevant provisions find application in any land, air or sea warfare which may affect the civilian population, individual civilians or civilian objects on land.[94] All these provisions further apply to all attacks from the sea or from the air against objectives on land, "but do not otherwise affect the rules of international law applicable in armed conflict at sea or in the air."[95] For example, as *lex specialis* the law of naval warfare provides a detailed regime governing the conduct of hostilities occurring at sea and allows for a more expansive understanding of the category of military objective.[96]

1.3.2 Combatants and Military Objectives

The negative definitions of civilian and civilian object work by opposition and elimination; a person who is not a combatant is a civilian, a target that is not military is a civilian object. This means that the concepts of combatant and military objective must necessarily be defined clearly.[97] In other words, the principle of distinction is practically pointless if at least one of the categories between which the attacker must distinguish is not properly defined.[98] Whilst, as discussed above, civilians are entitled to immunity from attack, unless and for such time as they take a direct part in hostilities, combatants on the other hand, "have the right to participate directly in hostilities",[99] entailing that they are also liable to attack during the entire duration of the conflict, unless they are *hors de combat* or otherwise fall into the power of an adverse party. Article 4(a) of the Third Geneva Convention (GCIII) provides a detailed definition of who can be a prisoner of war (POW), knowing that only combatants benefit from that status. Therefore, the list of categories enshrined in Article 4(a) offers significant insight on who shall be regarded as a combatant. API makes the secondary status of POW explicitly dependent on the primary status of "combatant". Thus, only combatants are entitled to take part in hostilities, and they cannot be punished merely for participation. Conversely, an individual who is not entitled to the status of combatant is liable to punishment under the criminal law

[93] Sassòli and Cameron 2006, p. 41.

[94] Ibid., pp. 41–43.

[95] API, Article 49(3), above n 42.

[96] Raina 2023.

[97] Van Engeland 2011, p. 30.

[98] Capone 2023, p. 746.

[99] API, Article 43(2), above n 42.

of the captor power for having committed acts in violation of its provisions, even if these acts would not constitute violations of IHL.[100] The relevant rules of API depart from earlier instruments in important respects. Article 43 of API reiterates existing principles, except that it discards the distinction between regular armed forces on one side and volunteer groups, militias and resistance movements, which featured in Article 4 of GC III, on the other. According to this most recent provision, the criteria for determining entitlement to combatant and POW status are the same for members of both groups. This obviously constitutes a novelty compared to pre–existing norms, but it appears to raise little controversy and has already been embedded into customary IHL.[101] Finally, Article 44, especially para 3, of API is also relevant as it relaxes the standards to be a combatant and extends the category to people belonging to armed groups. More in detail, this provision states that, if it is impossible for a combatant to distinguish himself as required, she/he may nevertheless retain her/his status as combatant, and therefore acquire POW status if captured, if she/he carries arms openly in the limited situations specified in the norm.[102]

Along the same lines and in reaction to the same needs, IHL treaties provide a positive definition of military objectives. The justification for this choice is based on the assumption that since "objects can become military objectives according to their current or potential use by the enemy", rather than due to their intrinsic character, "it was military objectives that were ultimately defined".[103] Under Article 52(2), an object must fulfil two cumulative criteria, that together satisfy a so-called "two-pronged test", in order to qualify as a military objective. To be labelled as military, a given object must: a) make an effective contribution to military action *by nature, location, purpose or use*; and b), offer *a definite military advantage* if destroyed, captured or neutralised, in the circumstances ruling at the time.[104] As far as dual-use objects are concerned, it is trivial to observe that they also need to satisfy both elements of the definition to be considered legitimate military objectives, taking into account the specific circumstances.

1.3.2.1 The First Prong of the Military Objective's Test

With regard to the first prong of the test, the "quadruple subdivision of military objectives by nature, purpose, use and location" is not as clear-cut as it appears *prima facie*, and obviously certain objectives can be catalogued within more than one subset.[105] The first criterion, i.e. "nature", refers to the intrinsic and permanent attributes of the object.[106] Although perhaps it sounds counterintuitive, it is not so obvious to

---

[100] Sommario 2016, pp. 150–151.

[101] Ibid.

[102] Aldrich 1991, p. 137.

[103] Lubell 2015, p. 79.

[104] Sassòli et al. 2011, p. 161 (emphasis added).

[105] Dinstein 2004, p. 92.

[106] Gill et al. 2014, p. 11.

identify the military objectives that belong to this category "by nature". The ICRC's 1987 Commentary, while seeking to shed light on the issue, has actually achieved the opposite effect by stating that this typology covers all objects "directly *used by the armed forces*: weapons, equipment, transports, fortifications, depots, buildings occupied by armed forces, staff headquarters, communications centres, etc.".[107] The ICRC's approach to the matter, as already noted by Henderson,[108] is quite problematic as it blurs the line between two criteria that must remain separate, or at least as separate as possible, i.e. "nature" and "use". The former, hence, refers to the native or inherent character of a thing, and not to the actor that owns or controls it. Also diving into the issue, the San Remo Manual on International Law Applicable to Armed Conflicts at Sea generally speaks of "targets having *obvious military value*",[109] and in doing so it separates them from "other objects" that can become military objectives, which include "enemy lines of communication used for military purposes, rail yards, bridges, rolling stock, barges, lighters, industrial installations producing war-fighting products, and power generation plants".[110] The Harvard Air and Missile Warfare Manual adds further details by explaining that military objectives by nature "must have an inherent characteristic or attribute which contributes to military action. Military equipment and facilities most clearly qualify on this basis, as do tanks, military aircraft, military airfields, or military barracks. Even when not in use, such objects always constitute lawful targets during armed conflict."[111] Despite the lack of an unequivocal and uniform approach, and notwithstanding a few attempts to stir the pot by expanding potential lists of military objectives,[112] dual-use objects do not qualify as a military objective under the nature criterion.

Location, purpose, and use show the dynamic nature of IHL and how civilian objects can become legitimate military objectives.[113] Concerning the "location" criterion, it must be factored in, irrespective of the nature, purpose and use of a given object, thus performing a task which is not always easy to undertake. Clearly "location" can refer also to "selected areas that have special importance to military operations",[114] although the doctrine agrees that the incidence of such locations cannot be too widespread. Military objectives by location have not attracted extensive research so far, with a few notable exceptions which address the topic from a

[107] Sandoz et al. 1987, para 2020.

[108] Henderson 2009, pp. 54–55.

[109] Doswald-Beck 1995 (emphasis added); Robertson 1998, p. 50.

[110] Ibid.

[111] Harvard Air and Missile Warfare Manual 2013, Rule 22, p. 116, where it further specifies that "[e]xamples of military objectives by nature include military aircraft (including military UAV/UCAVs); military vehicles (other than medical transport); missiles and other weapons; military equipment; military fortifications, facilities and depots; warships; ministries of defence and armaments factories."

[112] For example, the ICRC included radio and broadcasting stations in an annex list of legitimate military targets to its 1956 Draft Rules for the Limitation of the Dangers Incurred by the Civilian Population in Time of War. See Sassòli and Cameron 2006, p. 56.

[113] Jeangène Vilmer 2015, p. 88.

[114] Sandoz et al. 1987, para 2021.

practitioner's perspective.[115] For instance, Rynkeby Knudsen, in his attempt to dig out on the rationale for adding "location" to the criteria enshrined in Article 52(2) of API, reports that from the records of the diplomatic conferences leading up to the agreed text and paired with the ICRC Commentary on the Additional Protocols, very little light is shed on the matter. In fact, the ICRC Commentary even contains a footnote comment that the Working Group of Committee Three of the diplomatic conferences "gave no reasons for introducing the location criterion".[116] Despite the lack of significant insight, the ICRC Commentary does suggest that the core intention of including the location criteria has to do with sites, which are of special importance to military operations in view of their location. This is "either because it is a site that must be seized or because it is important to prevent the enemy from seizing it or otherwise because it is a matter of forcing the enemy to retreat from it".[117] As noted by Dinstein, there must be "a distinctive feature turning a piece of land into a military objective (e.g., a mountain pass, a specific hill of strategic value, a bridgehead etc…)".[118] In a note on Article 51(4)(a) the ICRC Commentary adds that if a belligerent wants to prevent an enemy army from establishing itself in a particular area or from passing through that area, there can be little doubt in such a case that "the area must be considered a military objective and treated as such".[119] At the same time the Commentary does not exclude that military objectives by location may include more than just sites or areas, in fact there is a reference to "a bridge or other construction".[120] Yet, the Commentary raises a very interesting, although overlooked, point, according to which the concept of "military objective by location" is only valid in the "combat area".[121] The ICRC Commentary further highlights that "outside the combat area the military character of objectives that are to be attacked must be clearly established and verified",[122] and the limits of such objectives must be precisely determined.[123] Rynkeby Knudsen stresses that this additional constraint placed on military objectives by location, in his view, does not make any sense.[124]

Other commentators, and in particular Henderson,[125] argue that this limitation does not appear in any of the State practice referred to in the section of the ICRC study on customary international humanitarian Law dealing with the definition of military objectives and areas of land. Moreover, he observes that there seems to be "no reason to read down 'location' as only applying in the combat area when such

---

115 Rynkeby Knudsen 2024, p. 2.

116 Sandoz et al. 1987, para 2021.

117 Ibid.

118 Dinstein 2002, p. 150.

119 Sandoz et al. 1987, para 1955.

120 Ibid., para 2021.

121 Ibid., para 1955.

122 Ibid., para 1954.

123 Ibid.

124 Rynkeby Knudsen 2024.

125 Henderson 2009, pp. 56–57.

a limitation is not applied to 'nature, purpose or use'".[126] It is worth noting that in current armed conflicts it is no longer possible to identify a defined combat area or a battle space, hence it would be pointless to restrict the application of the location criterion following the approach of the ICRC Commentary. At the same time, it is undeniable that while the location criterion needs to adapt to the new challenges of warfare, it is still necessary to read it in a restrictive way for it to be in compliance with other rules of IHL, in particular the prohibition to launch indiscriminate attacks ex Article 51(5)(a) of API, the rules governing the precautions to be taken by the attacker when planning and executing attacks (Article 57 of API), and the specific prohibitions addressed to the defender (Article 51(7) and Article 58 of API). Considering the above, it is logical to question the extent to which the assumption that "an object may become a military objective due to its location *if it obstructs[s] the field of fire for attack on another valid military objective*,"[127] can still be valid today. Thus, it seems plausible to argue that the location of an object can rarely transform it from a civilian one into a military objective, with the obvious exception of limited land areas or sites that have an evident strategic value.

In the case of dual-use objects, which as the present analysis will show are normally attacked for/in spite of their "function", a term "wider than use, while falling short of mere 'location'",[128] in this author's view the location criterion shall be carefully applied. This means that a dual-use object can be lawfully targeted as a military objective due to its location only if it is placed *within* an area of land that constitutes a military objective. Despite moving from opposite premises, Dinstein reaches the same conclusions when affirming that a bridge, i.e. a dual-use object usually qualified as a military objective "by location",[129] would fail to be a military objective when it is in "a residential area *away from the contact zone*".[130] Moreover, he further claims that "logic dictates that, if a civilian-by-nature object (like a supermarket) *is located within* a sprawling military base, it cannot be immune from attack".[131] Similarly, if a merchant vessel "is anchored *in a military port*, it becomes a military objective by location".[132] Therefore, it is hereby argued that the narrow and limited circumstance in which a civilian object can be transformed into a military one by location is when it is situated *inside* a site that can be classified as a military objective. This conclusion, in this author's opinion, shall be applied to all kinds of

[126] Ibid.

[127] Robertson 1998, p. 49 (emphasis added).

[128] Dinstein 2004, p. 164, commenting on the choice to use "function" in lieu of "use" in the text of Article 6 of the Second Protocol to the 1954 Hague Convention. See Second Protocol to the Hague Convention of 1954 for the Protection of Cultural Property in the Event of Armed Conflict, open for signature 26 March 1999, 38 ILM 76, entered into force 9 March 2004. See Chap. 4, Sect. 4.1 in this book.

[129] Sandoz et al. 1987, para 2021. On the classification of bridges as military objectives see also Milanovic and Schmitt 2022.

[130] Dinstein 2004, p. 93 (emphasis added).

[131] Dinstein 2002, pp. 149–150 (emphasis added).

[132] Ibid., p. 150 (emphasis added).

civilian objects, including dual-use objects, from electrical power systems to water systems and installations.

Traditionally, purpose and use are regarded as the most relevant criteria applicable to the classification of dual-use objects as military objectives. In relation to the first, the purpose is determined after the crystallisation of its original nature, yet prior to actual use. In other words, "the military purpose is assumed not to be stamped on the objective from the outset (otherwise, the target would be military by nature)".[133] Since purpose denotes "the intended future use of an object", it is not necessary for the attacker to wait until a civilian object is being used for military purposes before striking it. An object's purpose may be inferred using various forms of intelligence, such as observation with intelligence (human or signal), surveillance and reconnaissance (ISR) assets (manned or unmanned). However, when the intended future use of an object is not perfectly clear, the attacker "*must act reasonably* given the information available at the time of the strike".[134] A slightly different issue arises when an object or installation is not about to be used for military purposes but may be so used at any time. This is the case, for example, for means and installations of transport, including bridges. If an objective is military simply because at some point it could be converted into something useful for the military, the notion of military objectives could potentially become an all-encompassing one, leaving nothing to be regarded as civilian and thus protected under IHL. In spite of this, some authors claim that it is sufficient that the likelihood of military use is "reasonable and not remote".[135] However, as noted by Sassòli, according to the text of API, the object must "make" (in the present tense) an effective contribution to military action.[136] Admittedly, as according to Article 52(2) the purpose can turn an objective into a military one, Sassòli and Cameron conclude that an "intended future use" may be sufficient, but not a mere "possible future use".[137]

In this author's view the inclusion of the "purpose" criterion amongst the ones that can legitimately transform a civilian object into a military objective is at odds with other relevant IHL provisions. Just to provide an example, the inclusion of the purpose criterion is inconsistent with the presumption of civilian status enshrined in Article 52(3) of API. As already mentioned in the previous section, this provision represents an essential step to depart from the "shoot first and ask questions later" approach.[138] The wording is rather unambiguous as it refers to a doubt that can be instilled if a civilian object is actually "being used to make an effective contribution". The extent to which the presumption of the civilian status of an object can be considered compatible with the "purpose" criterion deserves, at the very least, to be questioned, as will be further discussed in Chap. 4.[139]

[133] Dinstein 2002, p. 148.

[134] Schmitt and Widmar 2016, p. 131 (emphasis added).

[135] Sandoz et al. 1987, p. 636, para 2022.

[136] Sassòli and Cameron 2006, p. 58.

[137] Ibid.

[138] Sandoz et al. 1987, p. 637, para 2030.

[139] See Chap. 4, Sect. 4.5.1 in this book.

Narrowing down the scope of the "purpose" criterion and *de facto* equating it to use, the International Criminal Tribunal for the Former Yugoslavia (ICTY) in the *Prosecutor v. Galić* case affirmed that a "[civilian] object shall not be attacked when it is not reasonable to believe, in the circumstances of the person contemplating the attack, including the information available to the latter, that *the object is being used to make an effective contribution to military action.*"[140] It is important to note that sweeping or anticipatory classification of objects would be inconsistent with the second prong of the definition of military objective. This approach would prevent an assessment of whether an object is military and would downplay the obligation to continually validate the nature of a proposed target. For example, it would be clearly contrary to IHL if all objects somewhat related to, owned by, or associated with the enemy were collectively considered military objectives. The "use" criterion, in line with the ICTY's decision, should be the one predominantly taken into consideration when assessing whether a dual-use object can be regarded as a lawful target as it refers to how an object is currently being employed.[141] As is well known, the category of "military objectives by use" covers civilian objects that are being employed for military purposes during the period of use. Most authors agree that a civilian object qualifies as a military objective "once it is converted to military use",[142] however slight that use is and regardless of how important its civilian function is. As stressed by the International Law Association (ILA) Study Group on the Conduct of Hostilities in the 21st Century, Article 52(2) API has "a clear temporal dimension, which works both ways".[143] An object, even a church or another place of worship, which is normally used for civilian purposes, may turn into a military objective if it is used for military purposes. An object, which has been used militarily, becomes (again) a civilian object when the military use is abandoned. In this sense, the definition of military objectives is "relativised", since there is "no fixed borderline between civilian objects and military objectives".[144] Thus, timely and reliable information of the military situation, and how the information is used by the relevant actors are crucial elements in the target selection and essential for the implementation of the principle of distinction.

1.3.2.2 The Second Prong of the Military Objective's Test

The second prong of the test enshrined in Article 52(2) refers to "a definite military advantage" that must result from the partial or complete destruction, capture, or neutralisation of a military objective. The expression "a definite military advantage", exactly like military objective, derives from the Hague Rules of Air Warfare, which

[140] ICTY *Prosecutor v Galic,* (5 December 2003) (Trial Chamber Judgement), Case No. IT-28-29-T, para 51.

[141] Schmitt and Widmar 2016, p. 131.

[142] Ibid.

[143] ILA Study Group 2017, p. 6.

[144] Randelzhofer 1992, p. 603.

used the formula "a distinct military advantage".[145] Experts agree on the fact that there is no apparent difference in the present context between the adjectives "distinct" and "definite" or, for that matter, many other alternatives taken into consideration by the drafters of Article 52(2). Whatever the adjective preferred, the idea conveyed is that of "a concrete and perceptible military advantage rather than a hypothetical and speculative one".[146] The advantage gained must be military and not, for instance, purely political, therefore, "forcing a change in the negotiating attitudes" of the adverse party cannot be deemed a proper military advantage.[147] It follows that the conclusion reached by the Eritrea-Ethiopia Claims Commission (EECC), according to which military advantage "must be considered in the context of its relation to the armed conflict *as a whole* at the time of the attack" and that "there can be few military advantages more evident than effective pressure to end an armed conflict",[148] must be rejected as it accepts that the military advantage may be purely political instead of essentially military. The assessment of the military advantage must be made against the background of the circumstances prevailing at the time. It should also be noted that the outlook of the attacking party is unlikely to match that of the party under attack in evaluating the long-term military advantage of any action planned. Because of this context-specific appraisal the same object may be legitimately attacked in one temporal framework but not in others.[149] Furthermore, the dominant view is that an assessment of the military benefits can be made in light of "an attack as a whole",[150] which involves a finite, circumscribed event, as distinct from "isolated or specific parts of the attack."[151] As the book will discuss in more detail in Chap. 3,[152] the notions of "military advantage" and "attack as a whole" represent crucial aspects to take in due consideration, both while applying the principle of distinction and for conducting a proportionality assessment. Although these elements are differently qualified in the two contexts,[153] it is important to highlight that their centrality will not go unnoticed in the process of identifying options to better address the unique features of dual-use objects.[154]

---

[145] Kalshoven 1978, p. 111.

[146] Fleck 1997, p. 48.

[147] Dinstein 2002, p. 144.

[148] Eritrea-Ethiopia Claims Commission, *Partial Award, Western Front, Aerial Bombardment and related claims – Eritrea's Claims 1, 3, 5, 9–13, 14, 21, 25 & 26* (Permanent Court of Arbitration, State of Eritrea vs Federal Democratic Republic of Ethiopia, 2005) paras 113, 121, https://pcacases.com/web/sendAttach/757 (accessed 4 March 2024) (emphasis added).

[149] Dinstein 2002, p. 145.

[150] Ibid.

[151] Oeter 2013, p. 442.

[152] See Chap. 3, Sect. 3.2 in this book.

[153] Solf 2013, p. 367; ILA Study Group 2017, pp. 32–33; Gillard 2018, pp. 9–10.

[154] See Chap. 3, Sects. 3.2.1 and 3.2.2 in this book.

1.3.2.3 The Past Attempts to Draft Lists of Military Objectives

As reported in the 1987 Commentary on API to the Geneva Conventions,[155] for a long time attempts have been made to go beyond a merely abstract definition of "military objective", starting with the non-exhaustive list contained in the Hague Convention IX of 1907 Concerning Bombardment by Naval Forces in Time of War.[156] In 1923 the Commission of Jurists made a further effort to distinguish between civilian objects and military objectives by incorporating into the Hague Rules of Air Warfare a practical approach, that ultimately led to singling out the following items, i.e. "military forces, military works, military establishments or depots, manufacturing plants constituting important and well-known centres for the production of arms, ammunition or characterized military supplies, lines of communication or transport *which are used for military purposes*".[157] Similarly, the Hague Convention of 1954 for the Protection of Cultural Property provided a list of military objects, such as "an aerodrome, broadcasting station, establishment engaged upon work of national defence, a port or railway station of relative importance or a main line of communication".[158] Notably, those lists, which contain several dual-use objects, do not mention water installations nor power infrastructures, thus inferring that perhaps the haste with which they are treated as military objectives should be reconsidered. In 1956 the ICRC submitted its Draft Rules for the Limitation of Dangers incurred by the Civilian Population in Time of War. Article 7 of the ICRC Draft Rules enshrines an abstract definition of military objectives, while an annex to the rules enumerates the categories of military objectives to which attacks may be lawfully directed.[159] The list of categories was drawn by the ICRC with the help of military experts, i.e. those who are called to make targeting decisions in the field. The scope of this endeavour is quite clear as providing the parties involved in an armed conflict with a precise catalogue would greatly simplify the practical implementation of the rules on distinction, allowing parties to overcome significant differences.[160]

However, as the work progressed, "it soon became clear that drawing up a list of military objectives or civilian objects would have raised insuperable problems, and the ICRC therefore abandoned the attempt".[161] Ultimately, the decision has

[155] Sandoz et al. 1987, p. 632.

[156] Article 2 of the Hague Convention IX of 1907 Concerning Bombardment by Naval Forces in Time of War (Hague Convention IX) opened for signature 18 October 1907 (entered into force 26 January 1910) includes in the category of military objectives the following: "military works, military or naval establishments, depots of arms or war matériel, workshops or plants which could be utilized for the needs of the hostile fleet or army, and the ships of war in the harbour, are not, however, included in this prohibition [...]."

[157] Article 24 of the Rules concerning the Control of Wireless Telegraphy in Time of War and Air Warfare. Drafted by a Commission of Jurists at The Hague, December 1922–February 1923.

[158] Article 8(1) of the Hague Convention for the Protection of Cultural Property in the Event of Armed Conflict opened for signature 14 May 1954, UNTS 249 (entered into force 7 August 1956).

[159] Capone 2023, pp. 746–748; Sandoz et al. 1987, pp. 630–632 (emphasis added).

[160] Ibid., p. 631.

[161] Ibid., p. 638.

received strong, although not so widely shared, criticism from authors like Dinstein who points out that "it is regrettable that the wording is abstract and generic, and no list of specific military objectives is provided (if only on an illustrative, non-exhaustive, basis)".[162] The text of Article 52(2) lends itself to "divergent interpretations" in application, and, as witnessed in many circumstances it is undeniable that "[a]mbiguous language encourages abuse".[163] An example of this is well represented by the US position, according to which "[e]conomic targets of the enemy that indirectly but effectively support and sustain the enemy's war-fighting capability may also be attacked".[164] More in detail, Dinstein believes, and this author agrees with his view, that in order to avoid vagueness and the inability to anticipate future scenarios, the drafters should have provided a so-called "composite definition", i.e. combining an abstract statement with a non-exhaustive catalogue of concrete illustrations. The rationale for this approach is that no abstract definition unaccompanied by actual examples can possibly offer a practical solution to real problems emerging on the battlefield.[165] One of these real problems is represented by the incessant resort to attacks on dual-use objects and the devastating impact of this military strategy on the civilian population, which, instead, should be spared and protected to the maximum extent possible.

1.3.3 *Dual-Use Objects:* Tertium non Datur*?*

Commenting on the excessively vague and potentially very broad formulation of Article 52(2) of API, Cassese's often-quoted take on the matter openly condemns the definition of military objectives for being "so sweeping that it can cover practically anything".[166] Due to the abstract character of the definition enshrined in Article 52(2) it is often argued that there are some objects that lie "within the grey area of protection as they serve both civilian and military functions".[167] When a certain object is used for both military and civilian purposes, it may be claimed that even a secondary or very limited military use renders it a military objective.[168] As is well

[162] Dinstein 2004, p. 84.

[163] Rosenblad 1979, p. 71.

[164] Dinstein 2004, pp. 95–96. The author refers to the U.S. Commander's Handbook on the Law of Naval Operations, which substitutes the words "military action" with the formulation "war-fighting or war-sustaining". The illustrative case offered is that of the destruction of raw cotton within Confederate territory by Union forces during the Civil War on the ground that sale of cotton provided funds for almost all Confederate arms and ammunition. U.S. Department of Defense, Law of War Manual (Office of General Counsel Department of Defense 2015) para 5.7.2, http://archive.defense.gov/pubs/law-of-war-manual-june-2015.pdf (accessed 18 February 2024). See also Goodman 2016, pp. 667–671.

[165] Dinstein 2004, pp. 84–85.

[166] Cassese 2001, p. 339.

[167] Waxman 2000, p. 20.

[168] Sassòli and Cameron 2006, p. 35.

known, this position decreases instead of increasing the level of protection afforded to the civilian population, especially in urban environments and populated areas, which contain plenty of shared military-civilian resources and house many dual-use facilities. Military and civilian populations often use common power sources, transportation networks, and telecommunications systems. Moreover, as already mentioned above, in the cyberspace the distinction between civilian objects and military objectives is pointless as the military deploys the very same cyber infrastructure that is used for civilian purposes and thus every component of the cyber infrastructure is *de facto* a "dual-use" object.[169]

Despite the self-evident relevance of this category of objects, as opposed to the definition of the terms "military objectives" and "civilian objects", there is no equivalent definition or even a reference to the term dual-use objects in the Geneva Conventions or their Additional Protocols. Greenwood, voicing the mainstream approach, sums up that "there is no intermediate category of 'dual use' objects: *either something is a military object, or it is not*".[170] Lacking a legal definition, or even a "working" one, these objects have been described in different ways. Some authors have depicted them as objects which are not "normally dedicated" to the civilian population, and hence do not immediately enjoy the benefit of doubt under API Article 52(3).[171] Yet, and quite interestingly, in the first Draft Protocol drawn up by the ICRC in 1970–1971, the phrase "installations and means of transport," which would have caught many "dual-use" objects, was included in the original provision prescribing the protection of civilian objects.[172] At the Diplomatic Conference, however, the Dutch delegation objected that "installations and means of transport [...] could subsequently contribute to part of the military effort and therefore be attacked". As the Dutch envoy suggested deleting any list of examples of civilian objects, the idea immediately found large support by many delegations. A working group then drafted a new provision, which no longer included "installations and means of transport", but retained the other examples currently mentioned in Article 52(3), i.e. "place of worship, a house or other dwelling or a school".

Leaving for a moment the question of the correct identification of the object aside, all the other IHL principles certainly apply when targeting a dual-use object. However, there is a lack of uniformity concerning the extent to which they can truly and effectively contribute to enhancing the protection of dual-use objects. In other words, the existing international legal framework blatantly fails to come to terms with the relevance of dual-use objects. Wider considerations based on State practice, theories advanced by the current doctrine and developments triggered by the rise of cyber warfare and new technologies, reveal a tendency to reconsider the legitimacy of attack on dual-use targets and demand consideration for the long-term, unintended effects of attacking them. Based on the observations already shared, which concern both the theoretical dimension as well as the more practical aspects of the issue,

---

[169] Geiß and Lahmann 2012, p. 383.

[170] Greenwood 1993, p. 73 (emphasis added).

[171] Chakrabarty 2020, p. 26.

[172] Sandoz et al. 1987, p. 633, para 2004.

in this author's view it is helpful to identify the objects that, more often than not, raise a number of question marks with respect to their status. This exercise, to a different degree and for different purposes, has already been carried out by authors like Dinstein, Sassòli and Schmitt,[173] but it is worth grappling with a more focussed analysis before seeking to lay down the foundations for the new paradigm presented in this book.

As a preliminary caveat, it is important to highlight that some objects shall be ruled out *tout court* from the list of "dual-use" objects, due to their objective and intrinsic impossibility to fulfil the criteria needed to be lawfully identified as military targets. The ban covers the civilian morale because, as it will be discussed more extensively later on,[174] under IHL it is not allowed to attack civilians (who are not directly participating in hostilities) or civilian targets for the purpose of undercutting morale. The ban applies also when the action could be explained along so-called "utilitarian" lines, e.g. if attacks designed to destroy civilian morale led to an early termination of the hostilities.[175] Also, some States, *in primis* the US, adopt a broad targeting practice which includes amongst the lawful targets economic objects whose financial revenue is used to sustain the enemy's war effort.[176] This strategy, strongly criticised by several authors,[177] is not in compliance with the law determining what constitutes a legitimate military objective. Furthermore, it is possible to exclude immaterial items too, e.g. computer data, which are not an "object" under IHL.[178]

There are several objects that are usually referred to as "dual-use", due to their ability to simultaneously fulfil both civilian and military functions. Notably, their inclusion in the target list of a belligerent party is justified on the basis of the definition of military objective that is enshrined in Article 52(2) as well as customary IHL. However, and specifically in relation to dual-use objects, there are a number of widely shared assumptions that will be punctually debunked in the course of this work. In the present introductory chapter, which mainly aims at setting the scene, some of these assumptions will be summarised while briefly presenting the objects that are traditionally considered as "dual-use":

- *Electrical power systems:* Historically, electric power production has been viewed as a critical target set in every war since the early German Zeppelin raids on England during WWI.[179] There are plenty of examples of attacks on power systems during armed conflict, the most recent one is represented by the attacks carried out by Russia against Ukrainian power grids,[180] with Russia's Ministry of Defence going as far as qualifying "energy systems" as on par with "military

[173] Dinstein 2004, pp. 94–99; Sassòli 2003, pp. 6–9; Schmitt 2006, pp. 280–288.
[174] See Chap. 3, Sect. 3.2.1 in this book.
[175] Harvard Air and Missile Warfare Manual 2013, Rule 18, p. 111.
[176] See Chap. 3, Sect. 3.2.1 in this book.
[177] Reetz 2022, pp. 441–446.
[178] Pompson 2023, pp. 356–363.
[179] Crawford 1997, p. 111.
[180] Capone 2023.

command systems" and "arsenals", both of which are unambiguously lawful military objectives by nature.[181] In addition to the most recent conflicts, the lineage of attacks against electrical power systems is certainly long,[182] including the 1952 US operation against North Korea, which led to the country's total black-out for over two weeks, with over 90% of its electric power supply eliminated. This resulted in the cutting off of the many thousands of small, virtually home-operated, industrial facilities across North Korea's territory.[183] During the First Gulf War, the Coalition's air campaign conducted in 1991 treated as a military target the integrated Iraqi national grid generating and distributing electricity, used by both the armed forces and civilians.[184] As reported by Schmitt,[185] to justify the attacks the US DoD at the time explained that

> electricity is vital to the functioning of a modern military and industrial power such as Iraq, and disrupting the electrical supply *can make destruction of other facilities unnecessary.* Disrupting the electricity supply to key Iraqi facilities degraded a wide variety of crucial capabilities, from the radar sites that warned of Coalition air strikes, to the refrigeration used to preserve biological weapons (BW), to nuclear weapons production facilities. To do this effectively required the disruption of virtually the entire Iraqi electric grid, to prevent the rerouting of power around damaged nodes.[186]

In other words, and according to the US DoD, the "dual-use" nature of the electric grid legitimised the attacks, despite the impact on the civilian population.[187] This view is still predominantly accepted and electrical power systems continue to appear in the targeted lists of belligerent parties.

- *Industrial plants in general:* Dinstein, alongside other authoritative voices, stresses that it is frequently difficult to "draw a stark distinction between military and civilian industries".[188] He provides the examples of tractors for agricultural use, which can swiftly be replaced on the assembly line by tanks, or even of children's toys factories that may become "tomorrow's leading manufacturer of electronic precision-guided munitions".[189] Besides their intended use and the fact that production *could be* switched to war materials during hostilities; the economic value of war-sustaining industries is also (mistakenly) used as a ground for attack, as it famously happened with the Confederate cotton production during the US Civil War.[190] It is worth recalling that most States already have in place a defense industrial base (DIB), meaning that in case of war they will

[181] Schmitt 2022.

[182] Ibid.

[183] Crawford 1997, pp. 119–120.

[184] Dinstein 2004, p. 96. See Chap. 2, Sect. 2.4 in this book.

[185] Schmitt 2022.

[186] US DoD 1992, p. 623.

[187] Ibid.

[188] Dinstein 2004, p. 96.

[189] Ibid.

[190] Schmitt 2006, p. 281.

expand their DIB capabilities domestically in order to increase the production of weapons and munitions, as it happened in Ukraine since Russia's full-scale invasion in 2022.[191] In spite of this, industrial plans remain a frequent target in armed conflicts. For instance, in the beginning of June 2022, it was reported that more than 25 big Ukrainian industrial companies were damaged or fully destroyed by Russian attacks. The most prominent, and discussed, examples are the ammonia producer AZOT, the Coke and Chemistry concern in Avdiivka and the centre of metallurgy AZOVSTAL in Mariupol.[192]

- *Oil refining, distribution and storage facilities:* According to Green, and other authors like Dinstein,[193] further assumptions are frequently made concerning oil installations of various types, as "there would seem to be little doubt that [they] are in fact legitimate military objectives open to destruction by any belligerent".[194] Oil, and more generally power sources of any nature, were also included in Hays Parks' famous list of legitimate targets attacked during the 1945 Allied strategic bombing campaign.[195] Furthermore, oil refineries, distribution, and storage are also encompassed amongst the "organic essentials" in Warden's Five Strategic Rings model, a theory that lays down the foundation for the modern approach to targeting and that will be examined in detail in Chap. 2 of this book.[196] The First Gulf War amounts to the most well-known example of armed conflict in which oil refining, distribution and storage facilities have been identified as the lawful targets of extensive air strikes. Commenting on the coalition forces' attacks against Iraqi oil refineries and major oil storage facilities, Gen. Schwarzkopf' statement to the press confirmed the US-led coalition's qualification of these items as military objectives, by explaining "I told you, *we went after militarily significant targets.* We didn't want to destroy their oil industry, but we certainly wanted to make sure they didn't have a lot of gasoline for their military vehicles".[197]
- *Broadcasting stations:* The Hague Cultural Property Convention of 1954 refers to any "broadcasting station"[198] as a military objective. The provision clearly includes civilian TV and radio stations, but it can be thought to refer to the media in general. Dinstein notes that in wartime, "control of civilian broadcasting stations can at any time be assumed by the military apparatus, which may wish to use it in communications (e.g., summoning reservists to service), in pursuit of psychological warfare, and for other purposes".[199] The ICRC in the context of its 1956

[191] Stepanenko et al. 2024.

[192] Shumilova et al. 2023, p. 580.

[193] Dinstein 2004, p. 96 "[i]n the final analysis, despite their civilian bearings, all of them can be deemed to constitute the infrastructure of the military industry".

[194] Green 1992, p. 233.

[195] Parks 1995, p. 145.

[196] See Chap. 2, Sect. 2.3 in this book.

[197] Human Rights Watch 1991, pp. 283–284 (emphasis added).

[198] Article 8(1) of the Hague Convention for the Protection of Cultural Property in the Event of Armed Conflict opened for signature 14 May 1954, UNTS 249 (entered into force 7 August 1956).

[199] Dinstein 2004, p. 98.

Draft Rules for the Limitation of the Dangers incurred by the Civilian Population in Time of War included in the list of military objectives also "installations of broadcasting and television stations".[200] Furthermore, several authors argue that the telecommunication network is "clearly of military importance".[201] Nonetheless, some prominent voices have questioned this approach. For example, Bothe rightly suggests that it is not always certain "whether each facility using telecommunications equipment that may be found in the country belongs to a network of military significance".[202] Hence, he asks if there is a kind of presumption that telecommunication facilities are always, unless the contrary is apparent, related to the military network.[203] This issue has been raised in the aftermath of the attack against the television facilities in Belgrade during the NATO bombing campaign,[204] which will be discussed in Chap. 2.

- *Traffic infrastructures:* This specific typology of objects, commonly labelled as "dual-use" in the context of an armed conflict, covers all the strategic arteries of transportation including roads, bridges, railways, airports, ports, tunnels etc… Also in this case, the widespread stance on the matter is that if not by nature, most lines of transportation may qualify as military objectives by purpose, use or—above all—location.[205] In particular, in relation to bridges there seems to exist a diffuse supposition that every "significant waterway or similar geophysical obstruction to traffic (like a deep ravine) must be perceived as a possible military barrier", and therefore "it comes a time when the strategy of either belligerent would dictate that all bridges (including pedestrian overpasses) across the obstacle have to be destroyed or neutralized".[206] Dinstein even claims that there "is nothing wrong in a military policy striving to effect a fragmentation of enemy land forces through the destruction of all bridges – however minor in themselves – spanning a wide river",[207] as happened in the Gulf War in 1991 with the destruction of the bridges over the Euphrates River. In furtherance of this view, Fenrick goes as far as affirming that "[i]f six bridges cross a river, and the armed forces only require two to function effectively, is it permissible to destroy all six? The answer is probably yes."[208]
- *Water systems and installations:* IHL applicable in armed conflicts contains no specific regulations on water protection, although it does enshrine a number of rules relating to the subject.[209] Notably, the general protection under the law applicable to armed conflicts extends to more than international watercourses,

[200] Ronzitti 2000, p. 1024.
[201] Bothe 2002, p. 179.
[202] Ibid.
[203] Ibid.
[204] See David 2000, p. 81; Sassòli and Cameron 2006, p. 55.
[205] Dinstein 2004, pp. 92–93.
[206] Ibid.
[207] Ibid., p. 93.
[208] Fenrick 2000, p. 72.
[209] Gleick 2019, p. 1737.

and, as reported by the Zemmali,[210] the four main prohibitions include: the ban on employing poison or poisonous weapons;[211] the ban on destroying, confiscating or expropriating enemy property;[212] the ban on destroying objects indispensable to the survival of the civilian population;[213] and the ban on attacking works or installations containing dangerous forces,[214] which covers dams, dykes and nuclear electrical generating sections. As noted by the ICRC, there has been a significant increase in attacks on water distribution systems and infrastructures—including dams, pipelines, water treatment plants—which make access to freshwater more and more difficult to achieve for the civilian population.[215] Water facilities, including water treatment plants, have been directly attacked during armed conflicts and/or they have been damaged or destroyed by indirect attacks.[216] For instance, in the course of the First Gulf War the destruction of the electrical power generating plants rendered the majority of water treatment plants in the country inoperable.[217] It has been reported that targeting electrical facilities in Iraq led to the deaths of between 40,000 and 110,000 civilians due to lack of access to water. Sassòli and Cameron rightly ask if this consequence should have been taken into account before launching the attacks? And, if so, how and by whom.[218] As expected, military planners of that campaign defended their actions, and when asked about the damage indirectly caused to water installations in Baghdad, maintained that the "water treatment facilities were never directly targeted", and that "[t]he electricity did impact on this problem and it was not foreseen".[219] Similarly, albeit still difficult to properly assess due to the ongoing conflict between Russia and Ukraine, many water infrastructures such as dams and

---

[210] Zemmali 1995, p. 605.

[211] Poisoning or rendering water resources unfit for use will jeopardize vital human needs. In fact, the Geneva Conventions of 1949, API and APII recognized the importance of water and sanitation for the health and survival of the persons they protect. Articles 20, 26, 29 and 46 Geneva Convention III; Articles 85, 89 and 127 Geneva Convention IV; Articles 54 and 55 API; and Articles 5 and 14 APII. See Tignino 2010, pp. 658-662; and Kebebew 2022, p. 1226.

[212] Articles 55 and 56 of the Geneva Convention IV.

[213] Article 54(1) and (2) of Additional Protocol I.

[214] Article 56 of Additional Protocol I.

[215] ICRC, Having Access to Water Is Increasingly a Matter of Survival in Conflict Zones, 21 March 2022, https://www.icrc.org/en/document/having-access-water-increasingly-matter-survival-conflict-zones (accessed 7 August 2024).

[216] Reported violence associated with freshwater resources and water infrastructure, from 2500 BC to the present, is tracked by the open-source database Water Conflict Chronology (Pacific Institute). At present, the database consists of more than 1300 entries, covering three separate categories: (1) water as a "trigger" (the control of or access to water leads to violence), (2) water as a "weapon" (water is used as a weapon during a conflict) and (3) water as a "casualty" (direct attack on water systems) of violence. See Pacific Institute, Water Conflict Chronology, https://www.worldwater.org/water-conflict/ (accessed 25 July 2024).

[217] Human Rights Watch 1991, p. 178.

[218] Sassòli and Cameron 2006, p. 65.

[219] Lewis 2003, p. 506.

reservoirs, water supply and treatment systems and subsurface mines in Ukraine have been impacted or are at risk from military actions.[220]

It should be noted that the list presented here does not aim at being exhaustive, but only at highlighting the typologies of objects that are traditionally regarded as dual-use ones. Also included in this category are space objects,[221] such as launch systems and satellites, that, due the widespread militarisation of space operations, are increasingly relied upon to support military activities.[222] Exactly like any other military operation conducted in the context of an armed conflict, military operations in, from, to or through outer space are bound by IHL and its principles.[223] Most commercial space systems nowadays serve military and civilian purposes simultaneously, providing services to the civilian population and militaries alike, such as communications or products of commercial space systems used by the military, including imagery and data from Earth observation satellites. The unprecedented progress made by commercial space actors in recent years has "dramatically expanded the landscape of options available to military actors seeking to engage in or enhance their space activities".[224] The ongoing armed conflict in Ukraine has been providing a highly relevant example of the practice of hosting, embedding, or obtaining military capabilities on or from otherwise civil/commercial satellites like the Starlink and OneWeb system. It has been reported that early in the war Ukraine's military forces actively relied on SpaceX's Starlink constellation to support a variety of military operations,[225] including "drop[ping] bombs on Russian forward positions".[226] Even though the dual-use of space systems does indeed pose specific challenges to the distinction between civilian objects and military objectives, the view shared by the majority of authors is based on the assumption that warfare, despite its ever-changing character, has a constant nature.[227] This means that, notwithstanding the "myriad challenges in identifying military objectives" during armed conflict in outer space,[228] the findings of this research and the paradigm shift can, indeed, be applied also to this scenario.

In conclusion, when it comes to so-called dual-use objects, the problem can be summarised as follows: there seems to be an "unofficial list" of objects qualifying as military objectives in most conflicts, if not all, fought around the world. It exists,

---

[220] Shumilova et al. 2023, p. 578.

[221] Schmitt and Tinkler 2020.

[222] Berrang 2023.

[223] Ibid.

[224] Beaulieu 2023, p. 3.

[225] More recently SpaceX has limited Ukraine's ability to use its satellite internet service for military purposes - after reports that Kyiv has used it to control drones. FitzGerald (2023) Ukraine war: Elon Musk's SpaceX firm bars Kyiv from using Starlink tech for drone control, https://www.bbc.com/news/world-europe-64579267# (accessed 23 February 2024).

[226] Beaulieu 2023, pp. 3–4.

[227] Klein 2016.

[228] Schmitt and Tinkler 2020.

hence, a ubiquitous "presumption of military status" extended to dual-use objects.[229] Therefore, deciding to exclude them *prima facie* from the group of potential targets is unacceptable from a military point of view. At the same time, including them in the group without any restrictions is in contrast with the overarching goal of protecting the civilian population.[230] Moving from these considerations, this work aims at challenging the mainstream approach to dual-use objects, dissecting the various factors and elements that have led to this mystification and building a new paradigm, more coherent with the key tenets of the IHL framework in force.

1.4 The Paradigm Shift in a Nutshell: Arguing for the Centrality of the Civilian Function of Dual-Use Objects and the Transversal Application of the Reasonable Military Commander Standard

The present book proposes a shift in the way dual-use objects are treated under IHL. The reasons for advocating for a novel approach are manifold. In part they have already been addressed in the previous (sub-)sections and they will be further discussed in the course of this analysis. At the heart of these efforts lies the unquestionable need to strengthen the protection of civilians and civilian objects in situations of armed conflicts, being mindful of the devastating effects of modern warfare and of the limits ascribable to the interpretation and implementation of the current legal framework. The paradigm shift that this book aims to unpack does not promote changes to the existing IHL set of principles and norms. In fact, the present work is mainly concerned with enhancing the *corpus juris* that is already in place. To this end the perspective *de lege ferenda* is incorporated only to the extent to which the term is not referred to "desirable" law, but rather to "emergent" law.[231] This expression, which was used by the ICJ in the *North Sea* case,[232] describes the phenomenon of accumulation of State practice which can already be observed, although it is not yet sufficient, or in any case lacks the accompanying *opinio juris*, to become binding customary law. Furthermore, the book relies on relevant examples, case law and the contribution of the doctrine to explain the paradigm shift and outline in detail its key elements.

This book will, hopefully, be filling a significant gap in the IHL scholarship. So far, the topic of dual-use objects has remained unexplored and only incidentally considered by academics and experts. Through an exhaustive and multilayered study, the present work will shed light on some crucial aspects. The first aspect concerns the

[229] Dinstein refers to this presumption when describing the situation of bridges under IHL, but the reasoning can be applied to all dual-use objects. Dinstein 2004, p. 93.

[230] Kalshoven and Zegveld 2011, p. 106.

[231] Thirlway 2001, p. 17.

[232] ICJ, *North Sea Continental Shelf Cases* (*Federal Republic of Germany v. Denmark; Federal Republic of Germany v. Netherlands*), 1969 ICJ Rep 3, p. 41, para 70.

mainstream approach to dual-use objects, that this book openly challenges, and its genesis. The development of the mainstream approach is arguably linked to different factors, including the militarisation of civilian activities, the changing characteristics of warfare and the rise of new military theories. This work focuses especially on the "Five Strategic Ring" model, advanced by Colonel John A. Warden USAF, which laid down the foundations for Operation Desert Storm, during the First Gulf War, and Operation Allied Force, during the NATO's bombing campaign against the Former Yugoslavia. As these two examples will show, the targeting of dual-use objects, including bridges, electrical power stations, oil refineries, and radio and television stations, is not an exception in armed conflicts, but rather a common strategy of warfare. This notwithstanding, the resort to this tactic does not leave experts indifferent. On the contrary, it has triggered extensive criticism and, overall, more questions than answers. The second main aspect that this book aims to discuss in as much detail as possible, is the problematic application of the notion of military objectives, as defined in Article 52(2) of API. Lying at the heart of the principle of distinction and representing the first bastion of IHL, the validity and accuracy of this concept is often taken for granted, ignoring most of the criticalities that are associated with its interpretation and implementation, which have a ripple effect when it comes to dual-use objects and their protection. To overcome some of the limitations stemming from the current understanding of what represents a lawful target, and, more broadly, from the ambiguous status of dual-use objects, this study proposes a working definition that will be presented at the culmination of the inquiry on the careless resort to the military objective label.

A third essential aspect tackled in this book is the importance of the civilian function that dual-use objects fulfil.[233] Although often mentioned, this crucial point rarely emerges in the discussion and in any case, it has never been duly examined against the backdrop of IHL. In order to do so, the present book analyses the civilian function of dual-use objects in relation with all the key IHL principles, i.e. distinction, precautions, proportionality and military necessity. Finally, this work sheds light on the "reasonableness military commander" standard—which in the past has been explicitly resorted to only to assess proportionality-[234] presenting it as an overarching and transversal test that must be applied to each of the core IHL principles. This marks a pivotal departure from the prevailing doctrine and represents a pillar of the paradigm shift, which, in line with the evolving process of the "humanisation of IHL",[235] considers individual actors in a highly prominent position. Consistently, those called to plan and/or execute an attack against a dual-use object are expected, and requested, to act in full compliance with the relevant IHL norms and with the reasonableness standard, that shall guide and inform their choices and actions.

---

[233] See Chap. 4, Sect. 4.1 of this book.

[234] Gillard 2018, pp. 21–22.

[235] Meron 2000.

1.5 Methodology and Structure of the Book

The present work, which aims at orienting the discussion on dual-use objects in a new direction, relies on methodological approaches specific to the international legal field.[236] This book boldly stands apart from the mainstreaming approach to "dual-use" objects under IHL, and in order to do so, it resorts to descriptive and doctrinal research methods. As is well known, the scope of descriptive research is depicting the state of the art in a specific field of research. Obviously, this methodological approach is closely intertwined with the doctrinal technique, as it refers to "what law is or what it is not".[237] Applying the doctrinal method requires a thorough review of both primary sources, i.e. legal documents encompassing laws and judicial decisions, and secondary ones, i.e. the existing scholarship. Doctrinal research is notably concerned with delving into the state of the art,[238] in particular in relation to the definition and application of legal concepts. This first chapter has already contributed to this achievement by presenting the definitions of civilian objects and military objectives that are essential to the development of the present research. This study, in fact, focuses on a category which is not (yet) legally defined, i.e. that of dual-use objects, but *de facto* exists within the current legal framework. This peculiar status calls for an analysis that combines a deductive exercise—giving substance to what the relevant international norms already say—and an inductive reasoning, drawing conclusions from specific cases to outline the mainstream and generalist approach to dual-use objects.

The latter task will be conducted in Chap. 2 of this work that retraces how the predominant approach to dual-use objects—which sees them merely as military objectives and only occasionally evokes their ability to fulfil civilian functions—has come to light and for which reasons. The analysis focuses first on the key elements and circumstances that have led to the current prevailing position, including the role played by the development of relevant theories which, from von Clausewitz's onwards, have constantly sought to emphasise the importance of the selection of certain targets. The primacy of aerial warfare has increasingly exacerbated the rise of *Blitzkrieg* first and "smart wars" later. Placing the "fog of victory"[239] at the forefront, early air power theorists, like Douhet, even argued that "the most humane way to end war was a swift attack on the most vulnerable element of society: the populace".[240] The tendency to look at the enemy as a "system" often prioritises efficiency over respect for IHL rules, culminating in the affirmation of Warden's Five Rings Model. The Five Rings theory represents the epitome of the dangerous gap between military strategy and IHL, which manifests itself especially in relation to dual-use objects. Unlike many of his predecessors, Warden was able to translate his ideas into actual combat planning for operations in the 1991 Persian Gulf War, leaving a footprint on

---

[236] Koskenniemi 2007; Deplano and Tsagouris 2021.

[237] Vibhute and Aynalem 2009, p. 16; Leontiev 2023, p. 38.

[238] Hutchinson and Duncan 2012.

[239] Blum 2013, p. 391.

[240] Chun 2006, p. 312.

subsequent military operations, like the NATO bombing campaign against the Federal Republic of Yugoslavia (FRY). Those two conflicts are analysed in Chap. 2 to provide an overview of the (very similar) military strategies adopted, their justifications, the legal assessments done *ex post*, and the growing critical voices that have been raised to condemn the inclusion in the targeting lists of objects essential for the survival of the civilian population. Although the disapproval triggered by attacks carried out against vital infrastructures, including electrical power grids and water installations, has emerged quite strongly,[241] so far it has never been unequivocal, with prominent authors like Dinstein supporting, at least to some degree, the mainstream approach to dual-use objects. Still grappling with the theoretical underpinnings of the key issues at stake, Chap. 3 questions the swift and uncritical qualification of dual-use objects as military objectives, starting with a thorough reflection on the limits connected to the definition and its application. Concerning the first aspect, the analysis tackles in particular the contested notions of "military advantage" and "attack as a whole" as they are essential to understand the shortcomings of the definition in force vis-a-vis the principle of distinction. In relation to the latter, the inquiry focuses on two examples of misapplication of the definition of military objectives. The two cases analysed, namely the Eritrea-Ethiopia Claims Commission's award on the aerial bombardment of the Hirgigo Power Station and the findings enshrined in the Goldstone Report issued by the United Nations Fact Finding Mission on the 2008–2009 Gaza Conflict, offer an interesting insight into the pervasiveness of considerations that are not of a military nature and that influence the understanding of what can be regarded as a legitimate target, and thus lawfully attacked, and what instead must be protected. Chapter 3 ends with the drafting of a "working definition" of dual-use objects, which obviously does not fill the normative vacuum, but has, nonetheless, an important role to play. The definition identifies the key elements that differentiate dual-use objects from military objectives, with the purpose of sharpening the distinction and triggering a more uniform and coherent approach to the matter.

Chapter 4 finally delves into the paradigm shift. It begins with an inquiry into the civilian function that dual-use objects play and the importance of this aspect to restate the necessity to set them apart from military objectives and to promote a more effective application of the existing IHL rules. The analysis covers the rules that are immediately associated with the protection of dual-use objects as well as the key principles at the heart of the entire IHL framework. Chapter 5 provides the reader with an in-depth examination of the other essential element of the paradigm shift, i.e. the "reasonable military commander standard". First, the inquiry delves into the notion of reasonableness, which doubles both as a theoretical concept and as a legal standard that can be applied in practical contexts, including situations of armed conflict. It is important to stress that the notion remains controversial and scantly analysed, despite being increasingly employed by international courts and tribunals, including the ICJ. In the IHL domain the reasonable military commander standard has

[241] Authors like Kalshoven, Sassòli, Gillard, Shue and Wippman, and Schmitt, have been vocal, to differing extents and moving from disparate perspectives, in advocating for strengthening the protection of dual-use objects.

received some attention, mainly thanks to the Report of the Committee established to review the NATO bombing campaign against the FRY,[242] and the case law of the ICTY. The standard, however, has been mainly considered in proportionality assessments, and rarely in different situations. Second, by rebutting this very limited approach and arguing for the relevance of the reasonableness standard as a transversal one, the present work develops a "sliding scale" of reasonableness, determining for each IHL principle a specific threshold. This effort does not only aim at satisfying a theoretical ambition, on the contrary it also serves the purpose of triggering practical consequences and contributing to the enhancement of a more uniform application of the reasonableness standard within the IHL framework.

Chapter 6 of this volume contains some concluding observations that aim both at providing an overview of the main findings of the book and pointing to the potential ramifications of this inquiry, by introducing the discussion on the new paradigm's application to new weapons and technologies.

References

Akande D (2010) Clearing the Fog of War? The ICRC's Interpretive Guidance on Direct Participation in Hostilities. International and Comparative Law Quarterly 59(1):180–192

Aldrich G H (1991) Why the United States of America should ratify additional Protocol I. In: Delissen A, Tanja G (eds) Humanitarian law and armed conflict: challenges ahead—Essays in Honour of Frits Kalshoven. Martinus Nijhoff Publishers, Dordrecht, pp 127–144

AOAV (2021) A Decade of Explosive Harm. https://aoav.org.uk/wp-content/uploads/2021/05/A-Decade-of-Explosive-Violence-Harm.pdf. Accessed 3 February 2024

Asi Y, Mills D, Greenough P G et al. (2024) 'Nowhere and no one is safe': spatial analysis of damage to critical civilian infrastructure in the Gaza Strip during the first phase of the Israeli military campaign, 7 October to 22 November 2023. Conflict and Health 18: 1–13

Bagshaw S (2023) The 2022 Political Declaration on the Use of Explosive Weapons in Populated Areas: A tool for protecting the environment in armed conflict? International Review of the Red Cross 105 (924): 1293–1312

Beaulieu D P (2023) State Practice and Military Objectives: International Humanitarian Law Regarding Military Applications of Otherwise Civil/Commercial Satellites. Duke Law, Essay Series Number 16, 9 January 2023, https://sites.duke.edu/lawfire/files/2023/01/Maj-Danny-Beaulieu-Civil-Commercial-Satellites-Paper.pdf. Accessed 10 February 2024

Belt SW (2000) Missiles over Kosovo: emergence, lex lata, of a customary norm requiring the use of precision guided munitions in urban areas. Netherlands Law Review 47:115–175

Berrang S (2023) How would IHL apply to hostilities in outer space?, 2 November 2023, https://blogs.icrc.org/law-and-policy/wp-content/uploads/sites/102/2023/11/How-would-IHL-apply-to-hostilities-in-outer-space_.pdf. Accessed 2 February 2024

Blum G (2013) The Fog of Victory. The European Journal of International Law 24 (1): 391–421

Boer R, Zwijnenburg W (2020) Exploring Environmental Harm from Explosive Weapons in Populated Areas, 28 May 2020, PAX. https://paxforpeace.nl/news/blogs/exploring-environmental-harm-from-explosive-weapons-in-populated-areas. Accessed 5 February 2024

[242] Final Report to the Prosecutor by the Committee Established to Review the NATO Bombing Campaign against the Federal Republic of Yugoslavia, (13 June 2000), (hereinafter OTP Report) reprinted in (2000) ILM 39:1257.

Bothe M (2002) Targeting. In: Wall A E (ed) Legal and Ethical Lessons in NATO's Kosovo Campaign, Volume 78, US Naval War College's International Law Studies, pp 173–187
Bothe M (ed) (2013) New Rules for Victims of Armed Conflicts: Commentary on the Two 1977 Protocols Additional to the Geneva Conventions of 1949. Brill | Nijhoff, The Hague
Byron C (2011) International Humanitarian Law and Bombing Campaigns: Legitimate Military Objectives and Excessive Collateral Damage. In: Schmitt M, Arimatsu L, McCormack T (eds) Yearbook of International Humanitarian Law - 2010. T.M.C. Asser Press, The Hague, pp 175–211
Byron C (2022) Direct participation in hostilities. In: Sayapin S, Atadjanov R, Kadam U, Kemp G, Zambrana-Tévar N, Quénivet N (eds) International Conflict and Security Law - A Research Handbook. T.M.C. Asser Press, The Hague, pp 277–300
Capone F (2023) The Wave of Russian Attacks on Ukraine's Power Infrastructures: An Opportunity to Infuse Meaningfulness into the Notion of "Dual-use Objects"? European Papers 8(2): 741–754
Cassese A (2001) International Law. Oxford University Press, Oxford
Chakrabarty I (2020) Reformulating Rules On Dual Object Targeting. NYU Journal of International Law & Politics Online, 52: 24–38
Chetail V (2002) The Fundamental Principles of Humanitarian Law Through the Case Law of the International Court of Justice. Refugee Survey Quarterly 21(3): 199–211
Chetail V (2003) The contribution of the International Court of Justice to international humanitarian law. International Review of the Red Cross 85(850): 235–289
Chun C K S (2006) John Warden's Five Ring Model and the Indirect Approach to War. Strategic Studies Institute, US Army War College. https://www.jstor.org/stable/pdf/resrep12025.30.pdf. Accessed 20 February 2024
Crawford J W (1997) The law of noncombatant immunity and the targeting of national electrical power systems. The Fletcher Forum of World Affairs 21(2): 101–119
David E (2000) Respect for the Principle of Distinction in the Kosovo War. Yearbook of International Humanitarian Law 3:81–107
Deplano R, Tsagouris N (eds) (2021) Research Methods in International Law A Handbook. Edward Elgar Publishing, Cheltenham Glos
Dinstein Y (2002) Legitimate Military Objectives Under the Current Jus in Bello. In: Wall A E (ed) Legal and Ethical Lessons in NATO's Kosovo Campaign, Volume 78, US Naval War College's International Law Studies, pp 139–172
Dinstein Y (2004) The conduct of hostilities under the law of international armed conflict. Cambridge University Press, Cambridge
Dörmann K (2002) Applicability of the Additional Protocols to Computer Network Attacks. In: Schmitt M N, O'Donnel B T (eds) Computer Network Attack and International Law: War Studies. Volume 76, US Naval War College's International Law Studies, pp 1–12
Doswald-Beck L (1995) San Remo Manual on International Law applicable to Armed Conflicts at Sea. Grotius Publications, Cambridge University Press, Cambridge
Doswald-Beck L (1997) International humanitarian law and the Advisory Opinion of the International Court of Justice on the legality of the threat or use of nuclear weapons. International Review of the Red Cross 316(2): 37–54
Drew P (2017) The Law of Maritime Blockade: Past, Present, and Future. Oxford University Press, Oxford
Fenrick W J (2000) The Law Applicable to Targeting and Proportionality after Operation Allied Force: a View from the Outside. Yearbook of International Humanitarian Law 3: 53–80
Fleck D (1997) Strategic Bombing and the Definition of Military Objectives. Israel Yearbook on Human Rights 27: 41–64
Geiß R, Lahmann H (2012) Cyber warfare: applying the principle of distinction in an interconnected space. Israel Law Review 45(3): 381–399
Gill T, Heinsch R, Geiss R (2014) ILA study group 'The conduct of hostilities and international humanitarian law: challenges of 21st century warfare' - Interim report. International

Law Association. https://www.ila-hq.org/en_GB/documents/ila-report-2014-conduct-of-hostilities-study-group-revised. Accessed 12 February 2024

Gillard EC (2018) Proportionality in the Conduct of Hostilities: The Incidental Harm Side of the Assessment. Research paper, Chatham House. https://www.chathamhouse.org/sites/default/files/publications/research/2018-12-10-proportionality-conduct-hostilities-incidental-harm-gillard-final.pdf. Accessed 5 February 2024

Gleick P H (2019) Water as a Weapon and Casualty of Conflict: Freshwater and International Humanitarian Law. Water Resources Management 33:1737–1751

Goodman R (2016) The Obama Administration and Targeting "War-Sustaining" Objects in Non-international Armed Conflict. American Journal of International Law 110(4): 663–679

Goodman R (2022) Clear Error in the Defense Department's Law of War Manual: On Presumptions of Civilian Status, 9 February 2022, https://www.justsecurity.org/80147/clear-error-in-the-defense-departments-law-of-war-manual-on-presumptions-of-civilian-status/. Accessed 4 March 2024

Green L C (1992) The Environment and the Law of Conventional Warfare. Canadian Yearbook of international Law/Annuaire canadien de droit international 29: 222–237

Greenwood C (1993) Customary International Law and the First Geneva Protocol of 1977 in the Gulf Conflict. In: Rowe P (ed) The Gulf War 1990–91 in International and English Law. Routledge, London, pp 63–86

Harvard Air and Missile Warfare Manual (2013) Program on Humanitarian Policy and Conflict Research at Harvard University (HPCR), Manual on International Law Applicable to Air and Missile Warfare. Cambridge University Press, Cambridge

Henckaerts J-M, Doswald-Beck L (2005) Customary International Humanitarian Law, Volume I: Rules. Cambridge University Press, Cambridge/Geneva

Henderson I (2009) The Contemporary Law of Targeting. Martinus Nijhoff Publishers, Leiden/Boston

Human Rights Watch (1991) Needless deaths in the Gulf War. Civilian Casualties During the Air Campaign and Violations of the Laws of War. Human Rights Watch, New York

Hutchinson T, Duncan N (2012) Defining and Describing What We Do: Doctrinal Legal Research. Deakin Law Review 17 (1): 83–119

ICRC (1987) Commentary on the Additional Protocols of 8 June 1977 to the Geneva Conventions of 12 August 1949. Martinus Nijhoff Publishers, Geneva

ICRC Reports and Documents (2008) Interpretive Guidance on the Notion of Direct Participation under International Humanitarian Law. International Review of the Red Cross 90 (872): 991–1047

IISS (2023) The Armed Conflict Survey 2023. https://www.iiss.org/publications/armed-conflict-survey/2023/editors-introduction/. Accessed 2 February 2024

ILA (2017) The Conduct of Hostilities and International Humanitarian Law: Challenges of 21st Century Warfare. International Law Association Study Group on the Conduct of Hostilities in the 21st Century. https://www.ila-hq.org/en_GB/documents/ila-final-report-25-june-2017. Accessed 4 March 2024

INEW (2016) Qasef: Escaping the bombing. The use of explosive weapons in populated areas and forced displacement: perspectives from Syrian refugees. https://www.inew.org/wp-content/uploads/2016/10/Qasef-Escaping-the-bombing-copy.pdf. Accessed 5 February 2024

Jeangène Vilmer J P (2015) Military objectives and lethal autonomous weapon systems. In: Greppi E (ed) Conduct of Hostilities: The Practice, the Law and the Future. International Institute of Humanitarian Law/FrancoAngeli, Milan, 86–94

Kalshoven F (1977) Reaffirmation and development of international humanitarian law applicable in armed conflicts: the Diplomatic Conference, Geneva, 1974–1977: Part I: combatants and civilians. Netherlands Yearbook of International Law 8:107–135

Kalshoven F (1978) Reaffirmation and Development of International Humanitarian Law Applicable in Armed Conflicts: The Diplomatic Conference, Geneva, 1974–1977, Part II. Netherlands Yearbook of International Law 9: 107–171

Kalshoven F, Zegveld L (2011) Constraints on the Waging of War, 4th edn. Cambridge University Press/ICRC, Cambridge/Geneva
Klein J J (2016) Space Warfare: Deterrence, Dissuasion and the Law of Armed Conflict, 30 August 2016, https://warontherocks.com/2016/08/space-warfare-deterrence-dissuasion-and-the-law-of-armed-conflict/. Accessed 26 February 2024
Koskenniemi M (2007) Methodology of International Law. In: Wolfrum R (ed) Max Planck Encyclopedia of International Law. Oxford University Press, Oxford
Lawless R (2023) 2023 DoD Manual Revision – The Civilian Presumption's Durability. 8 September 2023, https://lieber.westpoint.edu/civilian-presumptions-durability/. Accessed 23 February 2024
Leontiev L (2023) Jurisdiction of Territorial Non-State Entities in International Law. Ph.D. thesis, on file with author
Lewis M W (2003) The Law of Aerial Bombardment in the 1991 Gulf War. The American Journal of International Law 97(3): 481–509
Lubell N (2015) Current Challenges with regard to the Notion of Military Objective – Legal and Operational Perspectives. In: Greppi E (ed) Conduct of Hostilities: The Practice, the Law and the Future. International Institute of Humanitarian Law/FrancoAngeli, Milan, pp 79–85
Meron T (2000) The Humanization of Humanitarian Law. American Journal of International Law 94(2): 239–278
Milanovic M, Schmitt M N (2022) Ukraine Symposium - The Kerch Strait Bridge Attack, Retaliation and International Law. https://lieber.westpoint.edu/kerch-strait-bridge-attack-retaliation-international-law/. Accessed 9 August 2024
Neuman N (2018) A Precautionary Tale: The Theory and Practice of Precautions in Attack. Israel Yearbook of Human Rights 48(1): 19–41
Oeter S (2013) Methods and Means of Combat. In: Fleck D (ed) The Handbook of Humanitarian Law in Armed Conflict. Oxford University Press: Oxford, pp 401–488
Parks W H (1995) Precision' and 'area' bombing: Who did which, and when? Journal of Strategic Studies 18 (1): 145–174
Pompson O (2023) 'Objects'? The Legal Status of Computer Data under International Humanitarian Law. Journal of Conflict and Security Law 28(2): 349–387
Raina H (2023) Merchant Shipping as Military Objectives and Naval Economic Warfare, 7 August 2023. https://lieber.westpoint.edu/merchant-shipping-military-objectives-naval-economic-warfare/. Accessed 3 March 2024
Randelzhofer A (1992) Civilian Objects. In: Bernhardt R (ed) Encyclopedia of Public International Law. North Holland Publishing Company, Amsterdam, pp 93–96
Reetz N S (2022) Same Same but Different? Why War-Sustaining Objects Can Be Destroyed but Not Targeted. Journal of Conflict and Security Law 27(3): 439–469
Rizer K (2001) Bombing dual-use targets: legal, ethical, and doctrinal perspectives. Air & Space power journal—chronicles online journal. www.airpower.maxwell.af.mil/airchronicles/cc/Rizer.html Accessed 2 February 2024
Robertson Jr H (1998) The Principle of the Military Objective in the Law of Armed Conflict. United States Air Force Journal of Legal Studies 8: 35–69
Ronziti N (2000) Is the non liquet of the Final Report by the Committee Established to Review the NATO Bombing Campaign Against the Federal Republic of Yugoslavia acceptable? International Review of the Red Cross 840:1017–1027
Rosenblad E (1979) International Humanitarian Law. Henri Dunant Institute, Geneva
Ross WD (1930) The Right and the Good. Oxford University Press, Oxford
Rynkeby Knudsen J (2024) Military Objectives by Location. 9 February 2024. https://lieber.westpoint.edu/military-objectives-location/. Accessed 20 August 2024
Sandoz Y, Swinarski C, Zimmermann B (eds) (1987) Commentary on the Additional Protocols of 8 June 1977 to the Geneva Conventions of 12 August 1949. Martinus Nijhoff Publishers, Geneva

Sassòli M (2003) Legitimate targets of attacks under international humanitarian law. Background Paper prepared for the Informal High-Level Expert Meeting on the Reaffirmation and Development of International Humanitarian Law, Cambridge, January 27–29, 2003. https://hhi.harvard.edu/sites/hwpi.harvard.edu/files/humanitarianinitiative/files/session1_legitimate_targets_ihl.pdf?m=1615827575. Accessed 8 February 2024

Sassòli M, Cameron L (2006) The Protection of Civilian Objects: Current State of the Law and Issues de lege ferenda. In: Ronzitti N, Venturini G (eds) The Law of Air Warfare : Contemporary Issues. Eleven International, Utrecht, pp 35–74

Sassòli M, Bouvier AA, Quintin A (2011) How does law protect in war? Cases, Documents and Teaching Materials on Contemporary Practice in International Humanitarian Law. ICRC, Geneva

Schmitt M N (2002) Wired warfare: Computer network attack and jus in bello. International Review of the Red Cross 84(846): 365–399

Schmitt M N (2006) Faultlines in the Law of Attack. In: Breau S, Jachec-Neale A (eds) Testing the Boundaries of International Humanitarian Law. British Institute of International and Comparative Law, London, pp 277–307

Schmitt M N (2010) Deconstructing the Direct Participation in Hostilities: The Constitutive Elements. NYU Journal of International Law and Policy 42:697–739

Schmitt M N (ed) (2013) Tallinn Manual on the International Law Applicable to Cyber Warfare. Cambridge University Press, Cambridge

Schmitt M N (2019) Wired warfare 3.0: Protecting the civilian population during cyber operations. International Review of the Red Cross 101 (1): 333–355

Schmitt M N (2021) Targeting Dual-Use Structures: An Alternative Interpretation, 28 June 2021. https://lieber.westpoint.edu/targeting-dual-use-structures-alternative/. Accessed 21February 2024

Schmitt M N (2022) Ukraine-Symposium - Attacking Power Infrastructure under International Humanitarian Law, 20 October 2022, https://lieber.westpoint.edu/attacking-power-infrastructure-under-international-humanitarian-law/. Accessed 19 August 2024

Schmitt M N, Tinkler K (2020) War in Space: How International Humanitarian Law Might Apply, 9 March 2020. https://www.justsecurity.org/68906/war-in-space-how-international-humanitarian-law-might-apply/. Accessed 4 February 2024

Schmitt M N, Widmar E (2016) The Law of Targeting. In: Ducheine P A L, Schmitt M N, Osinga F P B (eds) Targeting: The Challenges of Modern Warfare. T.M.C. Asser Press, The Hague, pp 121–146

Shue H, Wippman D (2002) Limiting Attacks on Dual-Use Facilities Performing Indispensable Civilian Functions. Cornell International Law Journal 35(3): 553–579

Shumilova O, Tockner K, Sukhodolov A et al. (2023) Impact of the Russia–Ukraine armed conflict on water resources and water infrastructure. Nat Sustain 6: 578–586

Sivakumaran S (2012) The Law of Non-International Armed Conflict. Oxford University Press, Oxford

Solf W A (2013) Art. 52 API. In: Bothe M, Bartsch K J, Solf W A (eds) New Rules for Victims of Armed Conflicts. Martinus Nijhoff Publishers 2nd ed, Leiden, pp 318–327

Sommario E (2016) The Status of Foreign Fighters under International Humanitarian Law. In: de Guttry A, Capone F, Paulussen C (eds) Foreign Fighters under International Law and Beyond. T.M.C. Asser Press, The Hague, pp 142–159

Spaight JM (1911) War Rights on Land. London: Macmillan & Co.

Stepanenko K, Barros G, Kagan F W et al. (with Mappes G, Wolkov N, Evans A, Harward C, Stepanenko K, Barros G, Kagan F W, Mappes G, Wolkov N, Evans A, Harward C) (2024). Ukraine's Long-term Path to Success: Jumpstarting a Self-sufficient Defense Industrial Base With US and EU Support. Institute for the Study of War. https://www.understandingwar.org/backgrounder/ukraine's-long-term-path-success-jumpstarting-self-sufficient-defense-industrial-base. Accessed 4 August 2024

Thirlway H (2001) Reflections on lex ferenda. Netherlands Yearbook of International Law 32(1): 3–26

Tignino M (2010) Water, international peace, and security. International Review of the Red Cross 879: 647–674

Tignino M, Kebebew T (2022) The Legal Protection of Freshwater Resources and Related Installations during Warfare. Journal of International Criminal Justice 20: 1191–1228

UN Secretary-General (2024) Protection of civilians in armed conflict. Report of the Secretary-General UN Doc. S/2024/385

UN Security Council (2021) Resolution 2573 (2021), UN Doc. S/RES/2573 (2021)

US DoD (1992) Report to Congress on the Conduct of the Persian Gulf War - Appendix on the Role of the Law of War. International Legal Materials 31(3): 612–644

US DoD (2023) Law of War Manual (June 2015, updated July 2023). https://media.defense.gov/2023/Jul/31/2003271432/-1/-1/0/DOD-LAW-OF-WAR-MANUAL-JUNE-2015-UPDATED-JULY%202023.PDF. Accessed 4 September 2024

Van Coller A (2023) 2023 DoD Manual Revision - Redefining Doubt, 6 November 2023, https://lieber.westpoint.edu/redefining-doubt/#:~:text=In%20February%202023. Accessed 4 March 2024

Van Engeland A (2011) Civilian or combatant? A Challenge for the 21st Century. Oxford University Press, Oxford

Vibhute K, Aynalem F (2009) Legal Research Methods (Justice and Legal System Research Institute, 2009) https://chilot.wordpress.com/wp-content/uploads/2011/06/legal-research-methods.pdf. Accessed 10 February 2024

Waxman Matthew C (2000) International Law and the Politics of Air Operations. Rand, Santa Monica, CA

Wille C, Malaret Baldo B (2021) Reference Framework: Menu of Indicators to Measure the Reverberating Effects on Civilians of the Use of Explosive Weapons in Populated Areas, UNIDIR, Geneva. https://unidir.org/wp-content/uploads/2023/05/EWIPA-Research-Framework-Final.pdf. Accessed 5 February 2024

Zeitoun M, Talhami M (2016) The impact of explosive weapons on urban services: Direct and reverberating effects across space and time. International Review of the Red Cross 98(901): 53–70

Zemmali A (1995) La protection de l'eau en période de conflit armé. International Review of the Red Cross, 815: 601–615

Zimmerman MJ (1996) The concept of moral obligation. Cambridge University Press, Cambridge

Part I
Laying the Theoretical Foundations of Dual-Use Objects Under International Humanitarian Law

Chapter 2
The Mainstream Approach to Dual-Use Objects: A Legal/Historical Excursus

Contents

Abstract The present chapter aims to provide an overview of what can be described as the "mainstream approach" towards dual-use objects, focussing on two selected air campaigns that took place in the aftermath of WWII, i.e. the First Gulf War in 1991 and the NATO bombing campaign against the Federal Republic of Yugoslavia (FRY) in 1999. As is well known, the affirmation of the supremacy of air power in the twentieth century changed the reality of war and drastically transformed the dynamics of warfare. This evolution fuelled and was fuelled by the notion that targeting national infrastructures represents an effective way to attack the enemy from the "inside out", as advocated by the famous "Five Strategic Rings" theory developed by Colonel Warden. The implementation of this theory, which was tested during the First Gulf War and the NATO bombardment, results in a significant tension between IHL's key tenets and military strategies. The tension emerges between the (alleged) strategic value of hitting key infrastructures and the negative humanitarian impact that those military operations have on civilian life-support systems. After introducing and discussing the militarisation of civilian activities, as an essential precondition to the targeting of dual-use objects, the present chapter will reflect on the two selected examples and the theory that informed the choices made in both contexts, analysing the extent to which they have contributed to cementing the current, and still mainstream, approach to dual-use objects.

F. Capone, *Dual-use Objects under International Humanitarian Law: Towards a Paradigm Shift*, https://doi.org/10.1007/978-94-6265-679-6_2

Keywords Militarisation process · Centre of gravity · Five Strategic Rings · First Gulf War · NATO bombing campaign · Review Committee

2.1 The Implementation of the "Mainstream Approach" to Dual-Use Objects

The present chapter aims to provide an overview of the approach adopted towards dual-use objects so far, focussing in particular on two selected air campaigns that occurred in the aftermath of the Second World War (WWII), i.e. the First Gulf War in 1991 and the North Atlantic Treaty Organization (NATO) bombing campaign against the Federal Republic of Yugoslavia (FRY) in 1999. As is well known and documented, starting from WWII, factories, factory workers, and certain other civilian facilities and individuals began to have a tangible effect on armed conflict, in a way that can be described as unprecedented.[1] Although it is not surprising that belligerents felt compelled to attack those facilities directly, it is legitimate to question this choice, both from a military and a legal perspective. Together with the so-called "militarisation of civilian activities", rather than the "civilisation of armed conflict",[2] an additional crucial factor to take into consideration while delving into what has become the "mainstream" approach to dual-use objects is the expansion of aerial warfare,[3] which, together with technological advancement in general, has dramatically altered the targeting process.[4] The examples discussed in this chapter will be assessed from a legal perspective to better grasp the multifaceted challenges surrounding the targeting of dual-use objects and the implementation of the existing legal framework, hence further motivating the urge to develop a new paradigm.

Obviously, the context in which the analysis unfolds is a complex one. The English word "war" has its origin in the old Germanic term, *werra*, which can be loosely translated as "confusion" or "disorder".[5] In *On War*, Carl von Clausewitz famously introduced the readers to widely recognised axioms such as how the simplest things become hard in war and how the fog and friction of war transform minor difficulties into major, nearly insurmountable obstacles. Within many of these axioms, Clausewitz's theory of moral forces in war is founded on a basic observation: military action in armed conflicts always faces an enormous gap between theory and practice.[6] What seems to be very straightforward while planning a war becomes difficult to accomplish once the fighting erupts and can either not be doable at all or subject to significant changes. Clearly, similar gaps between theory and practice can be found

[1] Schmitt 2010, pp. 807–810.

[2] The civilisation of armed conflict refers to the increasingly important role that civilians play in armed conflicts. See Wenger and Mason 2008.

[3] McCoubrey 1995, p. 24.

[4] Danielsson and Ljungkvist 2023, p. 86.

[5] Kleemeier 2007, p. 109.

[6] Von Clausewitz 1989, p. 89.

in other areas, like economics, politics, and everyday life. However, since war represents the most extreme form of conflict, the gap between ideas and reality "is here more drastic and dramatic than in any other field of human action".[7]

Equally axiomatic is the premise that warfare is a constantly evolving phenomenon. Some authors, especially from the US, even argue that when the change in warfare proves fundamental, a "revolution in military affairs" (RMA) occurs.[8] The Gulf War in 1991 and the fighting over Kosovo are constantly regarded as relevant testament to an RMA,[9] which took place under the US technological and military leadership.[10] As is well known, both armed conflicts saw an unprecedented rise in attacks against dual-use objects, mainly resulting from air strikes. More in detail, although inaccurately hailed as the first "smart" war,[11] the 1991 Gulf War popularised a new era in "strategic bombing", mainly due to the resort to precision weaponry.[12] Similarly, the 1999 NATO coordinated strikes against Yugoslavia are remembered for the intensity of the aerial bombardment, the first of that magnitude for NATO and the third largest strategic application of air power by the United States since WWII.[13] Conflicting reactions were triggered by these two events, which on the one hand heavily shaped a new type of armed conflict, and on the other hand proved that aerial bombardments can still result in an unacceptably high level of civilian casualties, especially when compared with the low level of combatant casualties in the attacking force.[14]

A crucial aspect that concerns both conflicts is represented by the evolution of the application of the law of targeting under international humanitarian law (IHL), which covers the whole targeting process: the selection of targets, their prioritisation, planning, execution, and post-attack assessment. Military targeting is a crucial element to determine how armed conflicts unfold. It can be described as one of the "engines" of war, to the point where, if the targeting process stops, a war could effectively come to a halt. Authors look at targeting from different, but interrelated perspectives. From a military perspective "targeting is the process of making known, selecting, prioritising, and acting upon entities in the operational environment with the goal to reach certain ends".[15] Through the lenses of the critical scholarship on war and warfare, targeting is key to the constitution of military power, and it is productive of military violence. From a legal point of view, targeting lies at the very core of international

---

[7] Ibid.; Cole 2020, p. 43.

[8] Schmitt 1999, p. 143.

[9] Cordesman 2014.

[10] Neuneck 2008, p. 51.

[11] The definition of what exactly constitutes precision weaponry has changed over time as arms technology has evolved. Originally termed "smart bombs", the broader classification of "precision guided munitions" later became official. Mandel 2004, p. 174.

[12] Davis 1996; Lambeth 2000, pp. 72–73.

[13] Lambeth 2001, p. 1.

[14] Dinstein 2002, p. 219; Vierucci 2006, pp. 695–696.

[15] Danielsson and Ljungkvist 2023, p. 83.

humanitarian law.[16] While usually addressed in conjunction with the principles of distinction and proportionality,[17] as a matter of fact, targeting has a much broader scope, and its relevance emerges in relation to all the key IHL principles.[18]

Stricto sensu, and to use Ducheine's words, targeting can be defined as "the deliberate application of capabilities against targets to generate effects in order to achieve specific objectives".[19] Ducheine authoritatively goes on to explain that it "is about the application of means (weapons) of warfare to affect addressees (people or objects) using a variety of methods (tactics) that create effects contributing to designated goals. Targeting, accordingly, *represents the bridge between the ends and means of warfare*."[20] The targeting process is not an incipient one, although it has evolved significantly over time. Looking at the past, up to and including WWI, it is possible to infer that the destruction of enemy forces and equipment had been the primary, albeit not the only, means of securing ultimate victory. By weakening the enemy on the battlefield, it was possible to achieve the enemy's capitulation, either by rendering the enemy State unable to use its armed forces effectively or by pushing it to refrain from sending those forces into battle.[21] The introduction of air power in the twentieth century changed this reality and drastically transformed the dynamics of warfare. It allowed belligerent forces to "leap beyond the front line and thereby extend the conflict into the enemy's heartland".[22] By adding a third dimension, air warfare gave militaries the capability to target elements beyond the frontline engagement zones.[23]

This capability made it possible to adopt "targeting strategies that were non-linear, direct and sophisticated in design; [s]uch strategies shortened the link between targeting and the enemy's decision-making processes".[24] From this evolution stems the notion that targeting national infrastructures is an effective way to attack the enemy from the "inside out, using airpower to skip over military forces, such as armies in the field, to strike directly at state leadership".[25] Campaigns have been increasingly carried out against infrastructures of various kinds, that serve both the military forces and the civilian population and are, hence, swiftly labelled as dual-use objects. The targets are usually seen as lawful, or, if incidents occur, they are justified using the "euphemistic and apologetic term 'collateral damage' to suggest unintentionality, inevitability, adherence to humanitarian law",[26] and thus legitimacy. At the same time, attacks against dual-use objects are said to be of limited strategic value because they, so the argument goes, are of very limited or "unproven military utility,

[16] Schmitt 2009, p. 131.

[17] Bothe 2002, pp. 182–184; D'Aspremont and De Hemptinne 2012, pp. 201–203.

[18] Schmitt 2009, p. 134.

[19] Ducheine 2016, p. 203.

[20] Ibid., p. 204 (emphasis added).

[21] Ducheine et al. 2016, p. 2.

[22] Ibid.

[23] Osinga and Roorda 2016, p. 29.

[24] Ducheine et al. 2016, p. 2.

[25] Kuehl 1995, p. 251.

[26] Osinga and Roorda 2016, p. 58.

harken back to WWII morale bombing, put civilians unnecessarily in danger, and violate civilian immunity."[27] A significant tension thus arises between the fighter's perspective, according to which the military advantage gained by targeting critical infrastructures, e.g. national electric power systems, justifies the incidental civilian casualties, and the criticism triggered by the negative humanitarian impact resulting from the catastrophic reverberating effects on civilian life-support systems.[28]

Bearing in mind these premises and the purpose of shedding light on the multiple frictions briefly highlighted here, the next (sub-)sections will first discuss more at length the issue of the militarisation of civilian activities, as an essential precondition to the targeting of dual-use objects, and then it will reflect on the two selected examples, analysing the extent to which they have contributed to cementing the current, and still mainstream, approach to dual-use objects.

2.2 Towards the Militarisation of Civilian Activities

The research into what can be described as the "trilateral relationship between state, soldier, and society"[29] goes back a very long way. One can look as far as the "philosophical reflections of Plato, Machiavelli's counsels to the prince about statecraft, and von Clausewitz's theory of war",[30] to the early sociological explanations of the relationship between the military and society, thanks to the fundamental contribution of authors like Gaetano Mosca and Max Weber.[31] Modern social science research, however, began only in the 1940s and 1950s. The fragmentation of the research field into at least three different, albeit interrelated strands—i.e. military studies, comparative politics, and military sociology—persists to this day. Besides the fascinating and relevant theoretical implications, it is worth reflecting also on the practical consequences that the interplay between the civilian and the military spheres can carry from an IHL perspective. As noted by Schmitt "the concept of military objective will remain beleaguered as civilian activities are further militarized, and military activities are increasingly civilianized",[32] particularly in technologically advanced States. As a result of this, it is becoming more and more difficult to determine when an object, and the facility that makes it, can be legitimately regarded as military or not. It has been widely reported that the military increasingly uses civilian facilities and activities to reduce costs. Such arrangements range from sharing infrastructures, including for instance office space, runways, or port facilities, to using the Internet

[27] Ibid.

[28] Crawford 1997, p. 102.

[29] Pion-Berlin et al. 2024, p. 1.

[30] Carl von Clausewitz referred to a "paradoxical trinity" (*wunderliche Dreifaltigkeit*) between government, the armed forces, and society.

[31] Pion-Berlin et al. 2024, p. 1.

[32] Schmitt 1999, p. 159.

or initiating partnerships with commercial space entities and consortiums.[33] Aiming for savings and efficiencies, these practices have become quite common, although they risk diluting the prescriptive effect of the belligerents' obligations to "avoid locating military objectives within or near densely populated areas" and to "take the other necessary precautions to protect the civilian population".[34]

The actual intensification of civil–military relations in various ambits is part of the broader phenomenon of "militarisation", defined in a nutshell as "the spread of military influence or values into domains that are thought to constitute a separate civil sphere".[35] Some authors have described the militarisation process in more refined terms. Enloe, for example, explains that it includes any means by which societies come to "imagine military needs and militaristic presumptions to be not only valuable but also normal".[36] To further strengthen her intuition, Enloe grounds the concept of militarisation in both "material" and "ideational" processes. The former involve "the intrusion of military technologies into civilian domains", e.g. the resort to military weapons and vehicles in policing. The latter refers to the spread of military culture or military values, for instance when the language of war becomes commonplace in ordinary life.[37]

More recently, and stressing the multidimensional character of militarisation, Bayer et al. conducted an empirical study on the three different dimensions already identified by Bowman.[38] According to these authors, the first, i.e., "material militarisation", refers to the allocation of increasing material, economic, and social resources to the armed forces. The second dimension, namely "political militarisation" denotes the increase in military prerogatives, key decision-making power over policies, and influence in the inner workings of the ruling coalition. Finally, "social militarisation" refers to the expansion of the military's role in societal institutions and the daily lives of ordinary citizens.[39] The different dimensions of militarisation are clearly interconnected. Yet, empirical research has primarily focused on examining these three dimensions independently, with the third dimension, concerning military-society relations, receiving limited attention so far.[40] Overall, this is not surprising since societal militarisation is arguably the most complex among the three dimensions of militarisation as it covers a diverse range of factors. It encompasses, *inter alia*, forms of recruitment, entrepreneurial activities, and military's influence on educational and value system, political culture, legal system, and so on.[41]

---

[33] Ibid.

[34] Ibid., p. 182.

[35] Schulzke 2017, p. 97.

[36] Enloe 2000, p. 3.

[37] Ibid. See also Enloe 2010, p. 1107.

[38] Bowman 2002.

[39] Bayer et al. 2023, p. 4.

[40] Ibid.

[41] Ibid. See also Navajas et al. 2023, p. 133.

Whereas most experts maintain a critical stance vis-à-vis the militarisation process,[42] pointing out genuine problems that can and should be corrected, a few have started to question whether militarisation might, in some contexts, be unavoidable or even beneficial. Focussing on the US case, Schulzke notes that, at least to some extent, militarisation may even be necessary for two sets of reasons. First, some contact between the civilian and military domains may be useful for the society at large. They can be essential to encourage civil-military dialogue, which in turn "can prevent members of the military from feeling detached from civilians or even resenting them",[43] and ensure that civilian values continue to be relevant in military life. Second, it is important to observe that certain aspects of militarisation are simply inevitable. The most blatant motivation is represented by the necessity to have a national security infrastructure. Although these conditions are not universal nor persistent,[44] they do exist in most places and provide support for the argument that militarisation shall not necessarily be depicted only in negative terms and that "the degree of justified militarisation must be carefully evaluated on a case-by-case basis".[45]

The debate on the militarisation of civilian activities is particularly animated at the time of writing this book, due to the massive protests that are taking place across universities and academic institutions in Western countries, especially in the US and in Europe. Campuses have erupted with pro-Palestinian demonstrations because of the armed conflict between Israel and Hamas.[46] Besides opposing Israel's military campaign in Gaza,[47] which sits among the deadliest and most destructive in history, students/protestors contest the growth of the military-university nexus, oftentimes transcending the focus on Israel and its ties with various companies,[48] and calling for a broader reflection on the militarisation process in university settings. Such process, that includes a wide range of different activities, from disciplinary engagements with military institutions to flows of funding and knowledge,[49] has recently triggered attention also on research and development (R&D) involving technologies with "dual-use potential".[50] Notably, there is no common conceptualised definition of "dual use" in the context of R&D support, either internationally or at EU level. Regarding the EU, it is worth stressing that the Regulation on dual-use export control provides a definition of dual-use items and includes a list of several hundred of those items (and

[42] Schulzke 2017, pp. 95–98.

[43] Ibid.

[44] Of the 193 member states of the United Nations, only 20 do not have a military.

[45] Schulzke 2017, p. 96.

[46] Dill 2023.

[47] Pelham/BBC News, US college protests: Hundreds more arrested across US in Gaza campus protests https://www.bbc.com/news/world-us-canada-68895250 (accessed 2 May 2024).

[48] Delouya/CNN, Campus protesters are calling for divestment. Here's what that means, https://edition.cnn.com/2024/04/30/business/what-is-divestment-college-protests-israel/index.html (accessed 3 May 2024).

[49] Woodward et al. 2017, p. 203.

[50] European Commission 2024.

technical specifications) that covers not only tangible objects, but also intangible ones such as software or technology in the form of technical data or technical assistance.[51] This definition, however, has a limited scope, as it is designed in the context of export control and its specific goal is to avoid civil technology being misused or diverted for military purposes by countries, governments, or non-governmental bodies to undermine peace or security or in connection with internal repression or serious violations of human rights and international humanitarian law.[52]

Therefore, "technologies with dual-use potential" have not been yet defined in the EU research programmes. For the time being, the Horizon Europe Specific Programme focuses exclusively on civil applications, whereas defence research activities are carried out under another dedicated programme of Horizon Europe dealing solely with defence R&D.[53] Nonetheless, the intention set by the EU legislators, also in light of the current events, is to overturn its previous choice and facilitate cross-fertilisation between civil and defence R&D activities.[54] As a result of this, what emerges is that, beyond the need to strengthen and deepen the legal analysis in situations of armed conflict there are broader, and urgent considerations that inform the necessity to reflect on dual-use objects *lato sensu*. The present work, despite its focus on IHL, wishes to address some of the transversal issues at stake, without expecting to provide an exhaustive analysis and with the awareness that the topic could significantly benefit from a plurality of approaches and the adoption of different perspectives.

2.3 Introducing the Main Theory Behind the Targeting of Dual-Use Objects in the Two Selected Cases

In the case of an exclusively military environment, "such as forces dug in in the desert and far removed from civilians",[55] proportionality and distinction do not appear to be relevant. This does not rule out the application of other IHL rules, such as the prohibition to resort to certain weapons or the prohibition of unnecessary destruction, but clearly two armed forces fighting in the desert will not be able to trigger any observation with respect to dual-use objects. In fact, the issues tackled by the present work emerge exactly because all the armed conflicts fought around the world take place in urban and/or populated areas. It is worth to note that the pressure that this

---

[51] Regulation (EU) 2021/821 of 20 May 2021 setting up a Union regime for the control of exports, brokering, technical assistance, transit and transfer of dual-use items.

[52] Ibid., Article 2(1) which defines "dual-use items" as "items, including software and technology, which can be used for both civil and military purposes, and includes items which can be used for the design, development, production or use of nuclear, chemical or biological weapons or their means of delivery, including all items which can be used for both non-explosive uses and assisting in any way in the manufacture of nuclear weapons or other nuclear explosive devices".

[53] European Commission 2024, p. 7.

[54] Ibid., p. 2.

[55] Hampson 1992, p. 49.

approach to warfare puts on the principle of distinction, which lies at the heart of the whole IHL framework,[56] is only meant to grow if adequate actions are not taken by all the relevant actors. To better understand how moving from the "battlefield", i.e. geographically articulable lines where combat occurs, to the "battlespace", i.e. virtual and non-linear *loci* of combat,[57] has impacted civilians, it is necessary to delve into some of the most notorious events. As noted by Schmitt, the humanitarian effect of the ability to "strike anywhere and anytime" heightens the likelihood to hit civilians and civilian objects because of how much they have become intermingled with military objectives.[58] This agglomeration of military objectives and civilian objects is the consequence of both the presence of more civilians and civilian objects in the target area (i.e. the battlespace), and of the development of new technologies, which has made lawful targets easier to attack and thus more vulnerable. Since the targets that can be validly attacked multiply, so does the potential for collateral damage and incidental injuries to the civilian population. As a result of this transformation, it is possible to affirm that the "rules of war do not adequately reflect the reality of warfare"[59] anymore. Therefore, there is a need to dissect some of the milestones of this process, in order to understand how to challenge it, and possibly revert it, in a more effective way.

As explained above, both the Gulf War and the NATO bombardment of Yugoslavia represent relevant examples of how modern warfare has ultimately failed to limit considerable disruption of societal life.[60] Moreover, the two campaigns marked the occasion to translate some military theories into practice. This is especially true with regard to the "Five Strategic Rings" theory developed by Colonel John A. Warden USAF, which was applied during the 1991 Persian Gulf War and "perfected" during the NATO bombings against the FRY. An early exposition of this philosophy is usually attributed to the late Air Force general Curtis Lemay, who, in his 1965 memoir, raised the idea of destroying "every work of man in North Vietnam".[61] A preliminary caveat is needed before introducing Warden's model, as it blatantly relies on von Clausewitz's notion of "centre of gravity".[62] This term appears in *On War* in several passages of its eight books. However, it is perhaps in Book VIII that von Clausewitz provides a more detailed account of the concept, by emphasising the importance of identifying the right "centre of gravity" in the opponent to direct the effort against him most effectively.[63] In von Clausewitz's scheme, which notably theorises a "traditional" approach to war, the fielded forces, i.e. the enemy military, are the centre of gravity *par excellence*. Warden borrows from his intuition, but he clearly reverses this scheme, by claiming that trying to defeat an opposition's military

[56] Schmitt 1999, p. 181.

[57] Ibid., pp. 161–162.

[58] Ibid., p. 162.

[59] Kahn 1993, p. 425.

[60] Hampson 1992, p. 46.

[61] Lemay and MacKinlay 1965, p. 5.

[62] Echevarria 2007, p. 177.

[63] Meyer 2022, p. 327.

forces shall no longer be the primary objective in war, but rather the least important one.[64]

Ontologically, Warden refers to the "centre of gravity" notion, i.e. "the hub of all power and movement",[65] and further explains how this concept indicates "a point against which a level of effort, such as a push, will accomplish more than that same level of effort could accomplish if applied elsewhere".[66] Without aiming to untangle the relationship between the two theories and their authors, what is worth stressing here is that Warden relies on the centre of gravity in order to understand the enemy as a system, but he takes von Clausewitz's intuition several steps further, for example by specifying that in his theory the centre of gravity is also a ring of vulnerability. In addition to providing a framework to locate and designate von Clausewitz's centre of gravity—thus contributing to making the concept less nebulous and volatile—Warden clarifies that the centre of gravity/ring can only be physical, because he sees an actor's morale as "beyond the realm of the predictable".[67] This does not entail that Warden is not aware of how "morale factors" could change the physical dimension of warfare. However, his approach assumes that only the "appropriate" physical targets must be correctly identified and attacked, hence altering the morale of the population and affecting the ability of a rival to discern an attacker's intention.

From a more pragmatic perspective, the five rings model developed by Warden conceptualises a device for the employment of aerospace power.[68] Each ring refers to one of the key aspects of a nation's society; namely political leadership, economic systems, supporting infrastructure, population, and military forces. One could envision this model as a series of five concentric rings with the most important element, i.e. the political leadership, in the centre and the progressively less important ones moving outward. Colonel Warden's approach lays the foundation for the notion of attacking the enemy as a complex system,[69] from the "inside out, using airpower to skip over military forces such as armies in the field to strike directly at state leadership",[70] by disabling "the most important centre of gravity first and work outward to less important rings".[71]

Leadership is thus at the centre of Warden's ring model. In his biological system analogy, leadership equates to the brain of a living organism. Therefore, if the national leadership is isolated, disabled, or destroyed, then the country could not function. In the past, for example when William the Conqueror carried out his campaign to conquer England, the target had to be the centre, i.e. King Harold himself. Nowadays, the idea of directly capturing or killing the command element sounds impractical, to say the least, therefore the task has become to apply sufficient indirect pressure,

[64] Chun 2010, p. 313.

[65] Von Clausewitz 1989, pp. 595–596.

[66] Warden 2000, p. 7.

[67] Meyer 2022, pp. 330–331.

[68] Warden 1995, p. 40.

[69] Fenrick 2001, p. 491.

[70] Crawford 1997, p. 101.

[71] Chun and Bartholomees 2012, pp. 314–316.

i.e. by targeting the surrounding rings. This course of action is expected to push the commander to make concessions, or to realise that continuing combat is not feasible.[72] The second ring is represented by the economic systems, which can be described as the organism's raw materials that are necessary to live. This ring includes sources of energy, food, and financial resources to support the State's existence. In Warden's view, the degradation of a State's economic resources could indeed paralyse a modern State.[73] In an industrial State, for instance, the lack of energy can influence national leadership's behaviour and severely limit the actions of public and private actors.

The third ring depicts the skeleton and muscles of the living organism and consists of bridges, roads and rail networks, airports etc… Experts, including proponents of the Five Strategic Rings theory, note how disabling key infrastructures requires a careful analysis to find vital elements that, if struck, could disrupt operations. Warden himself warns of attacks perpetrated against infrastructures, stressing how destroying them could be extremely costly and could also impact the victor' side.[74]

The fourth ring is represented by the population. Similarly to a living organism that can survive even after the loss of many cells, the State can endure the loss of part of its population. Nonetheless, economic and military support might be severely impacted after an air attack if the public perceives that its losses are too high. Ethical considerations aside, Warden warns that it is difficult to attack the population directly. There are too many targets, and, in some instances, "the population may be willing to suffer grievously before it will turn on its own government".[75] Moreover, the effects of bombing the population are very difficult to anticipate.[76] Early air power theorists such as Douhet claimed that "the most humane way to end war was a swift attack on the most vulnerable element of society: the populace".[77] Douhet even argued that air forces could use poison gas against cities that "paralyzed all life" by killing civilians and that wars could be rapidly won by breaking the will of people through bombardment of cities.[78] On the contrary, Warden stresses that examples of increased morale under bombardment are indeed numerous. In fact, while early air theorists thought that casualties inflicted on the population would most certainly lead to surrender, during WWII the bombing of Great Britain and Germany ended up boosting the civilians' morale, with Germany's prolonged resistance until Hitler's death.[79] On a more cynical note, one should also consider that, if essential goods are limited, then a reduction in "unessential parts of the (enemy's) population

[72] Warden 1995, pp. 49–50.

[73] Ibid., p. 50.

[74] Ibid. See also Chun and Bartholomees 2012, p. 316.

[75] Warden 1995, p. 51.

[76] Fenrick 2001, p. 491.

[77] Douhet 1983, p. 56.

[78] Ibid.

[79] Warden 1995, p. 51.

may actually improve the state's ability to operate by relieving pressure on limited resources".[80]

Finally, the fifth element of the ring comprises the fielded military forces of the State. Fielded military forces represent the "fighting mechanism" that protects the State from attack and although one tends to think of the military forces as being the "most vital in war", in Warden's words "they are merely means to an end and not necessarily important in themselves".[81] In practical terms the fifth ring corresponds to a State's aircraft, ships, troops and, obviously, it is "the toughest to reduce, simply because it is designed to be tough". Warden makes an organic analogy to leukocytes or white blood cells that acts as the body's guardians by warding off viruses.[82] In Warden's opinion a campaign that focuses only on the fifth ring—either by choice or because no alternatives exist—is likely to be the longest and bloodiest for both sides. Instead of directly attacking this ring, strikes on the supporting/inner rings could sufficiently weaken the military forces to the point that they become incapable of resistance. This is, in a nutshell, the key argument advanced by Warden's theory, which rests on the idea that modern technology paved the way for new and more effective options that can put fielded forces into the category of means and not ends, thus allowing decision makers to separate, or better to distinguish more neatly, "the physical side of the enemy from its morale".[83]

As Warden notes, during WWII, Germans and Japanese managed to direct their attacks only towards the enemy's population and the fielded forces, respectively the fourth and the fifth rings, whereas the US and the Allies were able to target every German and Japanese rings of vulnerability.[84] Yet, in the context of WWII, and in light of the destruction of entire cities that stemmed from certain bombardments carried out with the aim of bringing an end to the war,[85] it is obviously impossible to speak of "strategic warfare" and consider the final outcome as a validation of Warden's model. When the Five Strategic Rings theory was developed, i.e. in the early 90', technology already made possible the "near simultaneous attack on every strategic- and operational-level vulnerability of the enemy".[86] At the time the theory emerged, "aircraft could attack several targets simultaneously with surprise. Precision guided munitions gave aircrews the ability to destroy or disable a target with a single mission instead of returning repeatedly to a target".[87] Ultimately, modern technology allowed a state's air forces to avoid having to go to battle against the military forces of their opponents, i.e. Warden's fifth ring. It was realised how attacks on several centres of gravity, or rings, resulted in more chaos and damage to an enemy than a single, direct clash between opposing militaries.

[80] Chun and Bartholomees 2012, p. 316.
[81] Warden 1995, p. 51.
[82] Ibid.
[83] Ibid., p. 43.
[84] Ibid., p. 51.
[85] Ledwidge 2018, pp. 98–100; Lambeth 2000.
[86] Warden 1995, p. 55.
[87] Chun 2010, p. 310.

Furthermore, Warden's theory reflected the change in the mindset of the decision makers. At the time the theory was developed, the principal question was not how many aircraft or systems could attack a target, but *which kind of target* should military forces damage or destroy? Commanders needed to consider not only the target itself, but also the consequences that the attack would have on the enemy' system, i.e. the extent to which striking certain targets could lead to the opponent' "strategic paralysis",[88] thus making it incapable of taking any physical action to conduct operations. When Warden's model emerged, what can be described as "a parallel process of war",[89] in contrast with the traditional "serial warfare",[90] had finally taken over. Obviously, whilst developing the Five Strategic Rings theory Warden could not predict the advancement of more groundbreaking technologies and the proliferation of multiple domains,[91] including cyber-space and outer space.[92] Thus, the model could not pass the test of time if its principal assumptions, i.e., (i) air power has almost unlimited access to attack enemy targets and (ii) a country's air force could strike the enemy at the onset of any hostilities,[93] are no longer valid.

The two selected cases that will be explored in the coming (sub-)sections have contributed to validating Warden's theory, which is still widely supported by everyone who envisions airpower as the primary determinant of victory.[94] Unlike most experts, John Warden was able to employ his ideas directly in the 1991 Persian Gulf War's campaign, hence translating his intuition into actual combat planning for operations.[95] Later on, the Five Strategic Rings theory was also heavily relied on during the NATO bombing campaign, another scenario in which air power played a decisive role and Western States bypassed the front line altogether. In both contexts the attacks, which targeted mainly dual-use objects, have been carried out through intense aerial bombardments. Besides representing an opportunity to apply and assess Warden's theory, both the Gulf War and the NATO campaign trigger significant legal questions about the characterisation of the selected targets as military objectives.

2.4 The First Gulf War: Operation Desert Storm

On 2 August 1990, Iraqi forces invaded and occupied Kuwait, beginning a seven-month long series of events known as the Persian Gulf War. Notably, the small emirate was an ally of the US, and a coalition was put together to drive Iraq back to

[88] Warden 1995, p. 43.
[89] McNaughton 2019, p. 49.
[90] Warden 2011, pp. 70–71.
[91] NATO 2022, pp. 2–5.
[92] Smith 2023, p. 2.38.
[93] Chun 2010, pp. 318–319.
[94] Fenrick 2001, pp. 490–491.
[95] Chun 2010, p. 310.

its borders.[96] As the diplomatic tensions quickly escalated after the Iraqi invasion, a planning cell within the US Air Force called "Checkmate" started to plan the military retaliation against Iraq. The plan for an air campaign entitled "Instant Thunder" was developed under Colonel Warden's leadership.[97] As anticipated above, this operation was based upon the Five Strategic Rings model, the theory developed by Warden himself. According to the original plan, in six days, US aircraft would strike 84 targets to neutralise Iraqi key leadership and military capabilities. The plan, however, was doomed to fail as it neglected to include the Iraqi military forces in Kuwait, i.e. the fifth and less relevant ring in Warden's theory. Instant Thunder was quietly rebranded into a more inclusive air campaign, famously known as Operation Desert Storm, that aimed at achieving four operational goals, described as phases: a strategic component, the suppression of the enemy's air defences in the Kuwaiti theatre of operations, preparation of the battlefield, and air support during the eventual ground assault.[98] In order to achieve these goals, the Joint Forces Air Component Commander (JFACC) identified a number of specific objectives:

> (1) to attack Iraqi political-military leadership and command and control (C2); (2) to gain and maintain air superiority; (3) to sever Iraqi supply lines; (4) to destroy known nuclear, biological and chemical (NBC) production, storage and delivery capabilities; (5) to destroy Republican Guard forces in the KTO (Kuwaiti theatre of operations); and (6) to liberate Kuwait City.[99]

The air campaign planners then choose 12 targets to achieve the objectives and implement the different phases of the operation. The selected targets were: (1) nuclear, biological, and chemical facilities (C); (2) Scud missile facilities/sites (SC); (3) military support, production, and research facilities (MS); (4) leadership (L); (5) command, control, and communications sites (CCC); (6) electrical power (E); (7) oil facilities (O); (8) railroads and bridges (RR); (9) airfields (A); (10) naval ports and facilities (N); (11) strategic air defenses (SAD); and (12) Republican Guards (RG).[100] The core of the strategic air campaign was represented by the first eight targets and it originally encompassed attacks against 295 objectives. During the war, the final list of 400 strategic targets, which was approved by the US Central Command (CENTCOM), and not by the White House as it happened in preparation for other wars,[101] almost doubled to over 700.[102] This occurred mainly due to two

---

[96] Ledwidge 2018, p. 143.

[97] Lewis 2003, p. 481.

[98] The US Department of Defense reported that ultimately the forces participating in Operation Desert Storm amounted to over 800,000 military personnel from 36 countries. The following ten countries participated in the air campaign: U.S., Britain, France, Italy, Canada, Kuwait, Saudi Arabia, Bahrain, United Arab Emirates, and Qatar. Human Rights Watch 1991, p. 1. See also Ledwidge 2018, p. 106.

[99] Lewis 2003, p. 488.

[100] Ibid.

[101] That was, for example, the case during the Vietnam war. See Human Rights Watch 1991, Chapter 4, p. 3.

[102] Lewis 2003, p. 488.

concurring factors: additional intelligence-gathering that identified more targets, and an increased number of B-52 and F-117A bombers available in the military theatre to attack those targets.[103]

Human Rights Watch (HRW) reported that for a full five months before the inception of the Gulf War, Iraq was subjected to a massive surveillance operation carried out primarily by the US.[104] The US focused its intelligence gathering capabilities on the whole country, covering in a capillary way the entire 170,000 square miles of Iraq's territory. By resorting to satellites, high-altitude aircraft, electronic eavesdropping equipment and state-of-the-art analysis techniques, the US patiently gathered information on its opponent. However, the validation of the objectives eventually placed on the target list was ultimately undertaken without the support of human intelligence, as the CIA reportedly lacked "even one skilled agent on the Iraqi soil".[105] As several news outlets mentioned in the aftermath of the Gulf War, the US Generals, especially Gen. Horner and Gen. Schwarzkopf praised the independence given to the military in developing the air war plan. In particular, the latter publicly claimed that he was responsible for the selection of the targets and that he would have been "overruled by civilians" only if they think he was doing "something particularly dumb".[106] Along these lines another relevant episode has been often cited by several commentators. An Air Force historian asked Gen. Glosson if, in his opinion, he and the other planners of the air campaign had complete autonomy in the target selection. Famously the answer to the question was a positive one, with Gen. Glosson stressing that they had "total" freedom.[107] Since there was a lack of oversight by senior principals, and since key agents did not believe there was anything wrong with the targeting strategy, there was no attempt to set "a level of acceptable non-combatant casualties",[108] which at that time was defined by the national leadership or established in some standing orders from the Joint Force Commander.[109] With these caveats in mind, it is worth exploring how the air campaign was ultimately carried out, especially with regard to the attacks against dual-use objects.

[103] Gellman 1991.

[104] Human Rights Watch 1991, Chapter 4, pp. 3–4.

[105] Ibid.

[106] Seib 1991.

[107] Ruby 2006, p. 21.

[108] Notably, the Pentagon removed the Non-Combatant Casualty Cut-Off Values (NCVs) from its doctrine in 2018, further info is available at https://www.defensedaily.com/pentagon-removed-non-combatant-casualty-cut-off-value-doctrine-2018/pentagon/ (accessed 11 June 2024).

[109] Deptula 1991; Mann 1995.

2.4.1 A Closer Look at the Selected Targets Qualifiable as Dual-Use Objects

Ultimately, the air campaign lasted 39 days and ended only after Iraq's withdrawal from Kuwait. Commentators from different backgrounds have already voiced their opinions on Operation Desert Storm, its objectives, its implications for the future use of military force, and the operation's degree of compliance with international norms,[110] therefore there is no need to linger on those aspects. The focus of this brief analysis will rather be on the targeting of dual-use objects through the aerial bombardments and the impact of the strategy on the Iraqi population. Based on the non-legal, but widely accepted and simplistic, definition of dual-use objects introduced in the previous chapter, i.e. "military objectives that play a relevant civilian function", it is possible to infer that at least four out of twelve of the targets selected by the coalition in the Gulf War can be instantly characterised as such, namely communication sites, electrical power, oil facilities, and railroads and bridges.

Regarding the first one, i.e. the communication sites, although the Western firms that had built the Iraqi telecommunications system assisted the coalition with the precision targeting, by the second week of the war it was clear that the strategy did not work as planned.[111] It is estimated that 40% of the attacks against "CCC", including the communication sites, were carried out using PGMs, either F-117s or F-111s with laser-guided bombs, Tomahawk or air-launched cruise missiles.[112] The coalition's approach was to search for weaker links in the Iraqi communications, in order to attack them and pursue the goals of "interrupting launch communications with the mobile Scud missile launchers, degrading communications within the Iraqi air defence network, and disrupting communications with the army in Kuwait".[113] Moreover, by shutting down television and radio transmitters, microwave relays, and telephone-switching facilities, the coalition sought to isolate and paralyse the Iraqi leadership, thus putting indirect pressure on the first ring of Warden's model. The information on the communication system that was gathered by US intelligence prior to the launch of the campaign, however, revealed that experience in its 1980-1988 war with Iran caused the Government of Iraq to develop a substantial and comprehensive degree of redundancy in its normal, civilian utilities as back-up for its national defence.[114] In practice this entailed that, in many domains, the Iraqi multilayered system included several built-in backups. The destruction of one layer could not lead to the disruption of service as other layers would be activated to replace the damaged one. In the case of the communication system, this meant that whilst the "civilian" telephone system carried more than half of the military's telecommunications, there

[110] Hampson 1992; Lambeth 2000, pp. 112–140; Fenrick 2001; Lewis 2003; Tucker-Jones 2014.

[111] Lewis 2003, p. 493.

[112] Ibid.

[113] Ibid. See also Tucker-Jones 2014, pp. 56–58.

[114] Department of Defense Report to Congress on the Conduct of the Persian Gulf War (Department of Defense Report), ILM, vol. 31 (3), 1992, p. 617, available at http://www.globalsecurity.org/military/library/report/1992 (accessed 12 June 2024).

were also special underground cables or radio transmissions that relied on "spread spectrum" technology.[115] As a result of this intricate web of doubles and backups, Senior Pentagon officials acknowledged that Iraqi military commanders were able to maintain their line of communication up and running (and were not forced to give orders by radio, where communications are vulnerable to US eavesdropping) because of the underground fibre optic cable that "ran from Baghdad to Basra and on to Kuwait".[116] The US officials further conceded that microwave communications towers had been bombed, including in remote villages, but that the fibre optic line continued to function throughout the conflict.[117] Ultimately, civilian communications were severely impacted, whilst the military channels remained almost unscathed.

With respect to the second target, namely electricity—according to Lewis—when the war began, the estimated capacity of the Iraqi electrical power system amounted to 9500 megawatts and it was established as a "modern" one, in light of the relative infrequency of service interruptions or brownouts.[118] When the Gulf War erupted, Iraq was notably reliant on electrical power for "essential services such as water purification and distribution, sewage removal and treatment, the operation of hospitals and medical laboratories, and agricultural production".[119] Yet, the choice to direct attacks against Iraq's electricity-generating plants, which resulted in their widespread destruction—including four of the country's five hydro-electric facilities—was the object of very limited discussion when the air campaign's plan was laid down and it was never questioned during the war.[120] Even though attacks against electricity set during Desert Storm represented only three per cent of the strategic air campaign and the PGMs were used to conduct most of these attacks, their secondary effects on the civilian population were devastating. The goal that the coalition hoped to achieve by targeting the Iraqi power grid was to impede communications and lower the morale of the Iraqi people, hence loosening Saddam's grip on the nation.[121] Apparently, the primary justification provided for attacking and destroying almost the entire electrical system in Iraq was that the system functioned "as an integrated grid, meaning that power could be shifted countrywide, including to military functions such as command-and-control centres and weapons-manufacturing facilities".[122] However, it should be noted that those crucial military targets had already been attacked during the opening days of the war. Furthermore, not only the planners of the attacks failed to outline the concrete and direct military advantages expected from the destruction of these facilities, and how these advantages were deemed to outweigh the obvious cost to the civilian population, but the "inconclusive battle damage assessment" during

[115] Human Rights Watch 1991, Chapter 4, p. 4.

[116] Atkinson 1991.

[117] Ibid.

[118] Lewis 2003, p. 495.

[119] Human Rights Watch 1991, Chapter 4, pp. 4–6.

[120] Ibid.

[121] Crawford 1997, p. 101; Lewis 2003, p. 495.

[122] Human Rights Watch 1991, Chapter 4, pp. 4–6.

the early days of the campaign also led to several unnecessary reattacks on some targets.[123]

An independent investigating mission organised by Harvard University visited Iraq for nine days in April and May 1991 and found that electricity was supplied at only 23% of the pre-war level.[124] This data was later confirmed by other sources,[125] alongside the widespread effects of the attacks which resulted in severe "deprivation of clean water and sewage removal for the civilian population and paralysed the country's entire health care system, exceeding the deprivations experienced by German civilians as a result of allied bombing during World War II".[126] Overall, Human Rights Watch noted how electrical-generating facilities were targeted not because the electricity directly supported the military effort but rather to harm the Iraqi population as part of a strategy that relied on civilian suffering in furtherance of military or political goals.[127]

In relation to the third dual-use target, i.e. oil facilities, it shall be observed that when the war began, Iraq's daily oil production of three million barrels was the second largest in the world, therefore the Iraqi military forces had a large stockpile of petroleum, oil, and lubricants (POL).[128] Reportedly, the attacks against the "O" set were limited due to President Bush's declared wish to minimise as much as possible long-term damage to Iraq's economic infrastructure. In line with this goal, initially the planners of the air campaign targeted the Iraqi refining capacity, rather than production sites, to deter the replenishment of POL stocks.[129] However, later the attacks hit also the oil industry's administrative facilities for their war-supporting capability, and several Jordanian oil tankers driven by civilians. Notably, the oil transported was taken by Jordan as repayment of loans; as such the oil shipments not only were not meant to refill the military' supply, but, moreover, they did not produce currency that could be used by Iraq to further its war effort.[130] The coalition sought to justify these attacks on the grounds that it was difficult to distinguish these civilian vehicles from trucks carrying materiel for military purposes. Nonetheless, the excuse appears to be weak since no warning had been issued to civilian drivers to stay off the highways in light of pilots' inability to distinguish civilian tankers from military vehicles. Furthermore, it has been ascertained that the Jordanian government

[123] Lewis 2003, p. 496.

[124] Harvard International Study Team on the Gulf Crisis (Harvard Study Team), Health and Welfare in Iraq after the Gulf Crisis an in-Depth Assessment, October 1991, available at: https://www.cesr.org/sites/default/files/Health_and_Welfare_in_Iraq_after_the_Gulf_Crisis_1991.pdf (accessed 13 June 2024).

[125] Crawford 1997, p. 113.

[126] Human Rights Watch 1991, Chapter 4, p. 4. Moreover, it is important to highlight that all of Iraq's water treatment plants operated on electricity. As reported by the World Health Organization (WHO), in March 1991 Baghdad's water supply was only at five per cent of its pre-war level.

[127] Human Rights Watch 1991, Chapter 4, p. 18.

[128] Lewis 2003, p. 495.

[129] Ibid.

[130] Human Rights Watch 1991, Chapter 4, p. 33.

had placed the allies on notice that Jordanian oil tankers were on the road and had been unlawfully attacked by allied planes.[131]

Finally, the fourth kind of dual-use objects attacked during the Gulf War is represented by Iraqi roads and bridges. The attacks carried out against the latter have been particularly devastating. It has been reported that Iraq's bridges were placed on the list of priority targets from the outset. According to the planners, the bombing of the bridges, particularly across the Euphrates River, was a key tactic in the coalition's effort to annihilate the supply lines to Iraqi troops massed in Kuwait and in the northern part of the Kuwait-Iraq border. Despite the military relevance of those targets, "relatively few" PGMs were used to launch attacks against bridges and roads.[132] Military officers provided details on this choice, by claiming that F-15E, F-16 and F/A-18 fighter-bombers flew over 100 missions against 42 key bridges in Iraq, but the aircraft used unguided bombs which ultimately failed to destroy the targets.[133] The decision not to use PGMs appears to be particularly striking, since the attacks on certain bridges, typically used by civilians,[134] were conducted in daytime and the ends of the bridges were near civilian communities.[135]

2.4.2 The Legal Assessment of the Attacks Against Dual-Use Objects

To this day, the First Gulf War is still described as "the conflict in which the potential of air power was fully realized".[136] It is usually argued that the reason behind the "successful" outcome of the war was, indeed, the unprecedented bombing campaign carried out by the coalition. There is no doubt that when the ground phase of the war finally started,[137] the job of US, UK, and French ground forces was made far easier by the "very great attrition air power had inflicted".[138] Furthermore, and this is indisputable, the air campaign played a major role in ensuring that coalition casualties were acceptably low.[139] At the end of the war "only" 154 coalition soldiers had been killed, many of them by "blue-on-blue" incidents, often known by the oxymoron "friendly fire".[140] Indeed, some authors even noted that it was "statistically safer to

---

131 Ibid.

132 Atkinson 1991.

133 Gordon and Schmitt 1991.

134 Hampson 1992, p. 48.

135 During a daytime attack on one of the bridges in Samawa, a city on the Euphrates River in southern Iraq, bombs fell near a crowded market, in an open area at the edge of the river, killing over 100 civilians and injuring others. Human Rights Watch 1991, Chapter 3, p. 7.

136 Ledwidge 2018, p. 146.

137 Smith 1992, p. 2.

138 Ledwidge 2018, p. 146.

139 Lewis 2003, p. 485.

140 Roberts 1993, p. 170.

be a soldier in the vast US and Allied army deployed to the combat theatre than to live in New York".[141]

In addition to the low number of coalition's losses, the Pentagon strongly promoted a one-sided narrative according to which the military campaign will be remembered for its effort, within the legal constraints of IHL, to be "humane".[142] According to the statements released by the US Department of Defense (DoD), the coalition airstrikes were designed to be as precise as possible, and the coalition pilots even took additional risks in order to minimise civilian casualties. Moreover:

> [T]he Coalition restricted the use of weapons employed near civilian areas, permitting some attacks only during the night when most civilians would be home and not near the target area. Other restrictions included not allowing attacks if targets could not be positively identified and avoiding valid military targets in close proximity to civilian areas, including combat aircraft parked in civilian housing areas or near historic sites.[143]

Public declarations also stressed that the meticulous targeting and expert use of technological superiority,[144] including PGMs, throughout the strategic air campaign achieved the scope of minimising collateral damage to the civilian population, thus fully reflecting the US policy's commitment that "Saddam Hussein and his military machine, not the Iraqi people, were the enemy".[145] Ultimately, while conceding that "some Iraqi civilian casualties and damage occurred", the Pentagon spoke deliberately in terms of Iraq's responsibility for the injuries and losses suffered by its own population.[146]

Several commentators over the years have endorsed this narrative, with authors like Lewis claiming that "there seems to be little doubt that the U.S. military took extraordinary measures to ensure that its air campaign complied with international law".[147] In Lewis' view, every action undertaken, from the approval of the targets to the sheer number of Judge Advocate General's Corps (JAG or JAG Corps) assigned to the theatre, is a testament to the "unprecedented pains that the military planners took

---

141 Ledwidge 2018, p. 146.

142 Department of Defense Report to Congress on the Conduct of the Persian Gulf War (Department of Defense Report), ILM, vol. 31 (3), 1992, p. 612, available at http://www.globalsecurity.org/military/library/report/1992 (accessed 12 June 2024).

143 Ibid.

144 Bartolini 2006, p. 230.

145 Final Report to Congress, Conduct of the Persian Gulf War, Pursuant to Title V of the Persian Gulf Conflict Supplemental Authorization and Personnel Benefits Act of 1991 (Public Law 102-25) APRIL 1992, p. 193, available at https://www.globalsecurity.org/military/library/report/1992/cpgw.pdf. Accessed 14 June 2024.

146 Ibid., p. 229. "The problem of collateral civilian casualties was worsened by Saddam Hussein's failure to carry out routine air raid precautions to protect the civilian population and his conscious use of civilians to shield military objectives from attack." From a theoretical perspective, this approach is supported by authors like Parks, according to whom "[i]n customary international law the primary responsibility for preventing collateral civilian casualties *rests with the defender and the individual civilian*, with little or no responsibility imposed upon an attacker." Parks 1998, p. 70 (emphasis added).

147 Lewis 2003, pp. 508–509.

to ensure legality".[148] Similarly, Kahn's words highlight how "the United States and allied forces conducted their operations in accordance with international law",[149] and despite the objections that the allied bombing campaign violated the law of proportionality, he regards this standard as "the weakest of all international law norms".[150]

Others, instead, have voiced their concerns with respect to the air campaign's compliance with international law. Crawford, for example, depicts the Gulf as a "real world laboratory within which the reality of collateral damage (casualties), based upon the lethality of 21st century warfare may be examined".[151] In his opinion, "never before has there been so much devastation visited upon a civilian population as a result of accurately placed munitions" and "civilian harm was exacerbated by the fact that noncombatants were otherwise spared the *direct effects* of urban aerial assault" thanks to the use of PGMs and other highly efficient techniques which eliminated the life support systems.[152] Notably, and contrary to popular belief, it was not until the war was over that the United States Air Force disclosed that the coalition relied overwhelmingly on unguided general-purpose bombs, i.e. "dumb bombs", to attack Iraqi targets. The Air Force chief of staff Gen. McPeak released information at a briefing in Washington, D.C., that PGMs accounted for only 7400 tons (or 8.8%) of the approximately 84,200 tons of ordnance dropped by the allies during Operation Desert Storm.[153]

In addition to the very limited use of PGMs during the air strikes—which ultimately caused somewhere between 1000 and approximately 3500 civilian deaths[154]—the indirect effects of the bombing campaign, which have been carefully overlooked by the US' assessment of the conflict, left a profound impact on all the essential infrastructures, including hospitals, water stations and wastewater stations. Also, agricultural production was significantly affected as the widespread destruction of the electric grid reduced irrigation capacity to Iraq's arable land resulting in decreased yields.[155] As a consequence of the lack of electricity across the country, Arkin, the director of the nuclear information unit of Greenpeace International, famously estimated between 70,000 and 90,000 deaths above the normal mortality rate over the period April–December 1991.[156]

---

[148] Ibid.

[149] Kahn 1993, p. 434.

[150] Ibid., p. 435.

[151] Crawford 1997, p. 115.

[152] Ibid.

[153] Some of these precision munitions reportedly were used against Iraqi military targets in the Kuwaiti theatre of operations, away from any civilian population, leaving an even smaller percentage for use in populated areas. Human Rights Watch 1991, p. 113.

[154] The broad range clearly suggests that the challenge to establish the precise number of deaths that were directly accountable to the air war has never been overcome. Larson and Savych 2006, p. 21.

[155] Human Rights Watch 1991, Chapter 4, p. 9.

[156] Arkin 1992, p. 63.

The legality of the operation, as explained above, has been proclaimed by many whilst challenged only by a few commentators. Narrowing down the focus on the dual-use targets that have been identified and briefly described above, it is useful to linger on the compliance of the air campaign with the key IHL tenets. The first one is the principle of distinction, according to which "[t]he parties to the conflict must always distinguish between civilian objects and military objectives. Attacks may only be directed against military objectives. Attacks must not be directed against civilian objects."[157] Iraqi communication sites, electrical power, oil facilities, and railroads and bridges have been characterised as potential "military objectives"[158] by most commentators on the Gulf War, regardless of whether they found the air campaign in line with the IHL framework in force or not. Some authors, however, have noted that although "a dual-use object clearly has a military function"[159]—at least according to the traditional approach—its status as a military objective still depends on whether its destruction or other debilitation offers a definite military advantage. In the case of some of the electricity-generating plants that have been hit later in the conflict, it has been argued that once the coalition had gained air supremacy the criterion of the definite military advantage could no longer be satisfied.[160] Similarly, in relation to the allied attacks on oil refineries and other production and storage facilities, it should be questioned first if it is permissible at all to attack the production of export items whose earnings are vital to finance an enemy's war effort,[161] and second, assuming that the first question shall be answered in the positive, where does the advantage lie since Iraq was not able to generate export earnings from its petroleum industry due to the Security Council-imposed sanctions on all trade with Iraq and occupied Kuwait? The issue does not even need to be raised with respect to the Jordan oil tankers which were owned and driven by private citizens of a State that was not a party to the conflict. The allied never asserted that Jordanian oil tankers were legitimate military targets, but instead excused these attacks on the grounds that it was "difficult" to distinguish these civilian vehicles from trucks carrying materiel for military purposes.[162]

This justification is not admissible inasmuch as IHL provides for "a presumption of civilian status" that applies to both persons and things.[163] This entails that in cases of doubt about how to classify a potential target, it shall be presumed that it is not being used to make an effective contribution to military action. In other words, it cannot be automatically assumed that any person or object that appears dubious may be subject

157 Henckaerts and Doswald-Beck 2005, Rule 1.

158 Military objectives are defined in Article 52(2) of Protocol I as "limited to those objects which by their nature, location, purpose or use make an effective contribution to military action and whose total or partial destruction, capture or neutralization, in the circumstances ruling at the time, offers a definite military advantage."

159 Hampson 1992, p. 50.

160 Human Rights Watch 1991, pp. 187–189.

161 Although still a controversial question, the present author shares the view that the inclusion of war-sustaining economic objects in the definition of military objectives is not correct. Reetz 2022, p. 462.

162 Human Rights Watch 1991, p. 218.

163 See Article 50(1) and 52(3) of API.

to lawful attack. This is also consistent with the principle of precautions, in particular with the obligation to verify that objects to be attacked are military objectives liable to attack and not civilian objects.[164] The presumption of civilian status, which was famously disputed in previous editions of the US DoD's Law of War Manual,[165] nowadays is expressly incorporated in its revised version.[166] This change, which according to some authors "adds nothing other than confusion to these meritorious standards already in place",[167] eliminates one of the major points of criticism against the DoD's Manual. Although it is difficult to assess the future developments of the United States' practice following the recognition of the presumption of civilian status, at the time of the Gulf War the US fiercely defended its controversial stance on the matter.[168] However, during the First Gulf War the rejection of the presumption had been somehow mitigated through the adoption of precautionary measures in attack. The Rules of Engagement (RoE) for US Military Forces in Iraq affirmed that positive identification (PI), i.e. a reasonable certainty that the proposed target is a legitimate military target, was required prior to engagement.[169] As a result of this, pilots attacking targets located in populated areas were directed to return to base with their munitions if they lacked positive identification of their target.[170] As reported by Lewis, this policy led to an approximately 25% of all combat missions returned to base with undelivered ordnance.[171] Notwithstanding these efforts, it is worth noting that the principle of precautions is a multifaceted one that consists of a number of different and obviously entwined obligations, which cannot be satisfied by merely verifying the military nature of the targets. Moreover, the presumption of civilian status, which did not find application in the Gulf War, is of particular relevance when it comes to assessing the lawfulness of attacks against dual-use objects, also because such rule shifts the burden of determining the precise use of an object from the defender to the attacker.[172]

With regard to the principle of proportionality—requiring that the expected incidental harm is not excessive in relation to the anticipated military advantage—this has been at the forefront of the discussion surrounding the legality of Operation

[164] Henckaerts and Doswald-Beck 2005, pp. 51.67.

[165] Van Schaack 2016.

[166] The US Department of Defense Law of War Manual (June 2015, Updated July 2023) https://media.defense.gov/2023/Jul/31/2003271432/-1/-1/0/DOD-LAW-OF-WAR-MANUAL-JUNE-2015-UPDATED-JULY%202023.PDF (accessed 23 June 2024). See Meier 2023.

[167] Richard 2022.

[168] Final Report to Congress, Conduct of the Persian Gulf War, Pursuant to Title V of the Persian Gulf Conflict Supplemental Authorization and Personnel Benefits Act of 1991 (Public Law 102-25) APRIL 1992 (hereinafter Final Report to Congress), p. 196, available at https://www.globalsecurity.org/military/library/report/1992/cpgw.pdf. Accessed 2 July 2024.

[169] Rules of Engagement for U.S. Military Forces in Iraq, issued by U.S. Central Command Combined Forces Land Component Commander, https://www.hrw.org/reports/2003/usa1203/11.htm (accessed 2 July 2024).

[170] U.S. Department of Defense 1991/2000, para 12-3.

[171] Lewis 2003, p. 501.

[172] Van Schaack 2016.

Desert Storm. Several authors have already discussed the matter and concluded that in some instances the coalition's attacks have failed the proportionality test.[173] It is not possible to delve into the manifold aspects raised by the practice of States in the Gulf conflict, but some considerations need to be reiterated in this work. In particular, the attacks carried out against dual-use objects, namely communication sites, railroads and bridges, oil facilities, and electrical power are emblematic of how the rule as it stands allows a considerable degree of latitude for interpretation.[174] The interpretation of this principle by the US forces, in fact, limits the legal obligation to minimise civilian casualties to the prohibition of attacks that are negligent in either the selection of the target or the conduct of the attack itself, resulting in such excessive losses as to amount to a direct attack on civilians.[175] This approach is at odds with the multiple elements that Article 51(5)(b) requires to take into consideration before an attack is launched,[176] and clearly ignores the reverberating effects that certain attacks have on the civilian population.

Concerning communication networks and sites, their disruption aimed at degrading communications within the Iraqi air defence network as well as communications with the army in Kuwait, thus pursuing, in principle, a legitimate military advantage gained from successful attacks. As discussed above, and despite the resort to PGMs for the attacks against those targets, the Iraqi national telecommunications system had not collapsed as had been anticipated. In relation to roads and bridges, it shall be noted that it is much more straightforward and thus easier to ascertain the amount of military benefit deriving from the dropping of a particular bridge or road.[177] With a few exceptions, it was concluded that the value of any individual bridge in Iraq was not great and that the proportionality assessment was done measuring the overall value of the "RR" set against the total casualties that such strikes were likely to cause.[178]

The attacks against Iraqi oil were set to prevent the Iraqi army from mounting a protracted ground war. Initially the strikes targeted only the Iraqi refining capacity, but later more strikes have been carried out against the large number of petroleum, oil and lubricants stocks in Iraq. Because of their size and separation from the civilian population, most "O" set targets were attacked with "dumb" bombs and did not result in civilian casualties, with the notable exception of the Jordanian oil tankers discussed above, which do not trigger a proportionality assessment due to their status as civilians and civilian objects.[179] With respect to the attacks against the Iraqi electrical infrastructures, the inconclusive battle damage assessment during the early days of the war left doubts in some of the air planners' minds as to the extent and permanence

[173] Gardam 1993; Roberts 1993; Lewis 2003.

[174] Gardam 1993, p. 407.

[175] Ibid., p. 409.

[176] Ibid., p. 408.

[177] Lewis 2003, p. 494.

[178] Ibid.

[179] See Sect. 2.4.1.

of the damage.[180] To use Crawford's words "some would argue that such is the price of war"; however, he points out that "this argument can only be justified if the nullification of electricity conferred a direct and concrete military advantage superior in its effect when balanced against the unintended casualties".[181] The unprecedented devastation of power infrastructures that characterised the coalition's air campaign resulted, indeed, from the targeting of objectives that, while apparently serving a military purpose—and thus being a legitimate military objective—were also essential to the survival of the civilian population. In line with the US approach to the issue,[182] the military advantage was calculated on a cumulative, rather than a case-by-case basis. That is, the attacks on dual-use targets were assessed solely in terms of their contribution to the weakening of the overall military forces of Iraq, rather than by considering the long-and short-term civilian casualties and balancing this factor against a direct immediate military advantage.[183] Since the Gulf War, the doctrine has widely endorsed the view that the proportionality equation should not be restricted to the immediate effects of an attack,[184] thus including also the reverberating effects of an attack, a notion that remains volatile to these days. The coalition's and especially the US' practice during the First Persian War, on the one hand undoubtedly cemented the mainstream position vis-à-vis dual-use objects. On the other hand, however, it drew significant attention to its shortcomings, triggering a much needed, albeit never settled, debate on how to improve the situation for the sake of the civilian population.

2.5 The NATO Bombing Campaign Against the Former Yugoslavia

On 24 March 1999 NATO, led by the United States, embarked in a 78-day air war against the FRY to halt and reverse the human-rights abuses that were being committed against the Albanian citizens of its Kosovo province. That air campaign, called Operation Allied Force, represents a further example in which air power proved pivotal in determining the outcome of a regional conflict during the 1990s. The war ended on 9 June 1999, after the FRY's President Milosevic finally acceded to NATO's demands and a withdrawal of Serb forces from Kosovo had begun.[185] It has been reported that during the bombing campaign, the NATO aircraft flew 38,004 sorties, including 10,484 strike sorties, and the NATO aircraft dropped a total of 6303 tons of munitions. Of the more than 23,000 bombs and missiles used during the operation, 35% were PGMs, a minority than nonetheless cemented the controversial notion of

[180] Lewis 2003, p. 496.
[181] Crawford 1997, p. 115.
[182] Gardam 1993, p. 409; Gillard 2018, pp. 8–9.
[183] Gardam 1993, p. 409.
[184] Crawford 1997, p. 114; Byron 2010, p. 201; ICRC 2016, pp. 43–46; Gillard 2018.
[185] Lambeth 2001.

"smart" wars.[186] As noted by Kritsiotis, such a robust application of armed force came on the eve of the 50th anniversary of NATO, an organisation which was established after WWII for the collective defence of its member States, and, remarkably, the air campaign constituted the first offensive operation launched against another sovereign State in the organisation's entire history.[187] Most commentators have focussed their attention on the examination of the NATO's claims and actions under the *jus ad bellum* perspective,[188] whereas least attention has been devoted to the international legal regulation of warfare and more specifically to the dual-use objects that have been attacked by the NATO forces.

2.5.1 The Attacks Carried out Against Dual-Use Objects

Given the effects of the Gulf War in 1991, the pressure to minimise civilian casualties and unintended damage to non-military structures was greater amongst NATO's member States than in any previous campaign involving US forces.[189] Arkin, sharing with the world the results of interviews conducted with some two dozen senior active and retired US Air Force generals, wrote about a collective sense of "disappointment that air power is being so poorly employed [and] frustration over the false promise of a perfect war and zero casualties."[190] There are multiple factors that played a role from the outset of the air campaign. In particular, NATO set specific strategic objectives for its use of force in Kosovo that later served as the basis for its stated conditions to Milosevic for stopping the air campaign. Those objectives were to: (i) demonstrate the seriousness of NATO's opposition to Belgrade's aggression in the Balkans; (ii) deter Milosevic from continuing and escalating his attacks on helpless civilians and create conditions to reverse his ethnic cleansing; and (iii) damage Serbia's capacity to wage war against Kosovo in the future or spread the war to neighbours by diminishing or degrading its ability to wage military operations.[191] Like in the case of Operation Desert Storm, the choice of targets during the NATO bombing must be viewed within the context of the prominent theory for the use of aerospace power developed by Warden and discussed above.[192] Although the model is hailed as strategic and

[186] Fenrick 2001, p. 489.

[187] Kritsiotis 2000, p. 330.

[188] See, *ex plurimis*, Cassese 1999; Simma 1999. Allegations have been made that, as NATO's resort to force was not authorized by the UN Security Council or in self-defence, forceful measures taken by NATO were unlawful.

[189] Lambeth 2001, p. 136.

[190] Arkin 1999.

[191] Final Report to the Prosecutor by the Committee Established to Review the NATO Bombing Campaign against the Federal Republic of Yugoslavia, (13 June 2000), (hereinafter OTP Report) reprinted in (2000) ILM 39:1257. For an assessment of the OTP's finding, see Ronzitti 2000, p. 1017.

[192] See Sect. 2.3.

highly effective, its main "unspoken-but-known result"[193] is the indirect targeting of the civilian population.[194]

Operation Allied Force was originally planned to be carried out in five phases under NATO's operational plan, whose development began in the summer of 1998. Phase 0 was the deployment of air assets into the European theatre. Phase 1 would establish air superiority over Kosovo and degrade command and control over the whole of the FRY. Phase 2 would attack military targets in Kosovo and those FRY forces which were providing reinforcement to Serbian forces inside Kosovo's territory. The goal was in fact to allow targeting of forces not only in Kosovo, but also in the south of Belgrade. Phase 3 would expand air operations against a wide range of high-value military and security force targets throughout the FRY. Phase 4 would redeploy forces as required. Within a few days of the start of NATO's campaign, alliance aircraft were striking both strategic and tactical targets throughout Serbia, as well as working to suppress and disrupt the FRY's integrated air defence system.[195] At the end of the operation, a widely cited report by Human Rights Watch concluded that there had been at least 90 incidents involving civilians, as a result of which "as few as 488 and as many as 527 Yugoslav civilians were killed. Between 62 and 66 per cent of the total registered civilian deaths occurred in just twelve incidents. These twelve incidents accounted for 303 to 352 civilian deaths."[196] The post-conflict casualties were presumably much higher, with estimates by the Yugoslav government varying between at least some 1200 and as many as 5000 civilians.[197]

The objects placed on the NATO list included: "military forces, security forces, command and control facilities, the integrated air defence system, military-industrial infrastructure, the media and broadcasting system, supply routes, lines of communications, bridges, government ministries and refineries".[198] According to the information released by NATO in the aftermath of the conflict, the selected targets were grouped into two distinct typologies, "tactical" vs "strategic" ones.[199] The first group encompassed military facilities, especially artillery and field headquarters. The second instead included "government ministries and refineries" to which the US statement also added media and other strategic targets.[200]

Dual-use objects attacked during the air campaign included a State-owned television and radio station in the centre of Belgrade and several elements of the country's transportation system. Concerning the former, on the early morning of 23 April 1999, the NATO attack on the headquarters and studio of Serbian state television and radio (RTS) in central Belgrade killed at least 16 civilians and injured 16 more. RTS was deliberately the object of the attack and this triggered extensive debate on whether it

[193] Fenrick 2001, p. 491.

[194] Crawford 1997, pp. 101–102.

[195] OTP Report, para 45 [n 191].

[196] Human Rights Watch 1999, pp. 12–13.

[197] Ibid.

[198] Fenrick 2001, p. 495.

[199] NATO 2000, pp. 14–15.

[200] OTP Report, para 47 [n 191].

was a legitimate military objective and, in the affirmative, if the incidental deaths and injuries were disproportionate or not.[201] With regard to the latter set of targets, the NATO's bombardment hit the Danube bridges, with 70% of roads bridges and 50% of the rail bridges reportedly destroyed, blocking the river traffic between Belgrade and Croatia; and the Kosovo corridors with 100% of the rail and over 50% of the road capacity interdicted.[202] One of the most famous and scrutinised incidents in the series of attacks that targeted the transportation system occurred on 2 April 1999, when a NATO aircraft launched two laser guided bombs at the Leskovac railway bridge over the Grdelica gorge and Juzna Morava river, in eastern Serbia. The designated target was the railway bridge, which was claimed to be part of a re-supply route being used for Serb forces in Kosovo. A five-carriage passenger train, travelling from Belgrade to Ristovac on the Macedonian border, was crossing the bridge at the time and was struck by both missiles. The attack killed at least 10 people and injured at least 15 individuals.[203] These two events over the years have been commented upon by practitioners and academics alike, in addition they have been analysed by an ad hoc committee (Review Committee) set up by the Prosecutor of the International Criminal Tribunal for the Former Yugoslavia (ICTY) to ascertain whether war crimes had been committed during the NATO bombing.[204] Notably, the Review Committee in its report, which was completed at the end of May 2000, formulated the recommendation that no investigation be commenced by the Office of the Prosecutor (OTP) in relation to the NATO bombing campaign.[205] Nonetheless, the findings of the Review Committee as well as the extensive debate triggered by these attacks provide a solid basis for a more thorough reflection on the dual-use nature of the targets and the problems (still) attached to the *non liquet* decision enshrined in the Review Committee's report.[206]

2.5.2 The Legal Assessment of the Attacks Against Dual-Use Objects

As a preliminary caveat, it is important to point out that, given the goal of the NATO intervention and the peculiar character of the conflict, two contrasting theories, both of them wrong, were put forward concerning the "different" reach of the rules of IHL, and, in particular the key principles of distinction and proportionality.[207] The first thesis claims that attacks carried out in order to undermine support amongst the enemy civilian population for the policy of its government would be lawful.

[201] Fenrick 2001, p. 496.

[202] Cordesman 2003, pp. 97–98.

[203] OTP Report, para 59 [n 191].

[204] Benvenuti 2001, p. 527.

[205] OTP Report, para 91 [n 191].

[206] Ronzitti 2000, pp. 1019–1020.

[207] Greenwood 2001, p. 114.

Consequently, a greater latitude in choosing the targets would be allowed. Those who endorsed this position suggested that military necessity and military advantage might be different for "humanitarian" interventions, since the scope of the bombing campaign was not to defeat the FRY armed forces (in the normal sense of that term, i.e., by successfully engaging them in battle) but to produce a change of policy on the part of the FRY Government.[208]

It has already been noted that one of the main challenges stemming from what can be easily described as a biased approach lies in defining the scope of application of such special rules compared to that of the normal rules and in abandoning the traditional equality of belligerents before IHL.[209] Furthermore, nothing in any of the treaties on the LOAC or the practice of States entails that a State's motives or the fact that it seeks to procure a change in its adversary's policy rather than that adversary's total defeat "can expand the range of targets which is lawfully open to it".[210] The second theory, equally misleading, proposes that in cases of humanitarian intervention "there must be even stricter adherence to the laws of war and international humanitarian law than in standard military operations."[211] Such an approach emerged, without finding much support, from the report of the Independent International Commission on Kosovo, namely an unofficial body of non-governmental commentators established at the initiative of the Prime Minister of Sweden. The Report does not appear to infer that the IHL norms applicable to a force engaging in humanitarian intervention should differ from those applicable to forces engaged in other military operations, but rather that those rules should be more strictly applied. The idea that the law can prescribe the same rules for all types of military operations but require a higher standard of compliance in some cases is, as rightly stressed by Greenwood, simply "untenable".[212]

None of the NATO governments engaged in the discussions triggered by these two theories, nor took the time to dismiss them. According to the NATO's official narrative "the selection of targets was carefully reviewed at multiple levels of command, as well as by the Allies carrying out the strikes. These reviews ensured they complied with international law, were militarily justified, and minimised the risk to civilian lives and property".[213] Several experts have contradicted this assessment of the targeting process by reporting that:

> [...] the joint air operations planning process didn't take the steps to ensure noncombatant protection. Rather, it skipped from determining objectives directly to picking targets without matching desired effects with weapons or platforms. The NATO chief of targets agreed, stating that targets were added so quickly in order to build a large list that there was not time to do a proper workup on them.[214]

---

208 Ibid.

209 See Sassòli 2005, pp. 199–200; Obradović 2000, p. 700.

210 Bothe 2001, pp. 533–534.

211 Greenwood 2001, p. 115.

212 Ibid., pp. 125–127.

213 NATO 2000, p. 15.

214 Gingras and Ruby 2000, p. 108.

Moreover, it is worth noting that NATO was criticised for directing its aircraft to fly above 15,000 feet early in the conflict as it was alleged that this would not permit the aircrew to adequately distinguish between military and civilian objects on the ground.[215] This restriction had clearly been imposed to protect NATO aircraft and pilots from FRY air defences; and in fact NATO lost no aircrews, realising the "zero-casualties policy" that was meant, from the outset, for its own forces rather than for the civilian population of its enemy.[216] Without lingering on the assessment of the entire air campaign, as mentioned above this work will focus solely on two relevant episodes concerned specifically dual-use objects. The first one is the attack against the RTS. The TV and radio station was attacked intentionally and the justification provided by NATO in press conferences, and denied by the FRY, was that the bombing of the RTS was part of a planned attack aimed at disrupting and degrading the FRY's C3 (Command, Control and Communication) network.[217] The decision to attack the RTS was borne out of NATO's classification of a media outlet as a military objective, an assumption that has been questioned at length.[218] In principle, the view that media are a legitimate military objective, or may become one, is supported implicitly by Article 8(1)(a) of the 1954 Hague Cultural Property Convention,[219] as well as by the compilation of military objectives made by the ICRC in the context of its 1956 Draft Rules for the Limitation of the Dangers incurred by the Civilian Population in Time of War. According to that list of military objectives, which should have become an annex to Article 7, para 2 of the Draft Rules, "installations of broadcasting and television stations" are military objectives.[220] Furthermore, it is undeniable that there are instances in which the media are used to incite the population to commit genocide, war crimes, and crimes against humanity, as happened in Rwanda in 1994. Yet, it is extremely rare for broadcasting networks to appear on a target list. Fenrick summarises the application of the principle of distinction to this specific category of objects as follows:

> RTS would be a military objective (only) if it was integrated into the military command, control or communications system. Whether it would be a legitimate military objective in other circumstances is more debatable. If RTS was merely a propaganda outlet, one might query its status as a military objective [...] The media would not constitute a legitimate military objective. If the state controls essentially all of the media and the political leadership directing the war effort uses that media as part of a system to control the civilian population, it is conceivable that media focal points could be regarded as legitimate military objectives.[221]

---

[215] Fenrick 2001, p. 501.

[216] Lambeth 2001, pp. 81–82.

[217] Benvenuti 2001, p. 522.

[218] As reported by HRW "[a]ccording to military sources, there was considerable disagreement between the United States and French governments regarding the legality and legitimacy of the target". Human Rights Watch 1999, p. 29.

[219] Convention for the Protection of Cultural Property in the Event of Armed Conflict with Regulations for the Execution of the Convention, opened for signature 14 May 1954, 3511 UNTS, entered into force 7 August 1956 (1954 Hague Convention).

[220] Ronzitti 2000, p. 1024.

[221] Fenrick 2001, p. 497.

In other words, being a symbol of the regime is not enough to qualify a media outlet as an element of the C3 or CCC system of a country, as this will imply that the media in a State with a free press could never be a legitimate military target.[222] In the case under scrutiny the RTS was controlled by the State only to a degree, therefore it could not be considered a part of the FRY's C3 system. Unfortunately, neither NATO nor the Review Committee reached this conclusion, with the former defending the choice to attack the RTS in several press statements[223] and the latter addressing the incident in a more critical, although inconclusive, way.[224] More in detail, the Review Committee found that "if the attack on the RTS was justified by reference to its propaganda purpose alone, its legality might well be questioned by some experts in the field of IHL".[225] Nonetheless, and assuming that with this sentence the Review Committee affirmed the violation of the principle of distinction, the report did not express strong condemnation for the attack.

In addition to the erroneous qualification of the target as a military objective, other considerations can be advanced with respect to the principle of precautions and given NATO's firm stance on the military nature of the broadcasting station, the principle of proportionality. As far as the principle of precautions is concerned, NATO failed to provide clear advance warning of the attacks, as required by Article 57(2) of Additional Protocol I.[226] It was reported that Western journalists, who were using the facility to forward material from Yugoslavia, had been warned by their employers to stay away from the television station before the attack, which was originally scheduled to take place on 12 April 1999. The attack was postponed because of rumours that foreign journalists ignored warnings to leave the buildings, and, only at that point, the Yugoslav Government had also received information about the planned operation. However, since the attack eventually took place 10 days later than originally scheduled, the FRY leadership dismissed the threat as no longer existing and local civilian workers and technicians ultimately stayed in the building.[227] The Review Committee also concluded that some doubts have been expressed as to the specificity of the warning given to civilians by NATO of its intended strike, and whether the notice would have constituted "effective warning [...] of attacks which may affect the civilian population".[228]

In relation to the principle of proportionality, which in any case would be relevant only if the RTS could be regarded as a military target, the question to answer would be whether the death of civilians had to be considered "collateral damage"

---

[222] Ibid.

[223] Accordingly, NATO stressed the dual-use to which such communications systems were put, describing civilian television as "heavily dependent on the military command and control system and military traffic is also routed through the civilian system". NATO press conference of 27 April 1999, cited in the OTP Report, para 72 [n 191].

[224] Benvenuti 2001, p. 522.

[225] OTP Report, para 76 [n 191].

[226] Human Rights Watch 1999, p. 30.

[227] Ibid., pp. 29–30.

[228] OTP Report, para 77 [n 191].

within the meaning of Article 51(5)(b) of API, i.e. damage which would not be "excessive in relation to the concrete and direct military advantage anticipated".[229] Concerning the "concrete and direct military advantage" stemming from the attack against the RTS, some additional considerations can be made. Both the NATO and the Review Committee shared an approach to the matter that is not in line with API and also contradicts the ICTY jurisprudence on the assessment of proportionality.[230] It is worth noting here that the attack on the RTS building was seen as forming part of an "integrated attack against numerous objects", including transmission towers and control buildings, which were "essential to Milosevic's ability to direct and control the repressive activities of his army and special police forces in Kosovo".[231] In other words, the proportionality assessment carried out by NATO was not focussed on the specific incident, but rather, as explained in the OTP Report, on the overall assessment of the totality of civilians victims against the goals of the military campaign.[232] Measured against this broad strategic military objective, one might be inclined to relax too much the second prong of the proportionality test. For this reason, there is little doubt on the necessity to apply a different approach, which takes into consideration the specific military advantage deriving from an attack against an individual military objective or at least from a given military operation, as it will be discussed in Chap. 4 of this book. In this case, several sources reported that after the strikes on the Belgrade and Novi Sad headquarters, Yugoslav State broadcasters were able to "easily move operations to other facilities".[233] Therefore, since broadcasting allegedly resumed within hours from the strike, it is legitimate to regard as negligible the importance of the military advantage gained by the attack vis-a-vis the civilian casualties incurred in the specific incident.

Regarding the attacks against the transportation system, the most discussed incident is the deadly attack against the Leskovac railway bridge, which caused also the destruction of a passenger train that was crossing it during the attack. In this instance the principle of distinction was blatantly violated as a civilian object, i.e. the passenger train, was hit whilst the pilot's mission was to take out the bridge, which was part of the integrated communications supply network in Serbia. The Review Committee considered the bridge to be a legitimate military objective,[234] and this view has been unequivocally supported also by the doctrine,[235] in line with the mainstream approach to dual-use objects that the present work seeks to challenge. As explained by Ronzitti "after the first bomb was dropped and the train hit, since the bridge was still intact, the pilot released a second bomb directed at the opposite end from where the train had come."[236] Therefore the issue has been

---

[229] Ronzitti 2000, p. 1023.

[230] Benvenuti 2001, p. 517.

[231] NATO press release 1 May 1999 cited in Benvenuti 2001, p. 524.

[232] OTP Report, para 78 [n 191].

[233] Human Rights Watch 1999, p. 30.

[234] OTP Report, para 62 [n 191].

[235] Ronzitti 2000, p. 1025; Benvenuti 2001, p. 521.

[236] Ibid.

analysed under the principles of precautions and proportionality. With regard to the former, the question is whether the pilot had the obligation to stop the attack when he realised that the train was crossing the bridge. According to Article 57(2)(b) of API an attack shall be cancelled or suspended if it becomes apparent that the objective is not a military one or if the attack violates the principle of proportionality, the norm is also part of customary international law as enshrined in Rule 19 of the ICRC study.[237] The Review Committee admittedly had "divided views concerning the attack with the second bomb in relation to whether there was an element of recklessness in the conduct of the pilot and/or the Weapons System Officer (WSO)".[238] Besides noting that the train was visible and on the bridge when the bridge itself was targeted a second time, the Committee concluded that the incident should not be investigated.[239] As stressed by a number of authors,[240] the Committee simply failed to assess the incident and in particular the individual responsibility attached to it.

Concerning the application of the principle of proportionality, since several civilians were killed or injured as a result of the attack, it is surprising that neither NATO nor the Review Committee manifested the need to carry out a proportionality assessment. Assuming that the bridge was a legitimate military objective, a reflection was due on whether the second attack fell under Article 51(5)(b) and it could be expected to cause incidental damage (loss of civilian life, injury to civilians and damage to civilian objects) that would be excessive in relation to the concrete and direct military advantage anticipated from the destruction of the bridge.[241] Concerning the expected military advantage of the attack, this has not been made clear by NATO. Moreover, due to the fact that the FRY and Croatia have not always maintained friendly relations, one might question the military significance of the strikes conducted to block the river traffic between Belgrade and Croatia.[242] Although the Review Committee's work was limited to an assessment of individual criminal responsibility for the purposes of exercising the ICTY's jurisdiction over the bombing campaign, which led to a much criticised *non liquet*,[243] it is striking to observe a one-sided attitude, an utter disregard for the ICTY case law, and widespread contradictions in the use of legal concepts.[244] However, and in spite of its many shortcomings, it is undeniable that the report of the Review Committee has contributed to shedding light on several important matters, starting with the famous statement that in some instances "the law is not sufficiently clear", especially when dealing with dual-use objects.[245]

---

[237] Henckaerts and Doswald-Beck 2005, p. 60.

[238] OTP Report, para 62 [n 191].

[239] Ibid.

[240] Ronzitti 2000, p. 1025; Benvenuti 2001, pp. 520–521.

[241] Ronzitti 2000, p. 1025.

[242] Fenrick 2001, p. 497.

[243] Ronzitti 2000.

[244] Benvenuti 2001, p. 526.

[245] OTP Report, para 90 [n 191].

2.6 Conclusion

The present chapter constitutes an essential bridge between the previous one, which laid down the research problem and pointed out the key main issues that this work aims at discussing, and the next one which will question the traditional understanding of the notion of "military objectives" and the repercussions that this definition has on dual-use objects. The analysis started with a thorough examination of the main factors which, in this author's view, affect the current approach to warfare. First, there is a widespread militarisation process that results in increasing interactions, at all levels, between a State's armed forces, and the other sectors of society in which the armed forces are more and more embedded.[246] It is difficult to disagree with the claim that the recent "epidemic of coups in parts of sub-Saharan Africa, the reliance of government in both democracies and autocracies on civil–military cooperation during the Covid-19 pandemic and the return of interstate war in Europe", have contributed to make militarisation the defining zeitgeist of a new "post-post-Cold War era".[247] A more IHL oriented view of the phenomenon triggers a perhaps narrower, but still crucial, reflection on the consequences that the militarisation process has on the conduct of hostilities, starting with the increasingly blurred lines between military objectives and civilian objects. The second main factor that needs to be considered is the supremacy of air power in modern warfare and the main theory that supported and informed the rise of strategic air warfare. The assessment made by Marshal Ferdinand Foch when, as a distinguished Professor of strategy at France's École Supérieure de guerre (war college) before World War I, affirmed that "[a]irplanes are interesting toys, but of no military value"[248] surely rings surreal now. The concrete implementation of Warden's "Five Strategic Rings" model, which educated Western leaders to look at the "enemy as a system" building on von Clausewitz' centres of gravity, took place in two distinct air campaigns that have been discussed in the present chapter and used as case studies to dissect the traditional approach to dual-use objects. Both the First Gulf War and the NATO bombing campaign against the FRY have been hailed as examples of operations that paid an unprecedented degree of attention to the applicable IHL framework. Without contradicting the *intentions* of the US-led coalition in Iraq and the NATO forces in FRY; it is blatant to observe that both episodes have resulted in what several commentators consider to be an unacceptably high level of civilian casualties.[249] Furthermore, both campaigns focussed extensively on key infrastructures, falling under the category of dual-use targets. On the one hand those two events have significantly contributed to cementing the current attitude towards dual-use objects. On the other hand, however, they have undisputably highlighted this approach's tension with IHL rules as well as the long-term consequences for the civilian population. The combination of these elements is essential to redirect the efforts in a new direction. As discussed in the previous (sub-)sections, which have

[246] Pion-Berlin et al. 2024, p. 1.

[247] Ibid., p. 3.

[248] Warden 2011, p. 64.

[249] Byron 2010, p. 176; Dinstein 2002, p. 219.

presented an analysis of the selected targets and of the legal questions raised by the attacks against them, it appears that the mainstream approach to dual-use objects warrants a significant, and urgent, paradigm shift.

References

Arkin W M (1992) Tactical Bombing of Iraqi Forces Outstripped Value of Strategic Hits, Analyst Contends. Aviation Week & Space Technology 4: 61–63

Arkin W M (1999) In the Air: Frustration with Expectations of a Perfect War. The Washington Post 25 April 1999. https://www.washingtonpost.com/wp-srv/national/dotmil/outlook042599.htm, Accessed 3 July 2024

Atkinson R (1991) Iraqis Called Vulnerable to Land Attack. The Washington Post, 15 February 1991. https://www.washingtonpost.com/wp-srv/inatl/longterm/fogofwar/archive/post021491_2.htm. Accessed 13 June 2024

Bartolini G (2006) Air Operations against Iraq (1991 and 2003). In: Ronzitti N, Venturini G (eds) The Law of Air Warfare: Contemporary Issues. Eleven International Publishing, The Hague, pp 227–272

Bayer M, Croissant A, Izadi R, Scheeder N (2023) Multidimensional Measures of Militarization (M3) – a Global Dataset. Armed Forces & Society: 1–25

Benvenuti P (2001) The ICTY Prosecutor and the Review of the NATO Bombing Campaign against the Federal Republic of Yugoslavia. European Journal of International Law 12(3): 503–529

Bothe M (2001) The Protection of the Civilian Population and NATO Bombing on Yugoslavia: Comments on a Report to the Prosecutor of the ICTY. European Journal of International Law1 2(3): 531–536

Bothe M (2002) Targeting. In: Wall A E (ed) Legal and Ethical Lessons in NATO's Kosovo Campaign. Volume 78, US Naval War College's International Law Studies, pp 173–187

Bowman KS (2002) Militarization, Democracy, and Development: The Perils of Praetorianism in Latin America. Pennsylvania State University Press

Byron C (2010) International Humanitarian Law and Bombing Campaigns: Legitimate Military Objectives and Excessive Collateral Damage. Yearbook of International Humanitarian Law 13: 175–211

Cassese A (1999) *Ex iniuria ius oritur*: Are We Moving towards International Legitimation of Forcible Humanitarian Countermeasures in the World Community? European Journal of International Law 10(1): 23–30

Chun C K S (2010) John Warden's Five Ring Model and the Indirect Approach to War. Theory of War and Strategy 1: 311–324

Chun C K S, Bartholomees J B (2012) John Warden's Five Ring Model and the Indirect Approach to War. Volume I: Theory of War and Strategy, Strategic Studies Institute, US Army War College, 2012, pp. 295–308. JSTOR, http://www.jstor.org/stable/resrep12116.24. Accessed 10 May 2024

Cole B (2020) Clausewitz's Wondrous Yet Paradoxical Trinity. The Nature of War as a Complex Adaptive System. Joint Force Quarterly 96. https://ndupress.ndu.edu/Media/News/News-Article-View/Article/2076059/clausewitzs-wondrous-yet-paradoxical-trinity-the-nature-of-war-as-a-complex-ada/. Accessed 23 March 2024

Cordesman A H (2003) The Lessons and Non-Lessons of the Air and Missile Campaign in Kosovo. https://csis-website-prod.s3.amazonaws.com/s3fs-public/legacy_files/files/media/csis/pubs/kosovolessons-full.pdf. Accessed 4 July 2024

Cordesman A H (2014) The Real Revolution in Military Affairs. https://www.csis.org/analysis/real-revolution-military-affairs. Accessed 23 March 2024

Crawford J W (1997) The Law of Noncombatant Immunity and the Targeting of National Electrical Power Systems. The Fletcher Forum of World Affairs 21(2): 101–119

Danielsson A, Ljungkvist K (2023) A Choking(?) Engine of War: Human Agency in Military Targeting Reconsidered. Review of International Studies 49(1): 83–103
Davis R G (1996) Decisive Force, Strategic Bombing in the Gulf War. https://www.rand.org/pubs/monograph_reports/MR1365.html. Accessed 24 March 2024
D'Aspremont J, De Hemptinne J (2012). Droit International Humanitaire. Pedone, Paris
Deptula D (1991) Transcript of Oral History Interview Conducted by Suzanne Gheri, Edward Mann, and Richard Reynolds. Air Force Historical Research Agency, Maxwell AFB, Alabama, Document Number K239.0472-85
Dill J (2023) Our Shared Horror. EJIL: Talk!, https://www.ejiltalk.org/our-shared-horror. Accessed 2 May 2024
Dinstein Y (2002) Discussion: Reasonable Military Commanders and Reasonable Civilians. In: Wall A E (ed) Legal and Ethical Lessons in NATO's Kosovo Campaign. Volume 78, US Naval War College's International Law Studies, pp 173–219
Douhet G (1983) The Command of the Air. Center for Air Force History, Washington DC
Ducheine P A L (2016) Non-kinetic Capabilities: Complementing the Kinetic Prevalence to Targeting. In: Ducheine P A L, Schmitt M N, Osinga F P B (eds) Targeting: The Challenges of Modern Warfare. T.M.C. Asser Press, The Hague, pp 201–230
Ducheine P A L, Schmitt M N, Osinga F P B (2016) Introduction. In: Ducheine P A L, Schmitt M N, Osinga F P B (eds) Targeting: The Challenges of Modern Warfare. T.M.C. Asser Press, The Hague, pp 1–5
Echevarria A J II (2007) Clausewitz and Contemporary War. Oxford University Press, Oxford
Enloe C (2000) Maneuvers: The International Politics of Militarizing Women's Lives. University of California Press, Berkeley
Enloe C (2010) The Risks of Scholarly Militarization: A Feminist Analysis. Perspectives on Politics 8(4): 1107–1111
European Commission (2024) White Paper on Options for Enhancing Support for Research and Development Involving Technologies with Dual-Use Potential. COM(2024) 27 final
Fenrick W J (2001) Targeting and Proportionality during the NATO Bombing Campaign against Yugoslavia. European Journal of International Law 12(3): 489–502
Gardam J G (1993) Proportionality and Force in International Law. The American Journal of International Law 87(3): 391–413
Gellman B (1991) Allied Air War Struck Broadly in Iraq. The Washington Post. https://www.washingtonpost.com/archive/politics/1991/06/23/allied-air-war-struck-broadly-in-iraq/e469877b-b1c1-44a9-bfe7-084da4e38e41/. Accessed 11 June 2024
Gillard E C (2018) Proportionality in the Conduct of Hostilities: The Incidental Harm Side of the Assessment. Research paper, Chatham House. https://www.chathamhouse.org/sites/default/files/publications/research/2018-12-10-proportionality-conduct-hostilities-incidental-harm-gillard-final.pdf. Accessed 5 February 2024
Gingras J L, Ruby T Z (2000) Morality and Modern Air War. JFQ 107–111. https://apps.dtic.mil/sti/tr/pdf/ADA525893.pdf. Accessed 4 July 2024
Gordon M R, Schmitt E (1991) Radios and Mine Sweepers: Problems in the Gulf. The New York Times 28 March. https://www.nytimes.com/1991/03/28/world/after-the-war-radios-and-mine-sweepers-problems-in-the-gulf.html. Accessed 14 June 2024
Greenwood C (2001) The Applicability of International Humanitarian Law and the Law of Neutrality to the Kosovo Campaign. Israel Yearbook on Human Rights 31: 111–144
Hampson F J (1992) Proportionality and Necessity in the Gulf Conflict. Proceedings of the ASIL Annual Meeting 86: 45–54
Henckaerts J-M, Doswald-Beck L (2005) Customary International Humanitarian Law, Volume I: Rules. Cambridge University Press/ICRC, Cambridge/Geneva
Human Rights Watch (1991) Needless Deaths in the Gulf War. Civilian Casualties During the Air Campaign and Violations of the Laws of War. Human Rights Watch, New York
Human Rights Watch (1999) Civilian Deaths in the NATO Air Campaign. Human Rights Watch, New York. https://www.hrw.org/reports/pdfs/g/general/natbm002.pdf. Accessed 3 July 2024

ICRC (2016) The Principle of Proportionality in the Rules Governing the Conduct of Hostilities under International Humanitarian Law. International Expert Meeting, 22–23 June 2016, Quebec. https://www.icrc.org/sites/default/files/document/file_list/4358_002_expert_meeting_report_web_1_0.pdf. Accessed 1 October 2024

Kahn P W (1993) Lessons for International Law from the Gulf War. Stanford Law Review 45: 425–441

Kleemeier U (2007) Moral Forces in War. In: Strachan H, Herberg-Rothe (eds) Clausewitz in the Twenty-First Century. Oxford University Press, Oxford, pp 107–121

Kritsiotis D (2000) The Kosovo Crisis and NATO's Application of Armed Force Against the Federal Republic of Yugoslavia. International and Comparative Law Quarterly 49: 330–359

Kuehl D T (1995) Airpower vs. Electricity: Electric Power as a Target for Strategic Air Operations. Journal of Strategic Studies 18(1): 237–266

Lambeth B S (2000) The Transformation of American Air Power. Cornell University Press, Ithaca

Lambeth B S (2001) NATO's Air War for Kosovo A Strategic and Operational Assessment. RAND Corporation. https://www.rand.org/pubs/monograph_reports/MR1365.html. Accessed 26 March 2024

Larson E V, Savych B (2006) Misfortunes of war. Press and Public Reactions to Civilian Deaths in Wartime. RAND Corporation, Santa Monica CA

Ledwidge F (2018) Aerial Warfare. The Battle for the Skies. Oxford University Press, Oxford

Lemay C E, MacKinlay K (1965) Mission with Lemay: My Story. Doubleday & Company, Garden City

Lewis M W (2003) The Law of Aerial Bombardment in the 1991 Gulf War. The American Journal of International Law 97(3): 481–509

Mandel R (2004) The Wartime Utility of Precision Versus Brute Force in Weaponry. Armed Forces & Society 30(2): 171–201

Mann EC (1995) Thunder and Lightning: Desert Storm and the Airpower Debates. Air University Press, Montgomery AL

McCoubrey H (1995) International Humanitarian Law and Air Warfare. International Law and Armed Conflict Commentary 2(1): 23–48

McNaughton A (2019) "Parallel Warfare" in Conflicts with Limited Political Aims. Canadian Military Journal 20(1): 49–57

Meier M V (2023) A Welcome Change to the Presumption of Civilian Status. https://lieber.westpoint.edu/whats-in-a-presumption/#:~:text=Specifically%2C%20the%20Manual%20now%20provides%20in%20Paragraph%205.4.3.2,that%20the%20persons%20or%20objects%20are%20military%20objectives. Accessed 29 June 2024

Meyer E L (2022) The Centre of Gravity Concept: Contemporary Theories, Comparison, and Implications. Defence Studies 22(3): 327–353

Navajas G E, López Villalba P A, Rossi M A, Vazquez A (2023) The Long-Term Effect of Military Conscription on Personality and Beliefs. The Review of Economics and Statistics, 104(1): 133–141

Neuneck N (2008) The Revolution in Military Affairs: Its Driving Forces, Elements, and Complexity. Physics Journal Complexity 50: 50–61

NATO (2000) Kosovo One Year on. Achievement and Challenge. https://archives.nato.int/uploads/r/null/1/3/137989/0346_Kosovo_one_year_on-Achievement_and_Challenge_2000_ENG.pdf. Accessed 4 July 2024

NATO Parliamentary Assembly (2022) The Future of Warfare, Preliminary Draft Report,025 STCTTS 22 E https://www.nato-pa.int/download-file?filename=/sites/default/files/2022-04/025%20STCTTS%2022%20E%20-%20THE%20FUTURE%20OF%20WARFARE%20-%20TRAUSTI%20FRIDBERTSSON%20REPORT.pdf. Accessed 4 June 2024

Obradović K (2000) International Humanitarian Law and the Kosovo Crisis. International Review of the Red Cross 82: 699–731

Osinga F P B, Roorda M P (2016) From Douhet to Drones, Air Warfare, and the Evolution of Targeting. In: Ducheine P A L, Schmitt M N, Osinga F P B (eds) Targeting: The Challenges of Modern Warfare. T.M.C. Asser Press, The Hague, pp 27–76

Parks W H (1998) The Protection of Civilians from Air Warfare. Israel Yearbook on Human Rights 27: 65–112

Pion-Berlin D, Croissant A, Kuehn D (2024) Introduction to the Research Handbook on Civil–Military Relations. In: Croissant A, Kuehn D, Pion-Berlin D (eds) Research Handbook on Civil–Military Relations. Edward Elgar, Cheltenham Glos

Reetz N (2022) Same but Different? Why War-Sustaining Objects Can Be Destroyed but Not Targeted. Journal of Conflict & Security Law 27(3):439

Richard T (2022) On the Legal Presumptions of Civilian Status: A Rebuttal in Support of the DoD Manual (Part I). https://sites.duke.edu/lawfire/2022/03/29/col-ted-richard-on-the-legal-presumptions-of-civilian-status-a-rebuttal-in-support-of-the-dod-manual-part-i/. Accessed 2 July 2024

Roberts A (1993) The Laws of War in the 1990–91 Gulf Conflict. International Security 18(3): 134–181

Ronzitti N (2000) Is the *non liquet* of the Final Report by the Committee Established to Review the NATO Bombing Campaign Against the Federal Republic of Yugoslavia Acceptable? International Review of the Red Cross 840: 1017–1027

Ruby T Z (2006) Making Moral Targeting Decisions in War: The Importance of Principal-Agent Motivation Alignment and Constraining Doctrine. Journal of Military Ethics, 5(1): 12–31

Sassòli M (2005) Targeting: The Scope and Utility of the Concept of "Military Objectives" for the Protection of Civilians in Contemporary Armed Conflicts. In: Wippman D, Evangelista M (eds) New Wars, New Laws? Applying Laws of War in 21st Century Conflicts. Brill/Nijhoff, Leiden, pp 181–210

Schmitt M N (1999) The Principle of Discrimination in 21st Century Warfare. Yale Human Rights and Development Law Journal 2: 143–182

Schmitt M N (2009) The law of targeting. In: Wilmshurst E, Breau S (eds) Perspectives on the ICRC Study on Customary International Humanitarian Law. Cambridge University Press, Cambridge, pp. 131–168

Schmitt M N (2010) Military Necessity and Humanity in International Humanitarian Law: Preserving the Delicate Balance. Virginia Journal of International Law 50(4): 796–837

Schulzke M (2017) Necessary and Surplus Militarisation: Rethinking Civil-Military Interactions and their Consequences. European Journal of International Security 3(1): 94–112

Seib G F (1991) Military Reform Has Given Field Commanders Decisive Roles and Reduced Interservice Rivalry. The Wall Street Journal, 21 January 1991

Simma B (1999) NATO, the UN and the Use of Force: Legal Aspects. European Journal of International Law 10(1): 1–22

Smith J (2023) Battle for Space: Statecraft, Diplomacy and Defence Strategy. Astronomy & Geophysics 64(2): 2.38–2.40

Smith R (1992) The Gulf War: The land battle. RUSI Journal 137(1): 1–5

Tucker-Jones A (2014) Modern Warfare. Gulf War Operation Desert Storm 1990-1991. Pen & Sword Military, Barnsley

U.S. Department of Defense (1991/2000) Pentagon Interim Report. Report to Congress: Kosovo/Operation ALLIED FORCE After Action Report, 31 January 2000, reprinted as JMO NWC 2102

Van Schaack B (2016) Evaluating Proportionality and Long-Term Civilian Harm under the Laws of War. https://www.justsecurity.org/32577/evaluating-proportionality-long-term-civilian-harm-law-war/. Accessed 23 June 2024

Vierucci L (2006) Sulla nozione di obiettivo militare nella guerra aerea: recenti sviluppi della giurisprudenza internazionale. Rivista di Diritto internazionale 89: 693–721

Von Clausewitz C (1989) On War (Howard M E (ed), Paret P (transl)). Princeton University Press, Princeton

Warden J A III (1995) The Enemy as a System. Air Power Journal 9(2): 40–55

Warden J A III (2000) The Air Campaign, 2nd edn. Excel Press, Lincoln
Warden J A III (2011) Strategy and Airpower. Air & Space Power Journal 25(1): 65–77
Wenger A, Mason S J A (2008) The Civilianization of Armed Conflict: Trends and Implications. International Review of the Red Cross 90(872): 835–852
Woodward R, Neil Jenkings K, Williams A J (2017) Militarisation, universities and the university armed service units. Political Geography 60(1): 203–212

Chapter 3
Redefining the Notion of Dual-Use Objects: Is "Military Objectives" the Right Label?

Contents

Abstract The present chapter, after providing an excursus of the milestones that led to the adoption of Article 52(2) of API, aims to address some crucial issues concerning the definition of military objectives, focusing in particular on the assessment of the "military advantage" and the controversial notion of "attack as a whole", which appear to be of particular relevance when dealing with dual-use objects. To this end, the chapter will discuss the difficulties of making clear determinations on how to plan and carry out military operations within the bounds of the law as enshrined in Article 52(2) of API and customary IHL. In this regard and to offer practical examples to rely on, the analysis will consider the controversial findings on the qualification of military objectives presented in the award on the aerial bombardment of the Hirgigo Power Station, issued by the Eritrea-Ethiopia Claims Commission (the Commission, or EECC), and in the so-called "Goldstone Report" released by the UN Fact Finding Mission on the Gaza Conflict. Furthermore, a working definition of "dual-use objects", which takes into consideration all the pressing issues discussed thus far, will be presented to lay the foundations for the paradigm shift discussed in the next chapters.

F. Capone, *Dual-use Objects under International Humanitarian Law: Towards a Paradigm Shift*, https://doi.org/10.1007/978-94-6265-679-6_3

Keywords Military objectives · Military advantage · Attack as a whole · Principle of distinction · Eritrea-Ethiopia Claims Commission · Hirgigo Power Station · UN Fact Finding Mission on the Gaza Conflict · Goldstone Report

3.1 Dissecting the Concept of Military Objectives Under IHL

Chapter 1 of this book has already offered an overview of the centrality of the principle of distinction in the inquiry on dual-use objects. It has done so by introducing the notion of civilian objects and military objectives,[1] and by providing an overview of the definition enshrined in the current legal framework and pointing out the main criticism triggered by it. As far as dual-use items are concerned, such as civilian means of transportation and communication which can be used for military purposes, practice considers that the classification of these objects depends, in the final analysis, on the application of the definition of a military objective.[2] Instead of adding more layers, the present chapter aims at further developing some of the issues already mentioned, discussing them more in depth. In order to quickly summarise the key aspects that shall be kept in mind in the course of this analysis, it is worth recalling here the definition of military objectives set forth in Article 52(2) of Additional Protocol I (API),[3] to which no reservations have been made; with the Mexican delegation even stating that Article 52(2) is so essential that it "cannot be the subject of any reservations whatsoever since these would be inconsistent with the aim and purpose of Protocol I and undermine its basis".[4] According to this provision

> Attacks shall be limited strictly to military objectives. In so far as objects are concerned, military objectives are limited to those objects which by their nature, location, purpose or use make an effective contribution to military action and whose total or partial destruction, capture or neutralization, in the circumstances ruling at the time, offers a definite military advantage.

Although this definition of military objectives was not included in Additional Protocol II (APII),[5] which applies to non-international armed conflicts (NIACs), and it does not appear in Common Article 3 either, it has subsequently been incorporated into treaties that find application also in this typology of conflicts, namely Amended

---

[1] See Chap. 1, Sect. 1.3.2 in this book.

[2] Henckaerts and Doswald-Beck 2005, Rule 8, p. 31.

[3] Protocol Additional to the Geneva Conventions of 12 August 1949, and relating to the Protection of Victims of International Armed Conflicts, opened for signature 8 June 1977, 1125 UNTS 3 (entered into force 7 December 1978) (Additional Protocol I or API).

[4] Henckaerts and Doswald-Beck 2005, Rule 8, p. 32.

[5] Protocol Additional to the Geneva Conventions of 12 August 1949, and relating to the Protection of Victims of Non-International Armed Conflicts, opened for signature 8 June 1977, 1125 UNTS 609, entered into force 7 December 1978, (Additional Protocol II or APII).

Protocol II to the Convention on Certain Conventional Weapons (CCW)[6] and the Second Protocol to the Hague Convention for the Protection of Cultural Property.[7] The ICRC study on customary IHL reports that military manuals, which are applicable or have been applied in NIACs, incorporate the same definition of military objectives applicable to IACs.[8] Said definition is also contained in some national legislation and included in official statements pertaining to non-international armed conflicts.[9]

As stressed by the "Review Committee" set up by the Prosecutor of the International Criminal Tribunal for the Former Yugoslavia (ICTY) to ascertain whether war crimes had been committed during the NATO bombing,[10] the definition, albeit far from perfect, is "generally accepted as part of customary law",[11] and as such it also binds countries, like the US, that are not parties to API.[12] Later on the ICRC comprehensive study of customary IHL, explicitly spelled out that "Article 52(2) in its entirety is evidence of customary IHL in international armed conflicts and non-international armed conflicts alike".[13] The API rule on military objectives must be read, understood, and applied in combination with other elements described in Article 52, including the presumption of civilian status incorporated in para 3 of the same provision.[14]

The characteristic of an object that may lead it to be considered as military either by nature, location, purpose, or use is just one of several criteria that must be considered. For instance, if an object constitutes a military objective by location, it may only be targeted if it makes "an effective contribution to military action and its destruction, capture, or neutralisation offers a definite military advantage owing to the circumstances ruling at the time of the attack".[15] When the above-mentioned criteria are satisfied, the object may be partially, or totally, destroyed, captured, or neutralised. Notably, as stressed by Rynkeby Knudsen, "may" is crucial here in light of two

---

[6] Protocol on Prohibitions or Restrictions on the Use of Mines, Booby-Traps and Other Devices as amended on 3 May 1996, opened for signature 3 May 1996, entered into force 3 December 1998, (Protocol II to the 1980 CCW Convention as amended on 3 May 1996), Article 2(6).

[7] Second Protocol to the Hague Convention of 1954 for the Protection of Cultural Property in the Event of Armed Conflict, The Hague, opened for signature 26 March 1999, entered into force 9 March 2004, Article 1(f).

[8] Henckaerts and Doswald-Beck 2005, Rule 8, p. 31.

[9] Ibid.

[10] See Chap. 2, Sect. 2.5.1 in this book.

[11] Final Report to the Prosecutor by the Committee Established to Review the NATO Bombing Campaign against the Federal Republic of Yugoslavia, (13 June 2000), (hereinafter OTP Report) reprinted in (2000) ILM 39:1257, para 42.

[12] Dinstein 2004, p. 83.

[13] Henckaerts and Doswald-Beck 2005, Rule 8, p. 32.

[14] See Chap. 1, Sect. 1.3.2; Chap. 4, Sect. 4.5.1 and Chap. 5, Sect. 5.3.1 in this book.

[15] Rynkeby Knudsen 2024.

reasons. First, there is always a choice to make, and second, attacks against a legitimate military objective still need to be proportionate pursuant to Articles 51(5)(b) and 57(2)(a)(iii) of API.[16]

Adopting a broader perspective and linking more directly the definition of military objectives to the principle of distinction, it is worth mentioning that although "new warfare" poses several challenges for its application exactly because of the absence of clearly defined boundaries between conflict areas and civilian areas, and thus between military objectives and civilian objects,[17] this does not mean that belligerents are absolved from their obligation to distinguish between legitimate targets and civilian ones.[18]

Furthermore, the need to clearly define the notion of military objectives also stems from the severe consequences attached to the violations of the principle of distinction. Article 85(a) of API declares that nearly all violations of the principle of distinction constitute "grave breaches"[19] of the Protocol, including:

> making the civilian population or individual civilians the object of attack; (b) launching an indiscriminate attack affecting the civilian population or *civilian objects* in the knowledge that such attack will cause excessive loss of life, injury to civilians or damage to civilian objects, as defined in Article 57, paragraph 2 (a)(iii).

The Rome Statute similarly criminalises attacks on civilians and indiscriminate attacks, more specifically of two types: intentional attacks directed against civilians and civilian objects, and attacks made in the knowledge that civilian casualties would be clearly excessive in relation to the military advantage gained, that is, attacks that violate the principle of proportionality.[20]

Consistently with the main approach of this book—which unlike other attempts to strengthen the protection of dual-use objects in armed conflict, does not seek to provide one final solution, but rather to propose a new paradigm that considers a multitude of different aspects and factors—the present chapter will not argue that the current definition of military objectives represents the main obstacle to overcoming the mainstream position. Also, as explained in Chap. 1,[21] the perspective *de lege ferenda* is incorporated in this work only to the extent to which the term refers to "emergent" law, i.e. law that is already grounded in empirical evidence. Therefore, albeit in this author's view introducing a so-called "composite definition" of military objectives, i.e. one that combines an abstract statement with a non-exhaustive catalogue of concrete examples,[22] would be the best option to limit abuses and controversial applications of the law, the next (sub-)sections will argue for an interpretation of the existing definition of military objectives that is more coherent with the key

---

[16] Ibid.

[17] See Chap. 2, Sect. 2.2 in this book.

[18] Blank 2009, pp. 353–354.

[19] Acquaviva 2014, pp. 103–108; Gaeta 2015, p. 615.

[20] Rome Statute of the International Criminal Court, opened for signature 17 July 1998, 2187 UNTS 3, entered into force 1 July 2002 (Rome Statute), Articles 8(2)(b)(i), 8(2)(b)(ii), 8(2)(b(iv).

[21] See Chap. 1, Sect. 1.4 in this book.

[22] See Chap. 1, Sect. 1.3.2 in this book. See also Dinstein 2004, pp. 84–85.

principles and with the scope of IHL. The importance of reaching a more uniform interpretation, and thus application, of this crucial definition is not purely speculative. There are practical and extremely dangerous consequences attached to the legal differences that have emerged so far. As reported by Lt Gen M. Short, NATO Air Commander during Operation Allied Force,[23] in a description that is still pertinent today:

> [s]o every day I put together what was called the air task order which is sent out to the thousand or more NATO airplanes indicating what targets they were going to strike the next day. I had to wait for the individual nations to answer back, having gone to their capitals and asked whether they should accept that target. And, indeed, in many capitals the answer was no—*we do not define that as a valid military target*. Now if I could get that answer back in a timely fashion, I could assign that target to a nation that had a less restrictive view of the law of armed conflict, but if I got that information late, and the aircraft were already airborne, then I ended up cancelling the strike.[24]

Reflecting further on the lack of a uniform approach and bearing in mind the premises succinctly described above, this chapter will first address some crucial issues concerning the definition of military objectives, focusing in particular on the assessment of the military advantage and the controversial notion of attack as a whole, which appear to be of particular relevance when dealing with dual-use objects. Then, the chapter will discuss the difficulties of making clear determinations on how to plan and carry out military operations within the bounds of the law as enshrined in Article 52(2) of API and customary IHL. In this regard and to offer practical examples to rely on, the analysis will consider the controversial findings on military objectives presented in the award on the aerial bombardment of the Hirgigo Power Station, issued by the Eritrea-Ethiopia Claims Commission (the Commission, or EECC), and in the so-called "Goldstone Report" released by the UN Fact Finding Mission on the Gaza Conflict. Furthermore, a working definition of "dual-use objects" that takes into consideration all the pressing issues discussed thus far will be presented to lay the foundations for the paradigm shift discussed in the next chapter. Finally, some conclusions will be drawn on how to strengthen the interpretation and application of the current definition of military objectives and include in the equation specific considerations on the status of dual-use objects.

3.2 The Most Challenging Aspects of the Current Definition of Military Objectives and Its Interpretation

In their commentary on the two 1977 Protocols Additional to the Geneva conventions of 1949, Bothe, Partsch, Solf et al. authoritatively note that the definition of "military objective", until the adoption of Article 52 of Protocol Additional I, "eluded all efforts

[23] See Chap. 2, Sect. 2.5 in this book.

[24] Short 2002, p. 25.

to arrive at a generally acceptable solution".[25] Although there have been some early intimations of the emergence of the principle of distinction in Canon Law's medieval period, the chivalric rules of the international order of knighthood, and the early war codes of certain European States,[26] the modern formulation of the principle of distinction has its origins in the late 19th and early 20th centuries, probably inspired by Rousseau's proclamation that wars could only be disputed between States and not between peoples.[27] This famous statement developed into the so-called "Rousseau–Portalis doctrine", which stipulated that "the law of nations does not permit the right of war […] to affect peaceful and unarmed citizens".[28]

Based on this assumption, military operations should be conducted exclusively between combatants in uniform, and unarmed civilians should be spared in their persons and property. Notably, the first formal recognition of the principle of distinction can be found in the 1863 Lieber's Instructions (or Code), promulgated during the United States Civil War by President Lincoln. Liber famously included in the provisions the universal rule that "the unarmed citizen is to be spared in person, property, and honor as much as the exigencies of war will admit".[29]

Without lingering on the various milestones that finally led to the incorporation of the principle of distinction in the modern law of armed conflict and ultimately in Additional Protocol I and Additional Protocol II to the Geneva Conventions,[30] what is interesting to point out here is that the earlier explicit reference to the "military objective" as a concrete rule of warfare can be found in the 1923 Hague Rules of Air Warfare.[31] Article 24(1) of the Rules, which never became legally binding but still contributed in a significant way to the evolution of customary international law on the subject,[32] affirms that aerial bombardment is legitimate "only when directed at a military objective", specifying that the notion refers to "an object of which the destruction or injury would constitute a distinct military advantage to the belligerent".[33] The validity of the Rules, which were considered "as an authoritative attempt to clarify and formulate rules of law governing the use of aircraft in war and they will

[25] Bothe et al. 1982, p. 321.

[26] Robertson 2012, p. 300.

[27] "[Wars] cannot subsist between man and man either in a state of nature […] or in a state of society", Rousseau 1997, p. 18.

[28] Talleyrand to Napoleon (20 November 1806) cited by Benvenisti 2022, p. 274.

[29] Instructions for the Government of Armies of the United States in the Field (Lieber Code). 24 April 1863. https://ihl-databases.icrc.org/assets/treaties/110-IHL-L-Code-EN.pdf (accessed on 19 July 2024).

[30] Article 13(2) of Additional Protocol II prohibits making the civilian population as such, as well as individual civilians, the object of attack.

[31] For a thorough excursus, see Jachec-Neale 2014, pp. 15–37; Benvenisti 2022.

[32] Piatkowski 2021, p. 507.

[33] Rules concerning the Control of Wireless Telegraphy in Time of War and Air Warfare. Drafted by a Commission of Jurists at the Hague, December 1922–February 1923, (the Hague Rules of Air Warfare). https://ihl-databases.icrc.org/assets/treaties/275-IHL-35-EN.pdf (accessed 19 July 2024). For a punctual assessment of the Rules, see Hanke 1993, pp. 34–35; Ronzitti 2006, p. 3; Scovazzi 2012, pp. 110–113.

doubtless prove a convenient starting point for any future steps in this direction",[34] could not be disregarded, "despite constant violations".[35]

As mentioned in Chap. 1 of this book,[36] the Hague Rules are amongst the few legal instruments that provide a composite definition of military objectives, although the list of objects is an exhaustive one and this poses excessive limitations also with respect to future technological developments. Furthermore, the Hague Rules on Air Warfare's definition distinguishes between the bombardment of towns "not situated in the immediate vicinity of the operations of the land forces", which was prohibited, and civilian areas in the vicinity of the operation of land forces, whose bombardment was legitimate if "the military concentration [was] important enough to justify" it.[37] In light of the current characteristics of the armed conflicts fought in different parts of the world, it is trivial to observe that this formulation ultimately fails to effectively protect the civilian population. A subsequent definition, which departs from Article 52(2) of API and deserves to be mentioned in this analysis, is the one included in the *Institut de Droit International*'s 1969 Resolution,[38] which heavily influenced the wording of Article 52(2). The formula developed by the *Institut* represents "the essential basis", in substance and form, of the corresponding definition in API,[39] and reads

> there can be considered as military objectives only those that, by their very nature or purpose or use, make an effective contribution to military action, or exhibit a generally recognized military significance, such that their total or partial destruction in the actual circumstances gives a *substantial, specific and immediate* military advantage to those who are in a position to destroy them.[40]

Although the 1987 ICRC Commentary on the Additional Protocols fails to acknowledge the significant influence of the *Institut* on the definition eventually adopted in API, several authors have recognised its relevance.[41] It is important to note that, in addition to its formula, the definition of the *Institut* also contains another essential element, which the doctrine has not taken into due consideration. At para 3 it declares that the "civilian population as such", and, in all circumstances, "*all the objects that are indispensable* for the survival of the civilian population" can never be considered as military objectives.[42]

This exclusion clause, that did not end up in the text of Article 52, has been incorporated, in a less straightforward and effective way, in Article 54(2) of Additional Protocol I, as a corollary to the prohibition of starvation.[43] Even though the ICRC

---

[34] Oppenheim 1955.

[35] Piatkowski 2021, p. 507.

[36] See Chap. 1, Sect. 1.3.2 in this book.

[37] Article 24(4) of the Hague Rules of Air Warfare.

[38] *Institut de Droit International* 1969.

[39] Schindler 1986, p. 209.

[40] *Institut de Droit International* 1969, p. 117 (emphasis added).

[41] Green 2008, p. 58; Benvenisti 2022, pp. 287–290.

[42] *Institut de Droit International* 1969, p. 117 (emphasis added).

[43] See Chap. 4, Sect. 4.4 in this book.

affirms the customary status of the prohibition on attacking, destroying, removing or rendering useless objects indispensable to the survival of the civilian population,[44] unfortunately several military manuals specify that in order to be illegal, the intent of the attack has to be "to prevent the civilian population from being supplied", a view that is perfectly aligned with the one expressed by France and the United Kingdom upon ratification of API.[45] Perhaps the language adopted by the ICRC in its study of customary international humanitarian law is too optimistic in light of the not so uniform military practice, with countries like France, Germany, Spain, Sweden and the US firmly anchored to the requirement of a specific purpose.[46] Moving towards a more homogenous approach to the matter would significantly increase the chance of strengthening the protection of dual-use objects that are or produce items that are crucial to guarantee the survival of the civilian population.[47] This topic will be discussed more in detail in Chap. 4 of this book. For now it is important to observe how, in the process of drafting the definition of military objectives included in Article 52(2) of API, the crucial exclusion of essential objects has been deliberately overlooked.

Before diving into the distinctive elements of the definition it is worth to clarify a few basic aspects that concern the interpretation of the norm. In order to determine the meaning of the term "military objectives" on the basis of the formal sources of international law, it is necessary to interpret it pursuant to the customary rules of treaty interpretation, as reflected in Articles 31–33 of the Vienna Convention on the Law of Treaties (VCLT).[48] Notably, the VCLT itself is not applicable to API, as the Protocol preceded the VCLT's entry into force. However, the customary rules of interpretation are still applicable to international treaties adopted prior to the VCLT. This follows from the doctrine of "intertemporal law",[49] pursuant to which a treaty should be interpreted according to the rules of interpretation existing "at the time of application, rather than at the time the treaty was concluded".[50] Furthermore, it is well established that the definition enshrined in Article 52(2) of API has evolved into custom,[51] and that the possibility that a norm "exists in parallel in both treaty law and customary law" is firmly settled in international law.[52] One may then raise the issue that the VCLT does not apply to norms of customary law; nonetheless, as Judge

44 Henckaerts and Doswald-Beck 2005, Rule 54, p. 189.

45 Ibid., p. 190.

46 Ibid.

47 See UN Security Council 2021, para 3.

48 Vienna Convention on the Law of Treaties, opened for signature 23 May 1969, 1155 UNTS 331, entered into force 27 January 1980 (VCLT).

49 Farnelli 2020; Linderfalk 2011, pp. 162–165; Kotzur 2008.

50 The intertemporal approach was shaped and further developed in the famous *Island of Palmas Case* of 1928. The renowned Swiss arbitrator Huber outlined the doctrine of intertemporal law pursuant to which a juridical fact must be appreciated in the light of the law contemporary with it, and not of the law in force at the time when the dispute in regard to it arises or falls to be settled. Island of Palmas (Netherlands/United States) (1928) 2 RIAA 829, 845.

51 Henckaerts and Doswald-Beck 2005, Rule 8, p. 32.

52 ICJ, *North Sea Continental Shelf*, Judgment, 20 February 1969, ICJ Reports 1969, p. 3, para 72.

Tanaka observed in the *North Sea* case before the ICJ, "[t]he method of logical and teleological interpretation can be applied in the case of customary law as in the case of written law".[53] Therefore, according to the "general rule" of interpretation set forth in Article 31(1) VCLT,[54] "[a] treaty shall be interpreted in good faith in accordance with the ordinary meaning to be given to the terms of the treaty in their context and in the light of its object and purpose". As authoritatively affirmed by the ICJ, these elements of interpretation, namely "ordinary meaning", "context", and "object and purpose" are to be considered "as a whole".[55] In this way, the interpretive elements contained in the VCLT form part of a single test to determine the meaning of the text. Indeed, the ordinary meaning of a text cannot be clear without understanding *why* that text was promulgated. As explained by Anzilotti

> [o]nly when it is known what the Contracting Parties intended to do and the aim they had in view is it possible to say either that the natural meaning of the terms used in a particular article corresponds with the real intention of the Parties, or that the natural meaning of the terms used falls short of or goes further than such intention.[56]

With respect to the ordinary meaning of the term "military objectives", the 1987 ICRC's Commentary explains that there is "no doubt that in this article both the English and French texts intended tangible and visible things by the word 'objective', and not the general objective (in the sense of aim or purpose) of a military operation".[57] Furthermore, it shall be mentioned that recourse to the *travaux preparatoires*, pursuant to Article 32 of the VCLT, is unnecessary in the present case, pursuant to the rules of treaty interpretation, as the meaning of the term "military objectives" based on Article 31 will be neither "ambiguous or obscure" nor one "which is manifestly absurd or unreasonable". The ordinary meaning of a term cannot be removed from its "context", which in the present instance refers to both the factual context, i.e. the conduct of hostilities, and the context in which the term "military objectives" appears and has been used throughout the Protocol. This aspect relates to the normative framework of which the interpreted provision forms a part in the treaty's "text, including its preamble and annexes".[58]

In relation to the last elements, i.e. the object and purpose of a treaty, it is useful to clarify that the doctrine is still divided on whether they are two separate notions or not.[59] Some authors affirm that the VCLT adopts this terminology to indicate two

---

[53] Ibid., Dissenting Opinion of Judge Tanaka, para 55.

[54] ILC, 'Report of the International Law Commission on the Work of its Eighteenth Session' (1966) UN Doc A/CN.4/191, 220.

[55] ICJ, *Maritime Delimitations in the Indian Ocean*, Preliminary Objections, 2 February 2017, ICJ Reports 2017, p. 3 para 64.

[56] PCIJ, *Interpretation of the Convention of 1919 Concerning Employment of Women During the Night*, Advisory Opinion of 15 November 1932, Dissenting Opinion of Judge Anzilotti, Rep Series A/B No 50, para 383.

[57] Sandoz et al. 1987, Article 52(2), para 2010.

[58] Pomson 2023, p. 361; Gardiner 2015, p. 194.

[59] Pompson 2023, p. 365.

distinct concepts.[60] The former refers to the legal position created for the parties by the provisions of the treaty as a whole, i.e. its subject-matter, while the latter indicates the aim which is to be achieved by the treaty.[61] Today the majority view is that the VCLT firmly established "object and purpose" as a "single standard expression: it consistently speaks of the 'object and purpose' together and in the singular";[62] meaning that they should be seen as "one whole rather than two distinct halves".[63] As is well known, there is no universally agreed method of determining the object and purpose of international treaties. Mačák and Policinski stress that the closest available document to such a source is the ILC's 2011 Guide to Practice on Reservations to Treaties.[64] The ILC Guide notes that "a fairly general approach is required: it is not a question of 'dissecting' the treaty in minute detail and examining its provisions one by one, but of extracting the 'essence', the overall 'mission' of the treaty".[65]

Scholars agree on the fact that the process of identifying the object and purpose of a treaty is by necessity inductive, and highlight that while "the preamble may be used as the source of a convenient summary of the object and purpose of a treaty, both the Vienna Convention (Article 31(2)) and practice make it clear that an interpreter needs to read the whole treaty".[66] With regard to API, its preamble *inter alia* sets forth that "[t]he High Contracting Parties [...] [b]eliev[ed] it necessary nevertheless to reaffirm and develop the provisions protecting the victims of armed conflicts and to supplement measures intended to reinforce their application". Several authors observe that the provisions of API as a whole demonstrate a constant attempt to strike a balance between humanitarian protection and the military exigencies of the parties to an armed conflict.[67] In their views, hence, striking a balance between those two driving forces represents the object and purpose of API. Other authors, in particular Kalshoven and Ronzitti, stress that the general protection of the civilian population is the major "object and purpose" of the Protocol.[68] Kalshoven further articulates this thought by explaining that the "rules in Part IV of Additional Protocol I focus specifically on civilians as a subcategory of victims of armed conflicts".[69] Therefore, it can be inferred that the main "object and purpose" of Article 52(2) in its normative context is the enhancement of the protection of civilians during situations of armed conflict.[70]

---

[60] Buffard and Zemanek 1998, p. 332.

[61] Ibid.

[62] Mačák and Policinski 2024, pp. 391–392.

[63] Ibid.

[64] Ibid., p. 402.

[65] ILC, 'Guide to Practice on Reservations to Treaties, Report of the ILC, 63rd Session' (26 April to 3 June and 4 July to 12 August 2011) UN Doc A/66/10/Add.1 (ILC Guide), commentary to guideline 3.1.5, para 3.

[66] Gardiner 2015, p. 218.

[67] Pomson 2023, p. 366; Crawford and Pert 2020, pp. 28–30.

[68] Kalshoven 1990, p. 78; Ronzitti 2017, p. 148.

[69] Kalshoven 2007, p. 448.

[70] Mačák 2015, p. 78.

Finally, a last consideration concerns the application of the evolutive method of interpretation to the terms of Additional Protocol I.[71] There are, indeed, certain instances in which the terms themselves of the treaty allow for the possibility that their interpretation may evolve over time,[72] resulting from the application of Article 31(1) of the VCLT. However, as noted by several authors, the doctrine of evolutionary interpretation does not represent a separate means of interpretation, hence it does not exist beyond the rules enshrined and reflected in the VCLT.[73] Rather, as pointed out by Pomson, if the "interpretation of a treaty changes over time, it must be a result of the application of the VCLT rules on interpretation to the treaty".[74] Some provisions in Article 31 of the VCLT explicitly refer to the possibility of changing interpretation as time goes by. Article 31(3)(a)–(b) mentions "subsequent agreement and practice" of the parties as a means of interpretation. Similarly, Article 31(3)(c) cites "relevant rules of international law", which can obviously be subjected to modification over time.[75] Hence, it would be necessary that all states parties to API "would participate in, or accept such, an agreement or practice for Article 31(3)(a)–(b) to be applicable",[76] something clearly lacking in regard to a purported evolutionary interpretation of "military objectives" in API.

Moving from this brief, but hopefully useful, analysis, the next sub-sections will discuss in detail two crucial aspects that, ever since the adoption of the definition of military objectives enshrined in Protocol I, have been prone to striking differences in the interpretation and application of this provision, as well as its enforcement. Notably, the "nature, location, use or purpose" criteria by which Article 52(2) qualifies the requirement of an effective contribution to military action will not be covered by this inquiry, first because the issue has already been addressed,[77] and second because in this author's view the "location" criterion (only when the dual-use object is situated inside a specific area that is lawfully designated as a military objective), and the "use" criterion should be the only ones taken into consideration when assessing whether a dual-use object can be regarded as a lawful target.[78] Therefore, the inquiry will focus on the issue of "definite military advantage", in order to clarify the breadth of this notion as well as its relationship with the requirement of an effective "contribution to military action";[79] and on the contentious notion of "attack as a whole", which is usually addressed with respect to the principle of proportionality, but is relevant, albeit overlooked, also when applying the principle of distinction.

---

[71] Ibid., p. 71.

[72] Turrini 2019.

[73] Arato 2010; Dupuy 2011, p. 125; Palchetti 2013, pp. 98–99, and 104; Bjorge 2014, pp. 139–141.

[74] Pomson 2023, p. 373.

[75] Ibid., p. 369.

[76] Ibid.

[77] See Chap. 1, Sect. 1.3.2 in this book.

[78] This view is also shared by other authors. See Benvenuti 2001, p. 516.

[79] Such an approach has already been adopted by Jachec-Neale 2014, p. 111.

3.2.1 A Further Reflection on the Assessment of the Military Advantage

The second criterion to qualify an object as a military one is the "definite military advantage" that needs to be offered by the object's (total or partial) destruction, capture or neutralisation, in the circumstances ruling at the time. Clearly, destruction refers to rendering the object permanently not usable. By "capture" an object is seized and the control/possession over it is maintained. Therefore, any use by the adverse party is avoided and the object can now even benefit the captor. "Neutralisation" concerns the act of disabling the military objectives, so that they are incapable of functioning as intended.[80] The challenge is not posed by the different ways in which the target can be rendered useless, but it rather stems from the notion of "military advantage", which is not singularly helpful, and from the phrase "in the circumstances ruling at the time", which may be prone to vague or controversial interpretations.[81] Watkin eloquently explains that

> [i]n terms of the attention paid to military advantage it is like another term introduced in the 1977 Additional Protocol I: "direct participation in hostilities." That latter term did not receive serious consideration regarding its meaning until after the attacks of 9/11. The same pressures that forced an analysis of direct participation in hostilities are also applicable to military advantage […].[82]

Lacking a more detailed definition across the key legal instruments that regulate IHL, military advantage for the purpose of the application of the principle of distinction has been defined in the Harvard Air and Missile Warfare Manual issued by the Program on Humanitarian Policy and Conflict Research at Harvard University (Harvard Air and Missile Warfare Manual) as to encompass "any consequence of an attack which directly enhances friendly military operations or hinders those of the enemy".[83]

The notion is essential also with regard to dual-use objects, which, as previously discussed, have increasingly become the targets of modern conflicts, in particular those that rely significantly on air campaigns.[84] Military advantage is a "value based concept", with the anticipated advantage being interpreted as "an indication of the importance of the target to the military effort".[85] Military advantage is determined at the time of planning or executing an attack. Anticipation of a military advantage is one of the key elements that can render the attack carried out against a target lawful or not.[86]

---

[80] Kolb 2015, p. 694.

[81] Dinstein 2004, p. 86.

[82] Watkin 2016, p. 279.

[83] Harvard Air and Missile Warfare Manual 2013, Rule 1, p. 34.

[84] See Chap. 2 in this book.

[85] Watkin 2016, p. 278.

[86] Harvard Air and Missile Warfare Manual 2013, Rule 1, p. 35.

The advantage, moreover, must necessarily be of military nature, requiring the existence of a clear belligerent nexus or other connection to ongoing or planned military operations. As stressed by Jachec-Neale, lawful examples of this kind of advantages are the gaining of ground and the weakening of enemy armed forces or their ability to fight; merely political or economic advantages do not suffice.[87] Surely, military advantage is not restricted to tactical gains. The spectrum is necessarily wide, and it extends to the security of the attacking force. Therefore, one of the problems triggered by the practical application of this notion is represented by the different perspectives of the belligerent parties. It is, in fact, unlikely that the outlook of the attacking party could exactly match that of the party under attack in evaluating the long-term military benefits of any action carried out.[88]

Furthermore, the issue is that the connection of some objects to an enemy's war effort may be "direct, indirect or even discrete".[89] A decision concerning the classification of an object as a military objective and the allocation of resources for its attack is dependent upon its *value* to an enemy nation, which for the US and a few other States cover also its war-sustaining efforts. According to this view, the category of military objectives encompasses also economic objects that are war-sustaining because the revenue they generate is used by the opponent to fund its fighting capacities.[90] As noted by Schmitt, the notion of war-sustaining objects refers to "economic targets that finance the war effort broadly", such as oil destined for export.[91] Based on this interpretation, even power generation and distribution infrastructures that support key industries generating income for the State that, in turn, can be used to support the war effort, would qualify.

In contrast to this, the ICRC argues that these war-sustaining economic objects need to be distinguished from other economic objects, such as arms factories that are military objectives "by nature", and must fall outside the scope of Article 52(2) of API. As noted by a report issued by the International Law Association Study Group (ILA-SG) in 2017 "[t]here is no indication in State practice that objects contributing to the enemy's war-sustaining effort qualify as such as military objectives and the SG believes that this position has no basis in the law as it stands today and should be clearly rejected".[92] Most States and international law experts actually agree with this reading of the existing norms and refuse to extend the military objective definition this far. Indeed, the danger of the war-sustaining approach is that States can exploit

[87] Jachec-Neale 2014, p. 113.

[88] Fleck 1997, p. 48.

[89] Parks 2007, p. 89.

[90] Reetz 2022, pp. 440–441.

[91] Schmitt 2022.

[92] International Law Association Study Group on the Conduct of Hostilities in the 21st Century, Final Report presented at the 77th ILA Conference in Johannesburg, South Africa (ILA-SG Report), https://www.ila-hq.org/en_GB/documents/ila-final-report-25-june-2017 (accessed 22 July 2024).

it to justify attacks against unlawful targets, as it happened during the 1991 Gulf War,[93] and as Russia appears to be currently doing in Ukraine.[94]

Besides the objects that have an economic, rather than military value, also the morale of the civilian population cannot be considered as a legitimate target in itself under the law as it stands.[95] The prohibition on shattering the morale of the enemy civilian population derives from the blind faith airpower advocates attached to "attacks on morale" from World War I through World War II.[96] For example, in the view of the Royal Air Force (RAF) harming the public morale was considered as a legitimate military goal. As Sir Hugh Trenchard, Marshal of the RAF, commented in May 1928 "air attacks will be directed against any objective which will contribute effectively towards the destruction of the enemy's means of resistance and the lowering of his determination to fight".[97] The same approach at the time was adopted also by other States, including Germany.

The lesson learnt from history is that military operations, directed exclusively at civilian morale, are ineffective and, ultimately, pointless, if not counterproductive.[98] As Dinstein reports, the cardinal point is that "even if a deliberate attack against civilians can truly bend the will of the enemy", it is proscribed.[99] This entails that the prohibition of direct attacks against civilians applies in absolute terms, irrespective of utilitarian considerations. Furthermore, the separate requirement that the attack must provide a definite military advantage presupposes that also an attack on an objective of a military nature would not be lawful if its main purpose is to affect the morale of the civilian population and not to reduce the military strength of the enemy.[100] In more practical terms, and to use Greenwood's words, "an object does not become a target simply because of its political significance or the effect which its destruction is likely to have on civilian morale and support for a hostile government".[101] Only an object that meets the two cumulative criteria of a military objective set forth under Article 52(2) may be lawfully attacked. According to the 1987 ICRC Commentary on the Additional Protocols, threats no less than acts are interdicted when the main scope is to intimidate or cause panic in the civilian population.[102] From a different, but complementary perspective, provided that the target is a military one, making it the object of an attack while concomitantly taking due account of the fact that it will also affect civilian morale, does not qualify as a breach of IHL.[103]

---

[93] See Chap. 2, Sect. 2.4.1 in this book.

[94] Capone 2023.

[95] Kolb 2015, p. 695.

[96] Parks 2007, p. 77.

[97] Benvenisti 2022, p. 276.

[98] See Mackay 2003.

[99] Dinstein 2004, p. 116.

[100] Sassòli 2015, p. 4.

[101] Greenwood 2001, p. 124.

[102] Sandoz et al. 1987, Article 51, p. 618.

[103] Greenwood 2001, p. 124; Dinstein 2004, p. 116; Jachec-Neale 2014, p. 137.

The pivotal aspect to clarify, hence, is how to interpret the adjective "definite", since this is what qualifies the advantage and allows us to legitimately exclude from the category of military objectives both war-sustaining objects and the civilian morale, often associated with attacks against dual-use objects that can have an economic value and/or an impact on the population's resilience. As noted by Benvenisti, at the Diplomatic Conference on the Reaffirmation and Development of International Humanitarian Law Applicable in Armed Conflict that led to the adoption of the Additional Protocols, the wording of the original draft, which defined the military advantage as "substantial, specific and immediate", was met with some resistance by several countries, *in primis* the US, and ultimately the adjectives were expunged from the definition and replaced with "definite".[104]

Albeit less specific than the original formulation, claiming that the advantage must be "definite" entails that it must be clearly defined, concrete, and not vague or general, or too distant in time and thus speculative.[105] As reported by the ILA-SG in 2017, the way in which the US Air and Missile Warfare Manual defines "definite" picks up on this interpretation, "indicating that the term 'definite' is employed to exclude advantages which are merely potential, speculative or indeterminate, and thus renders it very similar to the understanding of 'concrete'".[106] In other words, the common interpretation of the term "definite" rules out advantages that are "hardly perceptible" as well as those which would only materialise in the long run or advantages that are merely potential, indeterminate or based on hope.[107]

A further relevant issue is the necessary, although often overlooked, connection between the notions of definite military advantage and "effective contribution to military action", which qualifies the otherwise too vague words "nature, location and purpose or use" in the first prong of Article 52(2). As a result, an object cannot be attacked simply because the attack yields a military advantage, nor solely in light of the input by which the object adds to one's military action; both criteria must be satisfied for a target to be legitimate. The definition of a military objective requires both that the object in question makes an effective contribution to the enemy's military action and that the destruction or damage of the object offers a definite military advantage to the State whose forces attack it. Therefore, the two elements are cumulative and interconnected, and must be both met in the circumstances ruling at the time because the conditions of warfare change swiftly.[108] For this reason, while certain core objects will remain military objectives "by nature" in any conflict, the classification of dual-use objects is strictly "situation-dependent" and based upon various factors,[109] meaning that an "object may be a military objective here and now,

[104] Benvenisti 2022, p. 291.
[105] Jachec-Neale 2014, p. 137.
[106] ILA 2017, p. 32.
[107] Ibid.
[108] Dinstein 2010, p. 393; Watkin 2016, p. 346.
[109] Fenrick 2001, p. 494.

and not any more so some hours later, and then shift again back to being a lawful target".[110]

The requirement of effective contribution relates to military action in general. The adjective "effective" in this context means a manifest, not a hypothetical or possible, contribution. The contribution must not necessarily concern the adverse party, but it can also refer to the actions of the attacking party, e.g. conquering a piece of land to enhance the strategy of its own forces. According to Jachec-Neale, military action connotes the idea of military operations by the military personnel. It excludes the more vague notions of "war effort", which would expand the category of targetable objects into the realm of civilians. Yet, it is challenging to identify the exact reach of the link between the effective contribution and the military action. Authors like Dinstein argue that there need be no "direct connection with specific combat operations."[111] The ILA-SG reports that the generally accepted view is that "to qualify as a military objective, there must exist *a proximate nexus* to military action (or 'war-fighting')".[112] Departing from this view, Jachec-Neale considers that the extent to which the contribution must be "direct" can only be resolved under the banner of the "effectiveness" criterion, i.e. that the contribution must be discernible and real.[113] This requires a subjective assessment of the expected contribution of an attack to the military action.

In order to overcome the lack of a uniform and coherent approach towards this essential aspect and in furtherance of an interpretation coherent with IHL principles and rules, this author endorses the position expressed by the experts who drafted the Harvard Air and Missile Warfare Manual, according to which "[m]ilitary advantage refers only to advantage *which is directly related to military operations* and does not refer to other forms of advantage which may in some way relate to the conflict more generally".[114] Ultimately, it is a correct appraisal of the linkage between conflict goals, the effective contribution being sought, and the justification of the military advantage based on the "time and situation-specific circumstances" that contributes to better regulating the conduct of hostilities and enhancing the protection of dual-use objects.

---

[110] Kolb 2015, p. 694.

[111] Dinstein 2004, p. 87.

[112] ILA 2017, p. 6, (emphasis added). According to Dinstein the term "war-fighting" can be used as a synonym of military action, whereas "war-sustaining" is too broad and it would cover the controversial notion of war-sustaining objects. Dinstein 2004, p. 87.

[113] Jachec-Neale 2014, pp. 83–85.

[114] Harvard Air and Missile Warfare Manual 2013, Rule 1, p. 36 (emphasis added).

3.2.2 *The Problematic Notion of "Attack as a Whole" Applied to the Principle of Distinction*

The incipit of the provision enshrined in Article 52(2) of API famously claims that "attacks shall be limited strictly to military objectives". As already discussed in this book, the term "attack" is explicitly defined in Article 49 of the 1977 Additional Protocol I as "acts of violence against the adversary, whether in offence or in defence."[115] There is no need to further linger on the breadth of this definition, although it is useful to recall that nowadays the predominant approach supports the view that the "crux of the notion [of attacks] lies in the effects that are caused",[116] and therefore in the consequences caused by a given operation. This aspect is crucial for the purpose of the present inquiry, since, as emerged from the analysis of the air bombardments carried out in Iraq and in the former Yugoslavia against dual-use objects, a "consequence-based interpretation of 'attacks'" is essential to tackle the increasing use of new means and methods of warfare, and to recognise that the continuing evolution of civilian protection necessitates a broader and more expansive interpretation of the term than has traditionally been the case.[117]

The term "attack" includes both operations that result in violent effects, and those which were intended to, but failed. It excludes activities like intelligence gathering, propaganda, or any other military actions which do not cause (or were intended to cause) death, injury, damage or destruction of persons or objects,[118] consistently with the consequence-based interpretation of this notion. Such a definition of "attacks" also covers "non-kinetic" attacks, i.e., attacks that do not involve the physical transfer of energy but that may still result in death, injury, damage or destruction of persons or objects.[119]

In addition to the definition of attack, another essential piece of the puzzle is represented by how the reach of the attack influences the assessment of the military advantage for the purpose of applying the principle of distinction. The 1987 ICRC Commentary concisely states that "in the case of Article 52 there must be a definite military advantage *for every military objective that is attacked*".[120] This reading of Article 52 is mirrored and reinforced by the provision incorporated in Article 51(5) which prohibits indiscriminate attacks against the civilian population, including "an attack by bombardment by any methods or means which treats *as a single military objective* a number of clearly separated and distinct military objectives located in a city, town, village or other area containing a similar concentration of civilians or civilian objects." To put it simply, this means that the dangerous notion of "attack as a whole" against which the military advantage shall be weighed is blatantly not in

[115] See Chap. 1, Sect. 1.3.1 in this book.

[116] Schmitt 2013, pp. 92–94.

[117] Drew 2017, pp. 97–99.

[118] HPCR Manual 2013, Rule 1, pp. 11–12.

[119] Schmitt 2002, p. 377.

[120] Sandoz et al. 1987, Article 52, para 2028 (emphasis added).

compliance with the law. Yet, it appears that there is growing uncertainty concerning this key issue, fuelled by the misinterpretation and misapplication of this norm by several States and the lack of a consistent approach amongst the legal community. Dinstein explains that the dilemma whether to lump together as a single target several military objectives may be prompted "even by run-of-the-mill objects when they are located at a relatively small distance from each other".[121] In fact, while placing a reasonable limitation on the concept of "target area" bombing, Article 51(5)(a) does not categorically ban it. "Target area" bombing is still legitimate when the military objectives are not "clearly separated and distinct".[122] The choice of the words "clearly separated and distinct" leaves some degree of latitude to those planning an attack, especially since the prerequisite clarity can be interpreted both as a matter of objective determination or subjective appreciation.[123]

Furthermore, there is a tendency to forcibly draw similarities between the notion of military advantage in the two main domains where it is used under API, namely the principle of distinction (Article 52) and the principle of proportionality (Article 51(5)(b), and Article 57(2)(a)(iii) and (b)).[124] This problem has perhaps been exacerbated by the reference in Article 8(2)(b)(iv) of the Rome Statute to the notion of an "overall" military advantage.[125] However, it shall be noted that the provision in the Rome Statute concerns the war crime of intentionally launching an attack in the knowledge that such attack will violate the principle of proportionality by causing "incidental loss of life or injury to civilians or damage to civilian objects or widespread, long-term, and severe damage to the natural environment which would be clearly excessive in relation to the concrete and direct overall military advantage anticipated". Some authors, including Bothe, have expressed concerns with respect to the use of "overall" in the Rome Statute, since it "somewhat broadens the scope of military advantages which may be taken into account".[126] The conflation of the notions of military advantages and attacks in two different domains, i.e. the principle of distinction and the principle of proportionality, should be carefully avoided, as each of them serves a specific goal. Whereas, as it will be discussed in the next chapter, the notion of "attack as a whole" is accepted when applying the principle of proportionality, although with much needed caveats,[127] the same cannot be said with regard to the principle of distinction.

Concerning the latter, Sassòli reports that according to declarations of understanding by the United Kingdom, Canada, Belgium, France, Germany, New Zealand, the Netherlands, Italy, Spain, and the US "the military advantage anticipated from

[121] Dinstein 2004, p. 112.

[122] Ibid.

[123] Sandoz et al. 1987, Article 52, para 1972.

[124] See Chap. 4, Sects. 4.5.1 and. 4.5.3 in this book.

[125] Watkin 2016, p. 281.

[126] Bothe 2002, p. 399.

[127] See Chap. 4, Sect. 4.5.3 in this book.

an attack is intended to refer to the advantage anticipated from *the attack considered as a whole* and not only from isolated or particular parts of the attack [...]".[128] The Canadian approach of looking at the effect of the attack "as a whole" is broad enough to include as military objectives targets which indirectly make an effective contribution to an opposing party's military war effort.[129] Similarly, and as already discussed, the US includes in its list of lawful targets those that have an economic value, assessed in cumulative terms because obviously attacking a single oil facility cannot reduce an adversary's capability to finance and support the war effort.[130] This is not surprising, and it reflects the model theorised by Warden and previously analysed.[131] In Warden's words:

> Thus, an attack against industry or infrastructure is not primarily conducted because of the effect it might or might not have on fielded forces. Rather, it is undertaken for its direct effect *on the enemy system*, including its effect on national leaders and commanders who must assess the cost of rebuilding, the effect on the state's economic position in the postwar period, the internal political effect on their own survival, and whether the cost is worth the potential gain from continuing the war.[132]

What this theory suggests, in contrast with the existing norms, is that even though "not all targets will be purely military" they can still be attacked.[133] This is blatantly corroding the entire rationale of IHL. Although it is possible for an attack to have both military and political outcomes, belligerent parties must necessarily avoid what Watkin describes as a "tipping point at which the political purpose is seen to be dominant, and any possible military advantage fades into the background".[134] This happens in particular with the targeting of industry, infrastructure, and other dual-use objects, which, more often than not, is motivated by the impact that the attack will have on the population and/or on the national leaders. As soon as military commanders and airpower theorists place emphasis on that impact, rather than on the military advantage to be gained from targeting the objects themselves because of their contribution to military action, this approach renders the attack "an *impermissible political* rather than a lawful military one".[135] Therefore, in this author's view and in line with the approach clearly stated in the 1987 ICRC Commentary, for the purposes of correctly applying the notion of military objective enshrined in Article 52(2) of API and respecting the principle of distinction, the military advantage must be assessed for each individual attack and not for the attack as a whole.

---

128 Sassòli 2015, p. 4 (emphasis added).
129 Watkin 2005, p. 308.
130 Goodman 2016; Reetz 2022.
131 See Chap. 2, Sect. 2.3 in this book.
132 Warden 1995, p. 52 (emphasis added).
133 Watkin 2016, p. 335.
134 Ibid.
135 Ibid., p. 336 (emphasis added).

3.3 Relying on Practical Examples to Understand the Limits of the Definition of Military Objectives

As stressed so far, understanding what constitutes a military objective is central to realise how international humanitarian law governs the conduct of hostilities in armed conflicts and appreciate its protective regime. It is by now well known that under the two-pronged test of Article 52(2) an object must fulfil two cumulative criteria to be a military objective. Exclusively something that meets the criteria of a military objective laid down under IHL may be lawfully attacked.[136] In 2005, during an expert meeting on targeting military objectives organised by the University Centre for International Humanitarian Law of the University of Geneva, now known as the Geneva Academy of International Humanitarian Law and Human Rights, all (prominent) experts participating in the meeting agreed that the definition enshrined in Article 52(2), although far from perfect, was not controversial in itself.[137] It constitutes the standard definition of a military objective, which has been included into other international instruments and nowadays inspires countless definitions found in national legal texts.

Although the definition *per se* is not problematic, the two cases discussed below show how complex is the process of interpreting, applying, and enforcing IHL norms, in the specific instance Article 52(2) of API. Since it would be impossible to focus on the jurisprudence of national courts, the analysis will provide two examples from the international dimension. The analysis will show that, regardless of the level of authoritativeness of the body that undertakes the assessment of the lawfulness of a given target, the findings can easily blur the lines between civilian objects and military objectives. This further highlights the urge to strengthen the current framework to enhance the protection of the civilian population and of the dual-use objects that are needed for its survival.

3.3.1 The Eritrea-Ethiopia Claims Commission's Award on the Aerial Bombardment of the Hirgigo Power Station

In May 1998 an armed conflict erupted between Eritrea and Ethiopia that lasted over two years and caused substantial loss of life, personal injury, and economic damage to the civilian populations.[138] Through the work of the UN, the Organisation of African Unity (OAU),[139] the United States, and others, the conflict was finally brought to an

[136] Greenwood 2001, p. 135.

[137] Report of the Expert Meeting on Targeting Military Objectives, University Centre for International Humanitarian Law Geneva, 2005, p. 2.

[138] Matheson 2009.

[139] Nesi 1995.

end in June 2000 with the conclusion of an agreement for the cessation of hostilities, which established a security zone separating the opposing forces and requested the UN to deploy a peacekeeping force to help implement the temporal agreement.[140] This was followed in December 2000 by the Algiers Peace Agreement,[141] which, among other things, established three organs, an independent body to investigate the origins of the dispute,[142] and two arbitral bodies: a Boundary Commission to delimit and demarcate the disputed border; and the Eritrea-Ethiopia Claims Commission to decide claims for loss, damage and injury resulting from the conflict. The two Commissions had their seats in the Hague and worked with the assistance of the Permanent Court of Arbitration.

From the outset of its work in 2001 and continuing through 2005, the Claims Commission focused its efforts on determining the merits of the claims submitted by the two States. During that period, the Commission issued 15 separate awards that found Eritrea and Ethiopia liable for numerous international law violations. While both parties were found responsible for violations of *jus in bello*, Eritrea was additionally found in violation of *jus ad bellum*.[143] As is well known, during this liability phase, the Claims Commission made a number of findings of potentially great importance with respect to the use of force and the rules of warfare, including an elaboration of what provisions of existing agreements on IHL have attained the status of customary law; guidance on the application of various norms to wartime circumstances, such as target selection, treatment of prisoners, and actions against civilian property and economic activity; pronouncements on the applicability in wartime of peacetime treaties and human rights norms; and the lawfulness of the use of force in connection with boundary disputes.[144] Without discussing the work of the EECC at length, as it would fall outside the scope of the present study, what is especially relevant here is the Commission's interpretation of Article 52(2) of API and its key elements in the context of an attack against a dual-use object.

The Award on the aerial bombardment of the Hirgigo power station (HPS) was one of the claims decided by the EECC. It was issued on 19 December 2005 in a six-page decision, in which the Commission famously concluded that "[…]in the circumstances prevailing on May 28, 2000, the Hirgigo power station was a military objective, as defined in Article 52, para 2, of Geneva Protocol I and that Ethiopia's aerial bombardment of it was not unlawful".[145] Notably, and to highlight the fact that the decision reached was ultimately controversial, the Award is the only one where a decision was made by majority of votes; the rest of the Awards were decided

---

[140] Matheson 2009, p. 3.

[141] Greppi and Poli 2021, p. 67.

[142] However, since the "independent, impartial body" could not be established, the envisaged investigation never took place. See Venturini 2021, p. 346.

[143] Capone 2021, pp. 556–558. On the findings concerning the *jus ad bellum* violations, see Gray 2006.

[144] Matheson 2009, p. 4; Murphy 2012, p. 237.

[145] Partial Award: Western Front, Aerial Bombardment and related claims, Eritrea's Claims 1, 3, 5, 9–13, 14, 21, 25 & 26, (Partial Award) 19 December 2005, PCA Case No. 2001-02, para 121.

unanimously.[146] The merits of the claim are based on the following events occurred on 28 May 2000:

> [...] two Ethiopian jet aircraft dropped seven bombs that hit and seriously damaged the Hirgigo Power Station, which is located about ten kilometers from the port city of Massawa. At that time, construction was complete, and the power station was in the testing and commissioning phase. While not yet fully operational, the power station had successfully supplied some power briefly to Asmara and Mendefera. Eritrea asserted that the bombing of the plant was unlawful because the plant was not a legitimate military objective, and it requested that the Commission hold Ethiopia liable to compensate Eritrea for the damage caused to Eritrea by that violation of international humanitarian law.[147]

At the heart of the claim, obviously lies the classification of the HPS as a legitimate military target. The first step undertaken by the Claims Commission was to determine the applicable law, and hence to assess the status of the definition of military objectives enshrined in Article 52(2). The Commission concluded that, although the provision was not applicable as part of a treaty binding on both Parties to the conflict, it is widely accepted as an expression of customary international law.[148] As a second step of its reasoning, the EECC reflected on whether the criteria for the classification of the power station as a military objective had been met. Concerning the first criterion, if the power plant was an object that by its nature, location, purpose or use made an effective contribution to military action at the time it was attacked, the Commission found that the answer to this question was affirmative. Notably, the HPS had been under construction for a considerable time and the evidence indicated that "much of the related transformer and transmission facilities that would be necessary for it to transmit its power around the country were in place".[149] Yet, the power station at the time of the attack was not functioning and thus it was not producing energy. Despite the fact that the HPS was not in use, the Commission described the new and almost completed power station as "a suggestive example of the potential value to a country at war of a large".[150] The Commission's majority expressed no doubt that the near port and naval base at Massawa were military objectives. Along these lines of reasoning, the EECC affirmed that the generating facilities "potentially providing the electric power needed to operate them were objects that made an effective contribution to military action".[151] Even though, as discussed above, there are still discrepancies with respect to how to qualify the link between the effective contribution and a specific combat operation,[152] the adjective "effective" still means a manifest, not a hypothetical or possible, contribution. Therefore, and since the power station was not functioning at the time of the attack, the conclusion reached

---

[146] Andemariam et al. 2016.

[147] Partial Award para 111 (see n. 145 *supra*).

[148] Ibid., para 112.

[149] Ibid., para 118.

[150] Ibid., para 119.

[151] Ibid., para 120.

[152] See *supra* Sect. 3.2.1.

by the Commission cannot be said to be in line with the accepted interpretation of the first prong of the military objectives' test.

Subsequently, the EECC delved into the analysis of the term "military advantage", affirming that it can only be properly understood "in the context of the military operations between the Parties taken as a whole, not simply in the context of a specific attack".[153] Making reference again, and this time erroneously, to the customary character of the norm, the Claims Commission insisted that with respect to the claim under scrutiny "whether the attack on the power station offered a definite military advantage must be considered in the context of its relation *to the armed conflict as a whole at the time of the attack*".[154] As already discussed above, this reading of the provision is not in line with ICRC's interpretation, according to which there has to be a definite military advantage for every military objective that is targeted.[155] Although, as shown, some States depart from this approach, it is certainly a stretch to even suggest the emergence of a customary rule in this sense. Indeed, as noted by Sassòli, the EECC "went too far when it held that the advantage anticipated from the attack must be considered in the context of its relation to the armed conflict as a whole and includes the potential to end the conflict".[156] Furthermore, the Commission added that "[t]he infliction of economic losses from attacks against military objectives is *a lawful means of achieving a definite military advantage*, and there can be few military advantages more evident than effective pressure to end an armed conflict".[157] As already explained, the inclusion amongst lawful military objectives of war-sustaining targets is very controversial, and openly endorsed only by a handful of countries, spearheaded by the US.

In the Separate Opinion of the Claims Commission's President van Houtte, the criticalities of the majority's reasoning surfaced, further shedding light on its significant shortcomings. The EECC's President first underlined that Article 52(2) contains a "restricted definition" of military objectives, which requires, cumulatively, (1) that the objective makes an effective contribution to military action; and (2) that its destruction, capture or neutralisation provides a definite military advantage. In relation to the first prong of the test, he noted that the objective's contribution to the military action must be "effective" in the actual situation, not *in abstracto*. Otherwise, every object "potentially of use to enemy troops" could become a military objective. As already mentioned, the HPS was not a functioning power station when the attack occurred, hence the effective contribution stemming from its destruction was assessed on the basis of purely speculative considerations. Hence, Van Houtte, correctly stressed that the reference to "the hypothetical or speculative effect of the destruction of the military objective on the conduct of the war is […] not sufficient."[158]

[153] Ibid.

[154] Ibid., para 113.

[155] Sandoz et al. 1987, Article 52, para 2028.

[156] Sassòli 2015, p. 4.

[157] Partial Award para 121 (emphasis added) [n 145].

[158] Aerial Bombardment of Hirgigo Power Station (Eritrea's Claim 25)—Separate Opinion by President van Houtte (Separate Opinion by van Houtte), para 4.

Concerning the second prong, in his view, "a demonstration of the 'definite military advantage' of the attack is required by the party that must justify the military action."[159] On a procedural note, he stressed that the Ethiopian government failed to justify the attack, and the *modus operandi* of the EECC was not straightforward in this regard, as according to the Commission's rules of procedure "[e]ach party shall have the burden of proving the facts it relies on to support its claim or defense."[160] Ultimately, van Houtte reached the logical conclusion that, since the assessment made by the Commission's majority did not comply with the test of Article 52(2) of API, the HPS could not be classified as a military objective. Consequently, he went on noting, the "infliction of economic loss or the undermining of morale through the destruction of a civilian object, or the probability that the destruction may bring the decision-makers to the negotiation table,"[161] do not make that object a military objective.

3.3.2 The Goldstone Report's Take on Dual-Use Objects

On December 2008 Israel launched a deadly military operation in Gaza, named Operation Cast Lead, in response to the firing of rockets at the southern Israeli border and Hamas's use of tunnels to smuggle rockets into the strip. The Israel Defense Forces (IDF) carried out major air and ground operations against Hamas and other Palestinian armed groups in Gaza. The nature of the ensuing fighting draw attention to some complex legal issues regarding, *inter alia*, targeting, proportionality and the protection of civilians.[162]

On 3 April 2009, the President of the Human Rights Council established the United Nations Fact Finding Mission on the Gaza Conflict (Mission) with the mandate "to investigate all violations of international human rights law and international humanitarian law that might have been committed at any time in the context of the military operations that were conducted in Gaza during the period from 27 December 2008 and 18 January 2009, whether before, during or after."[163] The President appointed Justice Richard Goldstone, alongside other three members, namely Professor Christine Chinkin, Ms Hina Jilani, and Colonel Desmond Travers.[164]

The Mission, which interpreted the mandate as requiring it to place the civilian population of the region at the centre of its concerns regarding the violations of

---

[159] Ibid. (emphasis added).

[160] Eritrea-Ethiopia Claims Commission, Rules of Procedure, Article 14(1) (Oct. 2001), https://pcacases.com/web/sendAttach/774 (accessed 31 July 2024).

[161] Separate Opinion by van Houtte [n 158], para 8.

[162] Blank 2009, p. 347; Blank 2010, p. 279; Bartolini 2010, p. 185. On the violations committed by Hamas during Operation Cast Lead, see Pertile 2009.

[163] Human Rights in Palestine and Other Occupied Arab Territories, Report of the United Nations Fact Finding Mission on the Gaza Conflict, A/HRC/12/48, 15 September 2009 (hereinafter Goldstone Report), para 1.

[164] Ibid., para 2.

international law, convened in Geneva in May, July and August 2009, and conducted field visits to Gaza and Amman, in Jordan, during the summer of 2009. Notably, the government of Israel refused to cooperate with the investigations and to allow the Mission to enter Gaza through Israel. Eventually, Egypt granted the Mission permission to enter Gaza through the Rafah crossing. Furthermore, the Mission held public hearings in Gaza in June 2009 and in Geneva in July 2009. On 15 September 2009 the Mission issued its final report, entitled Human Rights in Palestine and Other Occupied Arab Territories: Report of the United Nations Fact Finding Mission on the Gaza Conflict (the Goldstone Report).

In its findings, the Goldstone Report described numerous violations of IHL and human rights law by Israel, Hamas, and other Palestinian armed groups. The report also made a number of recommendations, tackling crucial issues, such as accountability for IHL violations, redress measures, violations of human rights law, the blockade, the use of weapons and military procedures, and the protection of human rights organisations. Several authors have provided thorough assessments of the Goldstone Report with respect to many of the crucial aspects that the inquiry covered.[165] Amongst those, there is the fact that Operation Cast Lead, even more than previous asymmetrical conflicts, has demonstrated "the complexities of determining when buildings and other objects constitute military objectives".[166] The very nature of Hamas and the political context in Gaza exacerbated the challenge of how to identify lawful targets, in compliance with IHL principles and norms.[167] As stressed in the IDF report on Operation Cast Lead

> [w]hile Hamas operates ministries and is in charge of a variety of administrative and traditionally governmental functions in the Gaza Strip, it still remains a terrorist organisation. Many of the ostensibly civilian elements of its regime are in reality active components of its terrorist and military efforts. Indeed, *Hamas does not separate its civilian and military activities in the manner in which a legitimate government might*. Instead, Hamas uses apparatuses under its control, including quasi-governmental institutions, to promote its terrorist activity.[168]

Consistently with the alleged justification for blurring the lines, based on Hamas designation as a terrorist organisation, Israel identified and attacked military targets within the framework of a counter-terrorism operation, targeting Hamas ministries and other objects that appeared civilian in character. The Report, hence, concluded that the framing of the military objectives Israel sought to strike was "very wide indeed".[169] According to the Mission's findings there was, in particular, a lack of clarity about the concept of promoting "terrorist activity". Based on Israel's claim

---

165 Schmitt 2010, pp. 826–828; Bell 2010, pp. 80–86; Dajani 2010, p. 73; Wells-Greco 2010, p. 397; Barnette 2011, p. 123.

166 Blank 2009, p. 357.

167 Ibid., p. 357.

168 IDF, The operation in Gaza: factual and legal aspects, July 2009, para 235, https://www.gov.il/BlobFolder/generalpage/the-operation-in-gaza-factual-and-legal-aspects/en/English_Terrorism_GazaOperation%20w%20Links.pdf (accessed 31 July 2024).

169 Goldstone Report para 1210.

that there is no real division between civilian and military activities *because of Hamas's status*, it would appear that anyone who supports Hamas in any way may be considered as promoting terrorism. Ultimately, it was not far-fetched for the Mission to consider that, from Israel's perspective, very large sections of the Gazan civilian population could be regarded as part of Hamas' "supporting infrastructure".[170]

The Israeli approach has been extensively criticised, so there is no need to linger upon it,[171] besides adding that most of the criticisms still hold true in today's scenario.[172] In a nutshell, according to Israel's position all Hamas buildings were part of the terror infrastructure and therefore legitimate targets, clearly broadening the category of military objectives. Rather, what is worth analysing is how the Goldstone Report, a document certainly not immune to disapproval,[173] has interpreted the principle of distinction in this specific situation. In relation to government buildings and civilian political infrastructure in Gaza, including civilian ministries, the al-Saraya prison and the Palestinian Legislative Council building, the Goldstone Report rejected the argument that these targets could be military objectives by finding that they were not "war ministries",[174] nor did they have a "dual civilian-military use" and did not make an effective contribution to military operations.[175] On the "dual-use" status of these targets, the Mission further noted that IHL also recognises "a category of civilian objects which *may nonetheless be targeted in the course of armed conflict to the extent that they have a 'dual use'*".[176] This is not correct, as IHL treaties do not acknowledge the existence of an intermediate category between civilian objects and military objectives and do not suggest that civilian objects may lose their status because they have an intrinsic dual-use potential.[177] Nonetheless, the Mission went on to explain that

> [e]xamples often made for such dual-use objects, *which serve both civilian and military purposes, are civilian infrastructures such as telecommunications, power-generating stations or bridges, in so far as they are used by the military in addition to their civilian use.* There is no indication, nor any allegation of any such dual use of the Legislative Council building or of the Gaza main prison.[178]

Furthermore, the Mission found that the concept of what constitutes "supporting infrastructure" must be understood not only in the context of the military operations of December and January, but also in the tightening of the restrictions of access

[170] Ibid., para 1214.

[171] Blank 2009, p. 358.

[172] UN General Assembly, Report of the Independent International Commission of Inquiry on the Occupied Palestinian Territory, including East Jerusalem, and Israel, A/79/232, 11 September 2024.

[173] See Bell 2010, pp. 78–83.

[174] War Ministries traditionally encompass Ministries of Army, Navy, Air Force, National Defence, Supply, and other organs for the direction and administration of military operations. See ICRC 1956, Annex to the rules.

[175] Goldstone Report para 387.

[176] Ibid., para 388.

[177] See Chap. 1, Sect. 1.3.3 in this book.

[178] Goldstone Report para 388 (emphasis added).

to goods and people into and out of Gaza, especially since Hamas took power.[179] In the Mission's view the primary purpose was to bring about a situation in which the Palestinians would find life in Gaza so intolerable that, if given the possibility, they would leave or turn Hamas out of office, as well as to collectively punish the civilian population.[180] According to the Mission, and consistently with Israel's alleged goal, the military operations "destroyed a substantial part of the Gaza Strip's economic infrastructure and its capacity to support decent livelihoods for families. Many factories and businesses were directly targeted and destroyed or damaged. Poverty, unemployment, and food insecurity increased dramatically".[181] The Mission hence concluded that Israel had "*as one of its military objectives* the destruction of local industrial capacity so as to harm the prospects for an economic recovery in the Gaza Strip".[182] In the Mission's Report, therefore, military objectives are merged with political ones and they even become synonyms with the volatile notion of "supporting infrastructure". This, once again, proves how difficult it is to correctly interpret and apply even the key tenets of IHL when asymmetrical warfare poses challenges for distinction, precisely because of the lack of boundaries between conflict areas and civilian areas.[183]

3.4 Towards a "Working Definition" of Dual-Use Objects

As discussed in the previous sections of the present chapter, the correct qualification of certain targets as military or civilian is often not easy nor straightforward. The definition of military objectives that is contained in Article 52(2) of API, despite being considered by some as "too vague"[184] and by others as "too restrictive",[185] has unquestionably attained the status of customary law. Nonetheless, it is still prone to misinterpretation and misapplication that make compliance and enforcement very difficult to achieve, especially in a uniform way and even at the international level. The two examples analysed above have succinctly delineated some of the challenges faced by two international bodies, composed of renewed experts, that were tasked with shaping the contours of the definition of military objectives before ascertaining the lawfulness of its application by the belligerent parties. The controversial notion of "dual-use" objects has been addressed, implicitly or manifestly, by both the EECC and the United Nations Fact Finding Mission on the Gaza Conflict, thus showing that

[179] Ibid., para 1208 and para 1330 "Israel, rather than fighting the Palestinian armed groups operating in Gaza in a targeted way, has chosen to punish the whole Gaza Strip and the population in it with economic, political and military sanctions".

[180] Ibid.

[181] Ibid., paras 1228–1229.

[182] Ibid. (emphasis added).

[183] Blank 2009, p. 401.

[184] Kolb 2009, p. 248.

[185] Parks 1990, pp. 137–140.

this eery (non-)category has a practical relevance that is still unmatched under the IHL framework. Furthermore, besides not being the object of any legislative efforts at the international level, examples of domestic norms and policies dealing with dual-use objects are not so scant. The updated version of the US DoD's Law of War Manual affirms that

> Sometimes, "dual-use" is used to describe objects that are used by both the armed forces and the civilian population, such as power stations or communications facilities. However, from the legal perspective, such objects are either military objectives or they are not; there is no intermediate legal category. If an object is a military objective, it is not a civilian object and may be made the object of attack. However, it will be appropriate to consider in applying the principle of proportionality the harm to the civilian population that is expected to result from the attack on such a military objective.[186]

Similarly, the British Manual of the Law of Armed Conflict considers the peculiar status of dual-use objects when the assessment of the principle of proportionality comes into play. The Manual states that commanders "must bear in mind foreseeable effects of attack".[187] To this end, the British Manual provides the example of bombing petrol reserves and affirms that commanding officers must consider the possibility of burning liquid fuel flowing into nearby residential areas. This scenario has immediate foreseeable consequences, but it is certainly not the only case where attacks against dual-use objects can negatively impact the civilian population. As stressed by Sassòli and Cameron, it is perhaps noteworthy that the Manual does not refer instead to the much-discussed example of destroying electricity supply and thereby impeding access to health care and/or fresh water.[188] Sporadic examples of attempts to enhance the protection of dual-use objects without tying it to the issue of proportionality have also been reported. For instance, the National Liberation Army, *Ejército de Liberación Nacional* (ELN), an armed group in Colombia, enacted "El Codigo de Guerra" which mentions that "forces shall not target installations *more useful to the community than the enemy*".[189] However, the attention devoted to this topic is still very limited, even though dual-use objects keep generating and fuelling debate among scholars and military planners alike. Particularly concerning, in this author's view, is the lack of effort to define dual-use objects in any of the domains in which the subject bears some relevance.

In light of the many and complex issues raised and grappled with so far, it is clear that outlining at least a "working definition" of dual-use objects in the context of an armed conflict could contribute to enhancing the discussion and, hopefully, steering

[186] The US Department of Defense Law of War Manual (June 2015, Updated July 2023), para 5.6.1.2, https://media.defense.gov/2023/Jul/31/2003271432/-1/-1/0/DOD-LAW-OF-WAR-MANUAL-JUNE-2015-UPDATED-JULY%202023.PDF (accessed 23 June 2024).

[187] UK Ministry of Defence, The Manual of the Law of Armed Conflict, para 5.33.4. https://assets.publishing.service.gov.uk/government/uploads/system/uploads/attachment_data/file/27874/JSP3832004Edition.pdf (accessed 7 August 2024).

[188] Sassòli and Cameron 2006, pp. 64–65.

[189] National Liberation Army/Ejército de Liberación Nacional (ELN), Code of War (Unofficial Translation), http://theirwords.org/media/transfer/doc/ut_co_eln_1995_01_eng-07e5677b22c4cf06bdfc9f02eff206ef.pdf (accessed 7 August 2024). Cited in Tignino and Kebebew 2022, p. 1219.

it towards an approach that is more coherent with the LOAC's core principles and norms. To this end, the present book proposes a non-legal definition according to which dual-use objects are:

> objects, items, infrastructures, systems that fulfil a civilian function. Dual-use objects may become military objectives only when the following two cumulative criteria are satisfied in the circumstances ruling at the time: a) their *location* (when the dual-use object is situated inside a specific area that is lawfully designated as a military objective), and/or their *use* makes an *effective and direct contribution* to military action and b) a *definite military advantage* derives from the total or partial destruction, capture or neutralisation of *every dual-use object* that is attacked.

The definition clearly summarises and takes stock of all the issues discussed so far, providing what, in this author's view, amounts to a reading of the relevant rules and an interpretation of the key concepts able to reconcile the notion of dual-use objects with the current IHL framework, without revolutionising it or portraying developments that simply are not there yet.

3.5 Conclusion

The present chapter served the essential purpose of "sharpening the divide between objects that are military by their nature and dual-use objects".[190] To do so, the analysis carried out dealt in detail with a crucial topic, namely the definition of military objectives under the current international legal framework. Unfortunately, "[t]here has been relatively little discussion in the relevant literature of what constitutes a military objective and why, since the adoption of Protocol I in 1977",[191] and even less has been devoted to the concept of dual-use objects despite the wide recognition, in the past as well as today, of the importance of this issue.

As is well known, and as several authors have duly noted, a broad interpretation of military objectives is "insufficient to deliver the protection of civilian life" that a narrower interpretation would be able to bestow.[192] Schmitt reports that the most frequently cited disagreement regarding the distinction principle surrounds the reach of the term "military objective", a rather curious fact given that all sides, including non-contracting parties such as the United States, recognise the API textual definition as correct and accept its customary legal status.[193] The current definition of military objectives is supposed to enable a wide-ranging and effective protection of civilian life; yet, to use Dinstein's words, "[l]aw must not be confused with liturgy. It is not enough to prescribe and reiterate the law: to be meaningful, *norms must be adhered to in reality*".[194] As discussed above while analysing the EECC's award on the Aerial

[190] Sassòli and Cameron 2006, p. 59.
[191] Fenrick 2001, p. 495.
[192] Reetz 2022, p. 461.
[193] Schmitt 2006, p. 280.
[194] Dinstein 2004, p. 257 (emphasis added).

Bombardment of the Hirgigo Power Station and the Goldstone Report, even *super partes* bodies composed of renewed experts struggle to correctly interpret and apply the concept of military objectives, especially in light of a few, but central, aspects that have never been addressed in a uniform way and that, when misinterpreted, trigger ambiguous and potentially dangerous results. The challenge appears to be more difficult to face when the crux of the matter is to assess the legality of attacks against dual-use objects.

The present chapter has duly built on those findings, and it stirred away from the temptation of performing an untenable nomophylactic function aimed at providing an interpretation of the definition of military objectives that departs from the commonly accepted one. Rather, this analysis sought to shed light on the most critical aspects of the provision enshrined in Article 52(2), namely the controversial notion of military advantage and the equally problematic assessment of the reach of an attack. The inquiry ultimately led to a reading that is in line with the IHL framework and its key principles and values, pushing for an interpretation of military advantage that ties it to the other elements of the definition embedded in Article 52(2) of API and in particular to the effective contribution deriving from the (total or partial) destruction, capture or neutralisation of a military objective.

Furthermore, the analysis led to the conclusion that the military advantage must be assessed vis-à-vis the attack against an individual target and not by lumping together as a single target several military objectives, as it happens, under strict conditions, when assessing proportionality. Finally, this chapter provided a working definition of "dual-use" objects that takes into due account all the considerations shared so far and aims at reconciling this contentious notion with the normative framework to which the term does not formally belong, but in which it makes its presence unquestionably and increasingly felt.

References

Acquaviva G (2014) La repressione dei crimini di guerra nel diritto internazionale e nel diritto italiano. Giuffrè Editore, Milan

Andemariam S W, Tesfalidet I Y, Affa M (2016) Critiquing the Eritrea-Ethiopia Claims Commission's Interpretation of the Rules on Legitimate Military Objectives: Aerial Bombardment of the Hirgigo Electric Power Station. https://ssrn.com/abstract=2869126 or https://doi.org/10.2139/ssrn.2869126. Accessed 30 July 2024

Arato J (2010) Subsequent Practice and Evolutive Interpretation: Techniques of Treaty Interpretation over Time and Their Diverse Consequences. The Law and Practice of International Courts and Tribunals 9: 443–494

Barnette J (2011) Initial Reactions to the Goldstone Report and Reflections on Israeli Accountability. In: Meloni C, Tognoni G (eds) Is There a Court for Gaza? T.M.C. Asser Press, The Hague, pp 123–143

Bartolini G (2010) Il Rapporto Goldstone sull'operazione "Piombo fuso" a Gaza. Diritti Umani e Diritto Internazionale 4(1): 185–194

Bell A (2010) A Critique of the Goldstone Report and Its Treatment of International Humanitarian Law. Proceedings of the Annual Meeting (American Society of International Law) 104: 79–86

Benvenisti E (2022) The Birth and Life of the Definition of Military Objectives. International and Comparative Law Quarterly 71(2): 269–295

Benvenuti P (2001) The ICTY Prosecutor and the Review of the NATO Bombing Campaign against the Federal Republic of Yugoslavia. European Journal of International Law 12(3): 503–529

Bjorge E (2014) The Evolutionary Interpretation of Treaties. Oxford University Press, Oxford

Blank L R (2009) The Application of IHL in the Goldstone Report: A Critical Commentary. Yearbook of International Humanitarian Law, 12: 347–402

Blank L R (2010) Finding Facts but Missing the Law: The Goldstone Report, Gaza and Lawfare. Case Western Reserve Journal of International Law 43(1): 279–302

Bothe M (2002) War Crimes. In: Cassese A, Gaeta P, Jones J R W D (eds) The Rome Statute of the International Criminal Court: A Commentary, Vol. I. Oxford University Press, Oxford 379–399

Bothe M, Partsch K J, Solf W A (1982) New Rules for Victims of Armed Conflicts - Commentary on the Two 1977 Protocols Additional to the Geneva Conventions of 1949. Martinus Nijhoff Publishers, The Hague/Boston

Buffard I, Zemanek K (1998) The Object and Purpose of a Treaty: An Enigma? Austrian Review of International & European Law 3: 331–343

Capone F (2021) The 17 August 2009 Final Awards of the Eritrea-Ethiopia Claims Commission. In: de Guttry A, Post H H G, Venturini G (eds) The 1998–2000 Eritrea-Ethiopia War and Its Aftermath in International Legal Perspective. T.M.C. Asser Press, The Hague, pp 550–565

Capone F (2023) The Wave of Russian Attacks on Ukraine's Power Infrastructures: An Opportunity to Infuse Meaningfulness into the Notion of "Dual-use Objects"? European Papers 8(2): 741–754

Crawford E, Pert A (2020) International Humanitarian Law, 2nd edn. Cambridge University Press, Cambridge

Dajani O (2010) The Importance of the Goldstone Report. Proceedings of the Annual Meeting (American Society of International Law) 104: 73–79

Dinstein Y (2004) The Conduct of Hostilities under the Law of International Armed Conflict. Cambridge University Press, Cambridge

Dinstein Y (2010) The Conduct of Hostilities under the Law of International Armed Conflict, 2nd edn. Cambridge University, Cambridge

Drew P (2017) The Law of Maritime Blockade: Past, Present, and Future. Oxford University Press, Oxford

Dupuy P M (2011) Evolutionary Interpretation of Treaties: Between Memory and Prophecy. In: Cannizzaro E (ed) The Law of Treaties beyond the Vienna Convention. Oxford University Press, Oxford, pp 123–137

Farnelli G M (2020) I trattati nel tempo: considerazioni di diritto intertemporale alla luce della giurisprudenza internazionale. Bonomo editore, Bologna

Fenrick W J (2001) Targeting and Proportionality during the NATO Bombing Campaign against Yugoslavia. European Journal of International Law 12(3): 489–502

Fleck D (1997) Strategic Bombing and the Definition of Military Objectives. Israel Yearbook on Human Rights 27: 41–64

Gaeta P (2015) Grave Breaches of the Geneva Conventions. In: Clapham A, Gaeta P, Sassòli M (eds) The 1949 Geneva Conventions: A Commentary. Oxford Commentaries on International Law, Oxford University Press, Oxford pp 615–646

Gaeta P, Abhimanyu G J (2023) The Individualization of IHL Rules through Criminalization for War Crimes: Some (Un)Intended Consequences. In: Welsh J, Akande D, Rodin D (eds) The Individualization of War: Rights, Liability, and Accountability in Contemporary Armed Conflict. Oxford University Press, Oxford, pp 163–186

Gardiner R (2015) Treaty Interpretation, 2nd edn. Oxford University Press, Oxford

Goodman R (2016) The Obama Administration and Targeting War-Sustaining Objects in Non-international Armed Conflict. American Journal of International Law 110: 663–679

Gray C (2006) The Eritrea Ethiopia Claims Commission Oversteps its Boundaries: A Partial Award? European Journal of International Law 17:699–721

Green L C (2008) The Contemporary Law of Armed Conflict, 3rd edn. Manchester University Press, Manchester
Greenwood C (2001) The Applicability of International Humanitarian Law and the Law of Neutrality to the Kosovo Campaign. Israel Yearbook on Human Rights 31: 111–144
Greppi E, Poli L (2021) The 2000 Algiers Agreements. In: de Guttry A, Post H H G, Venturini G (eds) The 1998–2000 Eritrea-Ethiopia War and Its Aftermath in International Legal Perspective. T.M.C. Asser Press, The Hague, pp 67–88
Hanke HM (1993) The 1923 Hague Rules of Air Warfare—A Contribution to the Development of International Law Protecting Civilians from Air Attack. International Review of the Red Cross 33(292): 12–44
Harvard Air and Missile Warfare Manual (2013) Program on Humanitarian Policy and Conflict Research at Harvard University (HPCR), Manual on International Law Applicable to Air and Missile Warfare. Cambridge University Press, Cambridge
Henckaerts J-M, Doswald-Beck L (2005) Customary International Humanitarian Law, Volume I: Rules. Cambridge University Press, Cambridge/Geneva
ICRC (1956) Draft Rules for the Limitation of the Dangers incurred by the Civilian Population in Time of War. https://ihl-databases.icrc.org/assets/treaties/420-Draft-ICRC-Rules-1956-EN.pdf. Accessed 1 August 2024
ILA (2017) The Conduct of Hostilities and International Humanitarian Law: Challenges of 21st Century Warfare. International Law Association Study Group on the Conduct of Hostilities in the 21st Century. https://www.ila-hq.org/en_GB/documents/ila-final-report-25-june-2017. Accessed 4 March 2024
Institut de Droit International (1969) Sixième séance plénière: mardi 9 septembre 1969 (matin). Annuaire de l'Institut de Droit International 53(2): 116–126
Jachec-Neale A (2014) The Concept of Military Objectives in International Law and Targeting Practice. Routledge, London/New York
Kalshoven F (1990) Belligerent Reprisals Revisited. Netherlands Yearbook of International Law 21: 43–80
Kalshoven F (2007) Bombardment: From "Brussels 1874" to "Sarajevo 2003". In: Kalshoven F (ed) Reflections on the Law of War. Martinus Nijhoff, Leiden, pp 431–463
Kolb R (2009) Jus in Bello: Le Droit International des Conflits Armés. Helbing Lichtenhahn Verlag, Bâle
Kolb R (2015) Military Objectives in International Humanitarian Law. Leiden Journal of International Law 28: 691–700
Kotzur M (2008) Intertemporal Law. In: Wolfrum R (ed) Max Planck Encyclopedia of Public International Law. Oxford University Press, Oxford
Linderfalk U (2011) The Application of International Legal Norms Over Time: The Second Branch of Intertemporal Law. Netherlands International Law Review 58: 147–172
Mackay R (2003) Half the battle: Civilian morale in Britain during the Second World War. Manchester University Press, Manchester
Mačák K (2015) Military Objectives 2.0: The Case for Interpreting Computer Data as Objects under International Humanitarian Law. Israel Law Review 48: 55–80
Mačák K, Policinski E (2024) In Pursuit of a Treaty's Soul: A Study of the Object and Purpose of the Fourth Geneva Convention. International and Comparative Law Quarterly 73(2): 385–415
Matheson M J (2009) Eritrea-Ethiopia Claims Commission: Damage Awards. American Society of International Law Insights 13(13). https://asil.org/insights/volume/13/issue/13/eritrea-ethiopia-claims-commission-damage-awards. Accessed 30 July 2024
Murphy S D (2012) The Experience of the Eritrea-Ethiopia Claims Commission. Proceedings of the Annual Meeting (American Society of International Law 106: 237–241
Nesi G (1995) Organization of African Unity (O.A.U.). Digesto. Discipline pubblicistiche 10. UTET, Turin, pp 218–240
Oppenheim L (1955) International Law A Treatise: Vol II: War and Neutrality, 8th edn. In: Lauterpacht H (ed) Longmans, Green & Co, London

Palchetti P (2013) Interpreting "Generic Terms": Between Respect for the Parties' Original Intention and the Identification of the Ordinary Meaning. In: Boschiero N, Scovazzi T, Pitea C, Ragni C (eds) International Courts and the Development of International Law. T.M.C. Asser Press, The Hague, pp 91–105

Parks H W (1990) Air War and the Law of War. Air Force Law Review 32: 137–144

Parks H W (2007) Asymmetries and the Identification of Legitimate Military Objectives. In: von Heinegg W H, Epping V (eds) International Humanitarian Law Facing New Challenges - Symposium in Honour of Knut Ipsen. Springer-Verlag, Berlin/Heidelberg, pp 65–116

Pertile M (2009) Le violazioni del diritto umanitario commesse da Hamas durante l'operazione Piombo fuso. Diritti Umani e Diritto Internazionale 3(2): 333–344

Piatkowski M (2021) War in the Air from Spain to Yemen: The Challenges in Examining the Conduct of Air Bombardment. Journal of Conflict & Security Law 26(3): 493–524

Pompson O (2023) 'Objects'? The Legal Status of Computer Data under International Humanitarian Law. Journal of Conflict and Security Law 28(2): 349–387

Reetz N (2022) Same but Different? Why War-Sustaining Objects Can Be Destroyed but Not Targeted. Journal of Conflict & Security Law 27(3): 439–469

Robertson H B (2012) The Principle of the Military Objective in the Law of Armed Conflict. In: Schmitt M N, von Heinegg W H (eds) The Development and Principles of International Humanitarian Law. Routledge, London, pp

Ronzitti N (2006) The Codification of Aerial Warfare. In: Ronzitti N, Venturini G (eds) The Law of Air Warfare: Contemporary Issues. Eleven International Publishing, The Hague, pp 3–16

Ronzitti N (2017) Il diritto internazionale dei conflitti armati, 6th edn. Giappichelli Editore, Turin

Rousseau J (1997) The Social Contract (Gourevitch V (transl)). In: The Social Contract and Other Later Political Writings. Cambridge University Press, Cambridge

Rynkeby Knudsen J (2024) Military Objectives by Location. https://lieber.westpoint.edu/military-objectives-location/. Accessed 18 July 2024

Sandoz Y, Swinarski C, Zimmermann B (eds) (1987), Commentary on the Additional Protocols of 8 June 1977 to the Geneva Conventions of 12 August 1949. Martinus Nijhoff Publishers, Geneva

Sassòli M (2003) Legitimate Targets of Attacks under International Humanitarian Law. Background Paper prepared for the Informal High-Level Expert Meeting on the Reaffirmation and Development of International Humanitarian Law, Cambridge, January 27–29, 2003. https://hhi.harvard.edu/sites/hwpi.harvard.edu/files/humanitarianinitiative/files/session1_legitimate_targets_ihl.pdf?m=1615827575. Accessed 2 August 2024

Sassòli M (2015) Military Objectives. In: Wolfrum R (ed) Max Planck Encyclopedia of Public International Law. Oxford University Press, Oxford, pp 1–15

Sassòli M, Cameron L (2006) The Protection of Civilian Objects: Current State of the Law and Issues de lege ferenda. In: Ronzitti N, Venturini G (eds) The Law of Air Warfare: Contemporary Issues. Eleven International, Utrecht, pp 35–74

Schindler D (1986) Moderne Entwicklungen Im Kriegsvölkerrecht. Die Friedens-Warte 66(3): 205–215

Schmitt M N (2002) Wired Warfare: Computer Network Attack and Jus in Bello. International Review of the Red Cross 84(846): 365–399

Schmitt M N (2006) Faultlines in the Law of Attack. In: Breau S, Jachec-Neale A (eds) Testing the Boundaries of International Humanitarian Law. British Institute of International and Comparative Law, London, pp 277–307

Schmitt M N (2010) Military Necessity and Humanity in International Humanitarian Law: Preserving the Delicate Balance. Virginia Journal of International Law 50(4): 796–837

Schmitt M N (ed) (2013) Tallinn Manual on the International Law Applicable to Cyber Warfare. Cambridge University Press, Cambridge

Schmitt M N (2022) Ukraine Symposium - Attacking Power Infrastructure under International Humanitarian Law. https://lieber.westpoint.edu/attacking-power-infrastructure-under-international-humanitarian-law/. Accessed 22 July 2024

Scovazzi T (2012) Diritto internazionale e bombardamenti aerei: chi bombarda meglio degli altri ha più ragione degli altri? In: Annati M, Scovazzi T (eds) Diritto internazionale e bombardamenti aerei. Giuffrè, Milan, pp 83–130

Short M (2002) Operation Allied Force from the perspective of the NATO Air Commander. In: Wall AE (ed) Legal and ethical lessons of NATO's Kosovo campaign. United States Naval War College International Law Studies 78:19–26

Tignino M, Kebebew T (2022) The Legal Protection of Freshwater Resources and Related Installations during Warfare. Journal of International Criminal Justice 20: 1191–1228

Tsagourias N, Morrison A (2018) Enforcement of International Humanitarian Law. In: Tsagourias N, Morrison A (eds.) International Humanitarian Law: Cases, Materials and Commentary. Cambridge University Press, Cambridge, pp. 292–336

Turrini P (2019) Teoria e prassi dell'interpretazione evolutiva nel diritto internazionale. Editoriale Scientifica, Naples

UN Security Council (2021) Resolution 2573 (2021), UN Doc. S/RES/2573 (2021)

Venturini G (2021) International Humanitarian Law and the Conduct of Hostilities in the Case-Law of the Eritrea-Ethiopia Claims Commission. In: de Guttry A, Post H H G, Venturini G (eds) The 1998–2000 Eritrea-Ethiopia War and Its Aftermath in International Legal Perspective. T.M.C. Asser Press, The Hague, pp 345–371

Warden J A III (1995) The Enemy as a System. Air Power Journal 9(2): 40–55

Watkin K (2005) Canada/United States military interoperability and humanitarian law issues: land mines, terrorism, military objectives and targeting. Duke Journal of Comparative & International Law 15:281–314

Watkin K (2016) Military Advantage: A Matter of "Value", Strategy, and Tactics. In: Gill T, Geiß R, Krieger H, McCormack T, Paulussen C, Dorsey J (eds) Yearbook of International Humanitarian Law. T.M.C. Asser Press, The Hague, pp 277–364

Wells-Greco M (2010) Operation 'Cast Lead': *Jus in Bello* Proportionality. Netherlands International Law Review 57(3): 397–422

Part II
The Elements of the New Paradigm: Revisiting Dual-Use Objects Under International Humanitarian Law

Chapter 4
Shedding Light on the Civilian Function of Dual-Use Objects and Its Relevance for the Key IHL Principles

Contents

Abstract The present chapter investigates the civilian function of dual-use objects, a concept that has been often mentioned, without ever delving into its significance, nor into its practical implications. The analysis moves from the assumption that what makes an object more, or less, valuable than others boils down to the civilian function that it plays, especially in the context of an armed conflict. Function is defined by the Oxford English Dictionary as "an activity or mode of operation that is proper or natural to a person or thing, the *purpose* or *intended role of* a thing" and, despite not being a term of art in the legal sense, it is not alien to the IHL framework. Several authors over the years have noted how governments are uncomfortable with the notion that the civilian function of a dual-use facility can be so easily ignored in armed conflicts, yet efforts to fully and adequately take into account said function have been scant, if any. After reflecting on the civilian function of dual-use objects, the present chapter will provide a long overdue analysis that aims at finally reconciling this essential feature of dual-use objects with the relevant IHL rules and with the main principles of IHL.

Keywords Civilian function · Cultural property · ICTY · EECC · Enemy property · Starvation · Terrorism · Principle of distinction · Principle of

F. Capone, *Dual-use Objects under International Humanitarian Law: Towards a Paradigm Shift*, https://doi.org/10.1007/978-94-6265-679-6_4

precautions · Principle of proportionality · Principles of military necessity and humanity · Martens Clause

4.1 Introducing the Civilian Function of Dual-Use Objects as an Element of the Paradigm Shift

The previous chapter ultimately provided a working definition of dual-use objects, that serves the purpose of separating in a more neat and clear way that category of objects from military objectives.[1] According to this definition, dual-use objects in armed conflicts are

> objects, items, infrastructures, systems that fulfil a civilian function. Dual-use objects may become military objectives only when the following two cumulative criteria are satisfied in the circumstances ruling at the time: a) their *location* (when the dual-use object is situated inside a specific area that is lawfully designated as a military objective), and/or their *use* makes an *effective and direct* contribution to military action and b) a *definite military advantage* derives from the total or partial destruction, capture or neutralisation of *every* dual-use object that is attacked.[2]

Leaving aside the obvious asymmetry between "dual-use object", a term widely used but never properly defined, and "military objective", i.e. a fully-fledged legal notion that is part of the IHL terminology, the importance of finally connecting the dots and carrying out a thorough examination of what it entails for an object to be labelled as "dual-use" in the context of an armed conflict should not be overlooked. In addition to this significant achievement, the present work also aims at shedding light on a crucial matter, i.e. the civilian function that dual-use objects fulfil and that, at least *prima facie*, sets them apart from military objectives. In the past, the widespread "humanitarian" approach was to assume that "the avoidance of danger to civilian lives should be preferred over that of property".[3] This view was eventually challenged in the aftermath of the First Gulf War and the NATO bombing campaign in the Former Yugoslavia in light of the extensive damage caused not only to civilian property and dual-use objects (which were too swiftly and too lightly labelled by the attackers as legitimate military objectives) but indirectly also to the civilian population, as previously discussed.[4] The failure to duly take into consideration both the direct and indirect effects of the attacks carried out during the military operations in these two conflicts has planted the seed for a more thorough reflection on the value of dual-use objects. As noted by Henderson, if different objects "have different amounts of importance" the values of objects will vary from the perspective of the civilian population.[5] In this author's view, what makes an object more, or less, valuable than

---

[1] See Chap. 3, Sect. 3.4 in this book.

[2] See Chap. 3, Sect. 3.4 in this book.

[3] Bothe et al. 1982, pp. 368–369.

[4] See Chap. 2 of this book.

[5] Henderson 2009, p. 192.

others, especially during an armed conflict, ultimately boils down to the "civilian function" that it plays. Function is defined by the Oxford English Dictionary as "an activity or mode of operation that is proper or natural to a person or thing, the *purpose* or *intended role of* a thing".[6] Several authors over the years have noted how governments are increasingly uncomfortable with the notion that the civilian function of a dual-use facility can be so easily ignored in armed conflicts,[7] yet, efforts to fully and adequately take into account said function have been scant, if any. After reflecting on the civilian function of dual-use objects, the present chapter will provide the reader with a long overdue analysis of the existing legal framework, with the purpose of reconciling the essence of dual-use objects with the relevant IHL rules and with the main principles of IHL.

4.2 Shedding Light on Dual-Use Objects' Civilian Function

Under international law, references to function and "functionalism" as a paradigm commonly pertain to the law of international organisations.[8] Within the realm of IHL, there are provisions enshrined in the relevant treaties and in the ICRC study on customary international humanitarian law that specifically mention the "function" of an actor, e.g. authorised humanitarian relief personnel (Rule 56), as well as of an "object" e.g. medical transports (Rule 29) and laser weapons (Rule 86).[9] Nonetheless, the notion is not properly examined nor discussed with the exception of two main domains, i.e. civilians' direct participation in hostilities[10] and the protection of cultural property in armed conflict.

Regarding the second example, which is more relevant for the purposes of the present analysis since it deals with the "function" of (cultural) objects, the norm outlining this aspect is contained in the Second Protocol to the Hague Convention for the Protection of Cultural Property,[11] adopted by consensus in 1999. It is significant that the Second Protocol has maintained one of the major weaknesses of the 1954 Convention,[12] which is the notorious exception of military necessity: both the obligation not to use cultural property for military purposes and the obligation not to attack such property can be waived "in cases where military necessity imperatively

[6] Oxford English Dictionary, "function", https://www.oed.com/search/dictionary/?scope=Entries&q=function (accessed 11 August 2024).

[7] See Shue and Wippman 2002, p. 565; Byron 2011, pp. 184–185.

[8] See Gasbarri 2021, p. 17.

[9] Henckaerts and Doswald-Beck 2005.

[10] Melzer 2009, pp. 70–73, when explaining that members of organised armed groups belonging to a non-State party to an armed conflict cease to be civilians for as long as they assume their "continuous combat function".

[11] See Second Protocol to the Hague Convention of 1954 for the Protection of Cultural Property in the Event of Armed Conflict (Second Protocol to the 1954 Hague Convention), open for signature 26 March 1999, 38 ILM 76, entered into force 9 March 2004.

[12] Gioia 2003, p. 34.

requires such a waiver".[13] The Second Protocol provides that a waiver on the basis of imperative military necessity may only be invoked when and for as long as: (1) the cultural property in question has, *by its function*, been made into a military objective; and (2) there is no feasible alternative to obtain a similar military advantage to that offered by attacking that objective.[14]

Thus, the waiver comes into play when cultural property is used for purposes which are likely to expose it to destruction or damage, when and for as long as, no choice is possible between such use of the cultural property and another feasible method for obtaining a similar military advantage.[15] Furthermore, the decision to invoke imperative military necessity shall only be taken by an officer commanding a force the equivalent of a battalion in size or larger, or a force smaller in size where circumstances do not permit otherwise.[16] In any case, as far as attacks on cultural property are concerned, military necessity can only justify such attacks if the targeted properties legally qualify as a military objective. The definition of a "military objective" provided in Article 1(f) of the 1999 Protocol replicates the one included in Article 52(2) of API. Hence, on the one hand it clearly embraces any object which by "its nature, location, purpose, or use makes an effective contribution to military action and whose destruction offers a definite military advantage". On the other hand, it is impossible to overlook the fact that Article 6 of the 1999 Protocol refers specifically to cultural property which has been turned into a military objective *by its function*. Gioia explains how this ambiguous expression was coined:

> [it] is the result of a compromise between those (especially some NATO countries) who argued that cultural property could become a military objective by virtue of both its use and its location, and those (like Egypt and Greece, for example) who supported a restriction whereby only its use could turn cultural property into a legitimate target. *But it is at best doubtful that the present wording of Article 6 covers the mere location of cultural property, irrespective of its use.*[17,18]

During the Conference there was a clear understanding that "function" indicates "something that was in fact functioning" at that time, clearly alluding to the "use rather than to the nature, purpose, and, in most cases, location".[19] According to Drazewska, the choice to incorporate the criterion of "function" in Article 6 serves two different scopes. The first is to distinguish between "general protection" and

---

[13] Article 4(2) of the Convention for the Protection of Cultural Property in the Event of Armed Conflict, opened for signature 14 May 1954, UNTS 249, entered into force 7 August 1956.

[14] Article 6 of Second Protocol to the 1954 Hague Convention, above n. 11 (emphasis added).

[15] Venturini 2011, p 45; Venturini 2017, p. 107.

[16] Henckaerts and Doswald-Beck 2005, Rule 38, p. 130. The authors of the ICRC study on customary IHL report that "[d]uring the negotiation of the Second Protocol, this interpretation of the waiver in case of imperative military necessity was uncontroversial".

[17] Gioia 2003, p. 36 (emphasis added).

[18] Drazewska 2021.

[19] Ibid., p. 118.

"enhanced protection" in the Second Protocol;[20] the second is to "limit the possibility of invoking military necessity to attack cultural property *as compared to the broader customary standard based on the notion of military objective* used for other categories of civilian property".[21] Although "function" is not defined, it is possible to infer that the meaning of this criterion is broader than use and it also cover the purpose of an object, in line with the definition provided by the Oxford English Dictionary. By limiting the transformation of cultural property into a military objective to situations where the applicable criterion is that of the object's function, the drafters of the Second Protocol had in mind the goal of raising the threshold of protection of this specific category of civilian objects, by explicitly excluding both the nature and location criteria. The same reasoning could not be applied to dual-use objects, which on the contrary are attacked *because of* their capability to fulfil, at the same time, a civilian and a military function. Yet, in this author's view, this peculiarity shall be duly taken into consideration, and it shall represent the starting point of the paradigm shift that this book seeks to promote in order to enhance dual-use objects' protection. To duly incorporate the "civilian function" of dual-use objects into the current debate, the present chapter analyses the existing legal framework *in light of this feature*. Before delving into the relevant IHL norms and principles, it is worth exploring more in detail the civilian function that the dual-use objects described in Chap. 1, i.e. electrical power systems, industrial plants, oil refining, distribution and storage facilities, media, traffic infrastructures, water installations, usually perform.[22] Without aiming to provide an exhaustive overview of the specificities of each category, some additional reflections need to be shared with regard to the challenges connected to assessing the "value" of dual-use objects for the civilian population, also in judicial settings.

4.3 Assessing the Civilian Function of Dual-Use Objects

As far as electrical power systems are concerned there are strong and consistent arguments to depict their inherent relevance for the civilian population and the devastating short- and long-term impact of their damage and/or destruction.[23] Reporting on Russia's widespread attacks against Ukrainian electrical grids, the UN Independent International Commission of Inquiry on Ukraine affirmed that:

> The disruption of electric substations, power plants, and other installations which produce the energy and the heating indispensable to the survival of the population, has inflicted significant harm to civilians. Entire regions and millions of people have for periods been left without electricity or heating, particularly during winter, and consequently, with an impaired access

[20] On the distinction between general and enhanced protection, see Henckaerts 1999; Frulli 2011; Capone 2021, pp. 220–221.

[21] Drazewska 2021, pp. 118–119.

[22] See Chap. 1, Sect. 1.3.3 in this book.

[23] Crawford 1997, pp. 110–115.

> to, notably, water, sanitation, food, healthcare, and education. Despite public information about the civilian harm after the first few attacks, Russian armed forces continued to target energy infrastructure.[24]

Similarly, during the First Gulf War, the effects of the bombardments against the electrical infrastructure of the country have been closely scrutinised and widely condemned,[25] with authors and experts warning belligerent parties of current and future conflicts against the dangerous consequences that stem from cutting electricity.[26] Crawford in particular has been vocal in stressing the long term impact of the attacks, focusing on the electrical power stations' indirect role in supporting civilian infrastructures, including hospitals, which had to deal with "reduced capacity and the inability to refrigerate adequate quantities of vaccines/medicines".[27] Yet, the assessment of the civilian function of electrical infrastructures by a judicial body has rarely been undertaken in the aftermath of an armed conflict. One notable exception, which has already been discussed in Chap. 3 of this book, is represented by the Eritrea-Ethiopia Claims Commission's award on the aerial bombardment of the Hirgigo power station (HPS).[28]

As is well-known, the award was one of the claims decided by the EECC and was issued in 2005.[29] Whilst not specifically concerned with the civilian function of the power station, but rather with its military value, according to the decision "not all such power stations would qualify as military objectives".[30] In outlining the merits of the case, the Commission further stated that the sentence applies to "power stations that are known, or *should be known*, to be segregated from a general power grid and are limited to supplying power for humanitarian purposes, such as medical facilities, or other uses that could have no effect on the State's ability to wage war".[31] This statement, which might seem obvious, if not even trivial, is actually very relevant as it amounts to a valid, but still isolated attempt, to single out the dual-nature of power infrastructures. A more explicit recognition has been expressed in the Separate Opinion by President van Houtte, according to whom "the expected benefits of the Hirgigo power station to civilians and the expense and time required to repair the damage caused by the attack should also be taken into account" in the proportionality assessment.[32] Electrical grids are obviously not the only dual-use objects whose destruction or neutralisation can carry disruptive consequences for the civilian population. The same reasoning pertains to the other categories, in

24 Human Rights Council 2023, para 41.

25 See Chap. 2, Sect. 2.4 in this book.

26 Greenwood 1993; Sassòli and Cameron 2006, p. 65; Byron 2011, pp. 200–201.

27 Crawford 1997, p. 115.

28 See Chap. 3, Sect. 3.3.1 in this book.

29 Partial Award: Western Front, Aerial Bombardment and related claims, Eritrea's Claims 1, 3, 5, 9–13, 14, 21, 25 & 26, (Partial Award) 19 December 2005, PCA Case No. 2001-02.

30 Ibid., para 117.

31 Ibid.

32 Aerial Bombardment of Hirgigo Power Station (Eritrea's Claim 25)—Separate Opinion by President van Houtte (Separate Opinion by van Houtte), para 11.

consideration of the function that they fulfil. Although, unfortunately, so far this has never emerged in a sufficiently clear and straightforward way for most of them.

Regarding bridges, which in some instances in the past have been wrongly labelled as military objectives "by nature and/or location",[33] their civilian function and thus dual-use status has been noted by several authors. Shue and Wippman bring the example of a "bridge that is capable of allowing a farmer to truck produce across a river to the market and that is also capable of allowing a tank to cross is a dual-use object. One use is civilian (products to market) and one use is military (tanks to battle)."[34] Other authors have, controversially, claimed that "bridges are like schools",[35] i.e. they shall enjoy a presumption of civilian status that IHL seems to reserve only to a limited number of objects, even though the three examples included in Article 52(3) of API are simply illustrative.[36] Despite the lack of a uniform position, the prevailing scholarship recognises the inherent values of transportation arteries, especially when they are used to provide humanitarian aid to the civilians in need. An emblematic example in this sense is represented by the attack carried out in Yemen by the Saudi-led coalition on 11 August 2016, against a bridge located on the main road from the port city of Hodeidah to the capital of Sanaa.[37] Although it seemed plausible that the Houthi rebels would cross the bridge for "military purposes"—e.g. to transport material, armaments or personnel, given that it was on the main road between the port and the capital—when the attack occurred there was no evidence of military use. Instead, it was well known, also by the attackers, that the bridge in question at the time of the attack was used by the UN World Food Programme (WFP), as well as by other humanitarian actors, to deliver more than 90 per cent of the food *en route* to the civilian population.[38]

Similar situations have been disclosed elsewhere. For instance during the 2001–2003 conflict in Afghanistan, the executive director of Human Rights Watch reported that "certain roads, bridges and airports may ordinarily be legitimate military targets; in the case of Afghanistan they may also be essential to the delivery of humanitarian

33 See Chap. 1, Sect. 1.3.3 in this book; Dinstein 2004, pp. 92–93; Dinstein 2010; Dinstein and Dahl 2020, p. 76 "[b]ridges and tunnels are military objectives by 'nature' when they are a part of main railway lines or main roads, but they can be military objectives by 'nature' for other reasons as well."

34 See Shue and Wippman 2002, p. 562.

35 Kalshoven and Zegveld 2011, p. 101.

36 According to this provision "[i]n case of doubt whether an object which is normally dedicated to civilian purposes, such as a place of worship, a house or other dwelling or a school, is being used to make an effective contribution to military action, it shall be presumed not to be so used." Article 52(3) of Protocol Additional to the Geneva Conventions of 12 August 1949, and relating to the Protection of Victims of International Armed Conflicts (API), opened for signature 8 June 1977, 1125 UNTS 609, (entered into force 7 December 1978).

37 Van Schaack 2016.

38 Oxfam (2016) Yemeni people's ability to access food threatened as main supply route to Sanaa targeted by airstrikes, 12 August 2016, https://www.oxfamamerica.org/press/yemeni-peoples-ability-to-access-food-threatened-as-main-supply-route-to-sanaa-targeted-by-airstrikes/ (accessed 17 August 2024).

relief throughout the winter".[39] He went on by noting that "in such circumstances, the harm incurred to the civilian population by attacking them would be disproportionate to the military advantage gained".[40] Amnesty International made a similar point about the destruction of bridges and roads in the context of the conflict between Israel and Lebanon in 2006, and the effect that the attacks had "on civilians, especially the most vulnerable, such as those requiring urgent medical attention".[41]

Looking at the issue from a judicial body's perspective, also in the case of bridges there is limited evidence of efforts made to single out and assess their civilian function and value. The ICTY famously addressed the topic of the Old Bridge's destruction during the armed conflicts in the Former Yugoslavia in the case of *Prlić et al.*[42] The two decisions issued by the ICTY have been widely scrutinised, especially in light of the bridge's cultural importance.[43] However, it would be useful to pay attention also to a few additional considerations about the dual-use character of the bridge.[44] A preliminary caveat concerning the case is needed, to highlight also the complexity of the issues at stake. As is well known, during the ICTY's activity most of the convictions remained "undisturbed on appeal".[45] Yet, the *Prlić et al.* case represents a remarkable exception since the Appeals Chamber reversed the key legal findings on the destruction of the iconic Old Bridge by the HVO, i.e. the Bosnian Croat military forces, which occurred in November 1993.[46] In the first decision, the Trial Chamber recognised the bridge's exceptional character, noting its almost 500-year history and its symbolic role as a link between the communities of Bosnia-Herzegovina. The judges ultimately found that the destruction of the Old Bridge constituted the crimes of wanton destruction of cities, towns or villages or devastation not justified by military necessity, unlawful infliction of terror on a civilian population, and persecution.[47]

In its legal determination on the crime of wanton destruction, the Trial Chamber held that the Old Bridge was "essential to the ABiH [Army of Bosnia and Herzegovina] for combat activities of its units on the front line, for evacuations, for the

---

[39] Cited by Henderson 2009, p. 208.

[40] Ibid.

[41] Amnesty International (2006) Israel/Lebanon: Deliberate destruction or "collateral damage"? Israeli attacks on civilian infrastructure, 22 August 2006, https://www.amnesty.org/en/documents/MDE18/007/2006/en/ (accessed 17 August 2024).

[42] ICTY (TC), *Prosecutor v Prlić,* Judgment 9 May 2013, IT-04-74 (*Prlić et al.* TC Judgement); ICTY (AC) *Prosecutor v Prlić,* Judgment 29 November 2017, IT-04-74-A (*Prlić et al.* Appeal Judgement).

[43] See Fenrick 2004; Petrovic 2013; Moffett 2020.

[44] On this aspect, see also Cotter 2018.

[45] Ibid., p. 2.

[46] The shelling of the Old Bridge on 8 November rendered it completely unusable for either side by nightfall, the attack recommenced the following day, up until its eventual collapse into the Neretva River. See Drazewska 2021, p. 181.

[47] *Prlić et al.* TC Judgement, paras 1587, 1690, 1692, 1711, 1713.

sending of troops, food and material [sic]",[48] and that the ABiH was holding positions in its immediate vicinity. On this basis, the Chamber affirmed that the bridge was "a military objective" because of the HVO's "military interest" in its destruction.[49] Despite labelling the Old Bridge as a military objective, the Trial Chamber also noted that the destruction of the Old Bridge: a) had a significant psychological impact on the Muslim population of Mostar; and b) left the residents of Donja Mahala, the Muslim enclave on the right bank of the Neretva, in virtually total isolation.[50] The Chamber stressed that the inhabitants of Donja Mahala had only two remaining supply routes, namely the so-called Kamenica bridge, a makeshift construction erected by the ABiH in March 1993 which was also destroyed by the HVO a few days after the Old Bridge, and a treacherous mountain path toward Jablanica Municipality.[51] Hence, the majority of the Trial Chamber concluded that:

> although the destruction of the Old Bridge by the HVO may have been justified by military necessity, *the damage to the civilian population was indisputable and substantial* [...] the impact on the Muslim civilian population of Mostar was *disproportionate* to the concrete and direct military advantage expected by the destruction of the Old Bridge [...] the destruction of the Old Bridge, *in view of its immense cultural, historical and symbolic value* for the Muslims in particular, was extensive.[52]

There are, clearly, several different issues that emerge from the decision. Without aiming to provide a thorough examination, which has been carried out by authors like Moffett and Drazewska,[53] it is worth highlighting some substantial aspects. First, although the crime of destruction of cultural property was not directly charged in this case, the cultural and "symbolic" importance of the bridge for the Muslim population in Mostar was considered in the proportionality assessment, which followed the qualification of the bridge as a military objective. Second, both the military advantage anticipated by the HVO from the destruction of the Old Bridge and its impact on the civilian population are mentioned, but not properly assessed. As noted by Cotter, the judgment shows a lack of efforts to quantify (and qualify) both the military advantage (i.e. since the Old Bridge was relevant for the activities of the ABiH, how were these activities affected by its destruction?) and the humanitarian impact stemming from the isolation of the residents of Donja Mahala from the date of the destruction of the bridge (which were the consequences? How many people have been affected?).[54] Those crucial aspects are also essential to emphasise the civilian function of the Old Bridge, but unfortunately the limited attention devoted to them by the Trial Chamber is pointing, more broadly, to the challenges faced by "civilian judiciaries in assessing complex and specialised military/humanitarian considerations".[55]

[48] Ibid., paras 1582–1584.

[49] Cotter 2018, pp. 7–8.

[50] Ibid., p. 7.

[51] *Prlić et al.* TC Judgement, para 1583.

[52] Ibid., paras 1584–1586.

[53] Moffett 2020; Drazewska 2021, pp. 176–178.

[54] Cotter 2018, p. 8.

[55] Ibid.

In its subsequent decision, the Appeals Chamber also weighed on the matter. However, it did so without presenting a satisfactory analysis of its own findings and, thus, triggering extensive criticism in the form of an extremely detailed dissenting opinion by its own President, Judge Pocar.[56] The Appeals Chamber dedicated only a brief passage to the destruction of the Old Bridge in "stark contrast with the ca. 80 paragraphs devoted to it in the previous judgment".[57] In a nutshell, the Appeals Chamber held that the Trial Chamber erred in concluding that "the destruction of the Old Bridge of Mostar constituted the crime of wanton destruction not justified by military necessity as a violation of the laws or customs of war".[58] In an effort to bring clarity to a superficial analysis, Cotter, relying on Judge Pocar's dissenting opinion,[59] suggests the following reasoning on the part of the Majority

> the attack may have been disproportionate because of its attendant psychological harm and the humanitarian consequences for the residents of Donja Mahala, *but the destruction was nevertheless justified by military necessity because the bridge was a military objective.* In other words, the supposed key to the Majority's analysis is a distinction between attack and destruction. The legality of the former is determined by a proportionality assessment which may include factors such as downstream humanitarian consequences, but the legality of the latter always and only turns on whether the destroyed object was a military objective.[60]

The Appeals Chamber's legal reasoning is characterised by several shortcomings and inconsistencies that cannot be duly addressed in this work. In fact, many key aspects, such as the absence of any discussion of proportionality, the problematic and "convoluted distinction between 'destruction' and 'attack'",[61] and the illogical conflation of "military necessity" and "military objective",[62] have already been discussed elsewhere.[63] What deserves to be further noted, however, is that the Appeal judgment has abruptly excluded from the proportionality assessment the reverberating effects of the Old Bridge's destruction, in particular the psychological and humanitarian impacts on the civilian population. Thus, it can be claimed that the decision marks a dramatic reversal of the Trial Chamber's position which, at least within the broader context of the embryonic debate on dual-use objects, contributed to pointing to the right issues, albeit without offering any conclusive answer.[64] The significant gap between the Trial Chamber's decision and the one issued by the Appeals Chamber in the *Prlić et al.* case is indicative of the fact that judges themselves struggle to clarify the law on these matters. This is not surprising, and it

---

[56] *Prlić et al.* Appeal Judgement, Dissenting Opinions of Judge Fausto Pocar.

[57] *Prlić et al.* Appeal Judgement, para 411; Drazewska 2021, p. 179.

[58] *Prlić et al.* Appeal Judgement, para 411.

[59] Judge Pocar's dissenting opinion departs from the findings of majority on the grounds that the rest of the Chamber had "'erroneously' conflated the concept of military objective with that of military necessity, neglected an examination of proportionality, and failed to consider the bridge as cultural property with broader protection under international humanitarian law". See Moffett 2020, p. 238.

[60] Cotter 2018, p. 9 (emphasis added).

[61] Ibid.

[62] Moffett 2020, p. 239.

[63] Cotter 2018; Moffett 2020.

[64] Cotter 2018, p. 11.

certainly prompts a more in-depth analysis of how to factor in the civilian function of dual-use objects, also in judicial settings.

4.4 Reconsidering the Applicable Legal Framework in Light of the Civilian Function of Dual-Use Objects

There are several rules that can contribute to better framing the issue of enhancing the protection of dual-use objects in consideration of their civilian function, and that are often neglected or in any case only marginally discussed. First, IHL prohibits the destruction or seizure of the property of an adversary, "unless required by imperative military necessity".[65] This violation constitutes a war crime under the Rome Statute,[66] and, when "extensive", it amounts to a grave breach under the Geneva Conventions.[67] Since destruction of property qualifying as military objectives is, in principle, lawful, the practical scope of the rule concerns civilian property.[68] The prohibition against destruction of property is widely formulated and it encompasses both private and public property.[69] Moreover, the term "property" has a broader scope than "object" as traditionally understood in the context of IHL and referring solely to "visible and tangible" things. Differently from object, property includes, by the ordinary meaning given to the word, "a thing or things belonging to someone".[70] Thus, in consideration of the technological development "in the administration of valuables, as well as other identifiable possessions that it is possible for someone to own" and that, for example, only exists electronically, it would appear illogical to exclude certain intangible possessions from the term "property".[71] As noted by Johansen the decisive criterion should, indeed, be focused on the object's ownership.[72] The notion of ownership by an adversary also appears to have been central in the practice of the ICC, which affirmed in the *Mbarushimana* case that "the property in question may be moveable or immoveable, private or public, but must belong to individuals or entities aligned with, or having an allegiance to, a party to the conflict, adverse or hostile to the perpetrator".[73]

Furthermore, an important aspect that shall be considered is that the necessity to destroy enemy property is often motivated by the wish to prevent the enemy

---

[65] Henckaerts and Doswald-Beck 2005, Rule 50, p. 176.

[66] Article 8(2)(b)(xiii) of the Rome Statute.

[67] Article 50 of the First Geneva Convention, Article 51 of the Second Geneva Convention, Article 147 of the Fourth Geneva Convention.

[68] Johansen 2019, p. 342.

[69] Dinstein 2004, pp. 230–231.

[70] Johansen 2019, pp. 349–350.

[71] Ibid.

[72] Ibid. See also Salvadego 2016, pp. 127–130.

[73] ICC (PTC), *Prosecutor v Callixte Mbarushimana*, Prosecution's Application under Article 58, 20 August 2010, ICC-01/04-01/10-11-Red2, para 171.

armed forces from using it. The relevant examples from State practice and case law concern different forms of destruction of property, such as houses, food storages, crops, dwellings and livestock,[74] but obviously the list can be expanded to also cover industries, bridges, roads and other dual-use objects that perform a civilian function and belong to the enemy or to individuals/entities aligned with it. Notably, the destruction or seizure of enemy property is only permitted when justified by military necessity; however, there are several examples of incidental damage that may result from the movement and/or manoeuvre of military forces, both on land, at sea and in the air (or from the air) and that are considered as "an unavoidable consequence of warfare" and are thus "justified on the basis of military necessary".[75] The relevance of the rule with respect to dual-use objects emerges in those instances as well. First because it is essential to challenge the assumption that the destruction of railways or lines of communication during movement and/or manoeuvre of military forces *is a fortiori* lawful because they are military objectives,[76] and second because the commander's margin of appreciation includes "a great deal of latitude" that must, however, remain within the ambit of what is reasonable to expect when determining situations of necessity. Therefore, as it will be discussed in the next chapter, it is essential to ascertain more precisely the threshold of reasonableness on the part of the commander.[77]

Another relevant rule is represented by the prohibition on attacking, destroying, removing, or rendering useless objects indispensable to the survival of the civilian population, which amounts to a norm of customary international humanitarian law applicable both in IACs and NIACs. Although the 2005 ICRC study outlines the prohibition to deprive the civilian population of essential items as absolute, under Article 54(2) of API and in the practice of several States the intent of the attack still must be to prevent the civilian population from being supplied and the rule is still regarded as a corollary to the prohibition of starvation.[78] Article 14 of APII, also prohibits the "starvation of civilians as a method of combat" in NIACs, by means of "attack[ing], destroy[ing], remov[ing], or render[ing] useless, for that purpose, objects indispensable to the survival of the civilian population", and the provision further specifies that "foodstuffs, agricultural areas for the production of foodstuffs, crops, livestock, drinking water installation, and supplies, and irrigation works all qualify as protected civilian objects under the provision."[79] Since 1993 and starting with the war in the former Yugoslavia, there has been a series of UN resolutions condemning the widespread use of starvation in connection to sieges and related crimes incurring individual responsibility. As already mentioned,[80] the UN SC with

[74] For an overview of the relevant examples see https://ihl-databases.icrc.org/customary-ihl/eng/docs/v1_rul_rule50 (accessed 13 August 2024).

[75] Dinstein and Dahl 2020, p. 94.

[76] Johansen 2019, p. 357.

[77] Ibid. See Chap. 5, Sect. 5.3.4 in this book.

[78] Henckaerts and Doswald-Beck 2005, Rule 54, pp. 189–191.

[79] D'Alessandra and Gillett 2019, p. 819.

[80] See Chap. 1, Sect. 1.1 in this book.

the adoption of Resolution 2573 (2021) has strongly condemned attacks in situations of armed conflicts directed against civilians as such and other protected persons or civilian objects, as well as indiscriminate or disproportionate attacks, "resulting in the deprivation of the civilian population of objects indispensable to their survival".[81] Furthermore, and clearly detecting a growing tendency amongst belligerent parties to blur the contours of the principle of distinction, the Resolution asks Member States to increase their efforts to

> distinguishing between, on the one hand, civilian populations, civilian objects and all other persons and objects afforded protection, and, on the other hand, combatants and military objectives, prohibiting indiscriminate and disproportionate attacks, taking all feasible precautions in planning, deciding and conducting attacks to avoid, and in any event minimize, harm to civilians and civilian objects, and taking all feasible precautions to protect the civilian population and civilian objects within their control against the effects of attacks.[82]

The Resolution, additionally encourages all efforts to protect "objects indispensable to the survival of the civilian population and *civilian infrastructure that is critical to enable the delivery of essential services* in armed conflict [...]" to meet the basic needs of the civilian population, including by:

> (a) [protecting] civilians operating, maintaining or repairing these objects, as well as their movement for the purpose of maintaining, repairing or operating such objects; (b) allowing and facilitating safe passage of equipment, transport and supplies necessary for the reparation, maintenance or operation of such objects.[83]

Moreover, as noted when the destruction of the Nova Khakovka dam and hydroelectric power plant in Ukraine occurred,[84] the prohibition relating to objects indispensable to the survival of the civilian population is not confined to "attacks" but also proscribes destroying, removing or rendering useless such objects. As stressed by the 1987 ICRC Commentary these verbs are used in order to cover all possibilities, including pollution, by chemical or other agents, of water reservoirs, or destruction of crops by defoliants.[85] That means that even if, as suggested by some commentators,[86] "Russia blew the dam up from within", the conduct would still violate this special protection. Furthermore, the words "such as" included in the provision enshrined in Article 54(2) show that the list of protected objects is merely illustrative, because the idea of drawing an exhaustive list was quickly dismissed as it could have led to omissions and/or to an arbitrary selection.[87] As revealed by the text, the objects concerned are basically objects for subsistence. However, it cannot be excluded that as a result of climate or other circumstances, objects such as shelter, clothing, and heating must be considered as indispensable to survival.[88] Put it differently, and

[81] UN Security Council 2021, para 1.

[82] Ibid., para 2.

[83] Ibid., para 9.

[84] Tignino et al. 2023.

[85] Sandoz et al. 1987, p. 655, para 2101.

[86] Glanz et al. 2023.

[87] Sandoz et al. 1987, p. 655, para 2103.

[88] Ibid.

based on the recent UN SC Resolution, it seems quite clear that, to be meaningful and effective, the prohibition must cover both the objects and the infrastructures needed to produce and maintain them.

Another important rule that has been invoked in the aftermath of attacks against dual-use objects is the prohibition to spread terror amongst the civilian population. This rule also gained momentum on the occasion of the widespread attacks carried out by Russia against the Ukrainian electrical infrastructures,[89] with Schmitt stressing that "the attacks have gone on for so long, are so widespread, and are so intense, that it is difficult to attribute any purpose to them *other than terrorizing the civilian population*", and ultimately "*they have had little impact on ongoing Ukrainian military operations*".[90] According to Rule 2 of the ICRC study on customary IHL, acts or threats of violence the primary purpose of which is to spread terror among the civilian population are prohibited.[91] This norm is enshrined in both Article 51(2) of Additional Protocol I and Article 13(2) of Additional Protocol II. Additionally, the prohibition of acts or threats of violence aimed at terrorising the civilian population is set forth in many military manuals.[92] Notwithstanding the apparent lack of controversies surrounding this norm and the recognition of its customary status, it appears that its practical application is still rather problematic.

Looking at the case law of international courts and tribunals, it has been noted that judicial consideration of the prohibition of inflicting terror on the civilian population has been piecemeal, at times partial, and never concerned with factoring in the civilian function of certain objects. The ICTY represents the most relevant, although still limited, exception. As is well known, the ICTY handled a series of cases that focused on attacks against civilians and civilian objects, and the "novel" war crime of inflicting terror on a civilian population.[93] In the *Prosecutor v. Galić* case, the ICTY faced the issue at length as it dealt with the protracted campaign of shelling and sniping upon civilian areas in Sarajevo, which "had no discernable significance in military terms" and "served to instill a state of extreme fear in the population".[94] The ICTY put together for the first time the essential elements of a still oblivious international crime, distinguishing between the *actus reus* and the *mens rea*. As far as the former is concerned, the Appeals Chamber found that the sniping and shelling in question undoubtedly fell within the scope of "acts of violence" contemplated under IHL. Elaborating on the content of the rule against terror as a method of warfare, the Appeals Chamber concluded that the acts or threats of violence constitutive of the crime of terror are not limited to direct attacks against civilians or threats thereof but may include indiscriminate or disproportionate attacks (or threats thereof). Moreover,

---

[89] Schmitt 2022a; Capone 2022; Capone 2023.

[90] Schmitt 2022b (emphasis added).

[91] Henckaerts and Doswald-Beck 2005, pp. 8–9.

[92] Ibid., p. 8.

[93] See Darcy 2014, in particular Chapter 5.

[94] ICTY (TC) *Prosecutor v. Galić*, 5 December 2003, IT-98-29-T, para 593 (*Prosecutor v. Galić*, TC Judgment).

the nature of the acts or threats “may vary if they are committed with the specific intent to spread terror among the civilian population”.[95]

With regard to the *mens rea* of the crime, the ICTY found that it is composed of the specific intent to spread terror among the civilian population. Obviously, there are significant challenges in defining the *mens rea* of a crime that is so evidently hinging on the state of mind of both the accused and the impacted civilians.[96] Regarding the intent of the perpetrators, the ICTY affirmed that it could be determined from the “nature, manner, timing and duration of the acts or threats”.[97] Notably, the Appeals Chamber also stated that other purposes might have “coexisted simultaneously” with that of spreading terror, which, according also to the 1987 Commentary, shall be the primary, but not necessarily the only purpose.[98] In the *Dragomir Milošević* case the ICTY provided further insight on the *mens rea* element of the crime. The use of modified air bombs was considered proof of the intent to spread terror, because of the psychological effects that would be caused by their highly destructive force.[99] The Trial Chamber affirmed that according to the witnesses “the delays between the shelling occurred on the purpose of terrorising the population who had no idea of when the next bomb would be dropped, or the attack would end”.[100] Concerning the impact of the crime on the civilians, the Appeals Chamber in the *Galić* case clarified that the offense specifically concerns instances of “extensive trauma and psychological damage” as resulting from attacks “designed to keep the inhabitants in a constant state of terror”.[101] In the Appeal Judgment of the *Dragomir Milošević* case the judges also explained that causing death or serious injury to body or health represents “only one of the possible modes of commission of the crime of terror”, and thus is not an element of the offence *per se*.[102] What is required is that the victims suffer grave consequences resulting from the acts or threats of violence; such grave consequences include, but are not limited to, death or serious injury to body or health.[103] Finally, according to the ICTY, the “actual terrorisation of the civilian population is not an element of the crime”,[104] although “evidence of actual

---

[95] ICTY (AC) *Prosecutor v. Galić*, 30 November 2006, IT-98-29-A, para.102 (*Prosecutor v. Galić*, Appeal Judgment).

[96] Darcy 2014, pp. 212–213.

[97] *Prosecutor v. Galić,* Appeal Judgment, para 104.

[98] Ibid., para 104. In the Prosecutor v. Radovan Karadzic case, the ICTY further stressed that “the co-existence of other purposes behind the acts or threats of violence would not disprove the charge of terror, so long as the intent to spread terror was the ‘principal among the aims’”. ICTY (TC) *Prosecutor v. Radovan Karadzic*, 24 March 2016, IT-95-5/18-T, para 461 (*Prosecutor v. Radovan Karadzic*, TC Judgment).

[99] Darcy 2014, p. 214.

[100] ICTY (TC) *Prosecutor v Dragomir Milošević*, 12 December 2007, IT-98-29/1-T, paras 970-971 (*Prosecutor v Dragomir Milošević*. TC Judgment).

[101] Ibid.

[102] ICTY (AC) *Prosecutor v Dragomir Milošević*, Judgment 12 November 2009, IT-98-29/1-A, para 33 (*Prosecutor v Dragomir Milošević*, Appeal Judgment).

[103] Ibid.

[104] Ibid., para 35.

terrorisation may contribute to establishing other elements of the crime of terror, including the specific intent to terrorise".[105]

Despite its important role in shedding light on the crime of terrorism in armed conflict, the legacy of the ICTY has not been picked up. Notably, the Rome Statute of the ICC presents a large, although far from exhaustive, list of war crimes in Article 8 which deals with IACs and NIACs and divides grave breaches of the Geneva Conventions and Additional Protocol I from common Article 3 violations and other serious violations of IHL.[106] It is remarkable, and not immune to criticism, that the Rome Statute does not criminalise acts or threats of violence the primary purpose of which is to spread terror among the civilian population. Although such acts might be partly covered by intentionally directing attacks against the civilian population, this absence marks a departure, and perhaps a step backward from the ICTY, which in its case law was able to consider attacks on the civilian population and acts of terror as separate charges, finding that both constituted existing war crimes.

In the case of Russia's attacks against Ukrainian power installations, it would be interesting to see if, and how, the application of this rule will unfold as well as its consequences in terms of individual accountability. The attacks against essential infrastructures that fulfil a civilian function by providing electricity and heating to the Ukrainian people caused extensive damage, including "a toll on the mental health of Ukrainians, [who are] at risk of mental disorders such as acute stress, anxiety, depression, substance use and post-traumatic stress disorder (PTSD)".[107] Indeed, the role of international judicial bodies, including the ICC, will probably be very limited, whereas, since the military manuals of both countries contain a specific prohibition on spreading terror among the civilian population, domestic courts could be better suited to hold trials dealing with the conduct of hostilities, including this violation of IHL.[108]

---

[105] *Prosecutor v. Radovan Karadzic*, TC Judgment, para 466.

[106] Thynne 2021, p. 241; Cassese 1998.

[107] Statement by Dr Hans Henri P. Kluge, WHO Regional Director for Europe (2022) Winter in Ukraine: people's health cannot be held hostage, 21 November 2022, https://www.who.int/europe/news/item/21-11-2022-statement---winter-in-ukraine--people-s-health-cannot-be-held-hostage (accessed 20 September 2024).

[108] For an overview of the practice relating to Rule 2 of the ICRC study on customary IHL see https://ihl-databases.icrc.org/en/customary-ihl/v2/rule2 (accessed 20 September 2024).

4.5 Looking at the International Humanitarian Law's Key Principles through the Prism of the Civilian Function of Dual-Use Objects

Being a "second best" to eradicating the use of force globally,[109] IHL aims at limiting destruction and suffering in armed conflict. Therefore, IHL comprises those principles and rules of international law which establish minimum standards of humanity that must be implemented in any situation of armed conflict. Given its specific focus and scope, it is not admissible for the belligerents to justify the failure to abide by IHL norms by blaming the "harsh nature" of war.[110] IHL thereby provides the yardstick by which to measure the legality and justifiability of the acts committed in war. As noted by Kalshoven and Zegveld, the limits, or legal restraints, "do not purport to turn armed conflict into a socially acceptable activity like the medieval jousting tournament".[111] On the contrary, the overarching goals are to prevent wanton cruelty and ruthlessness—which may all too easily degenerate into utter barbarism—and to guarantee essential protection to those most directly affected by the conflict.[112] In order to achieve those noble purposes, it is essential to overcome some superficial assumptions that justify the targeting of vital infrastructures and may even result in dangerous claims, such as, for example, that dual-use objects "presumptively qualify as military objectives",[113] or that dual-use objects will "always constitute lawful military objectives in light of the fact that one component of the duality involves an effective contribution to the military effort".[114] Establishing the notion that dual-use objects must be set apart from military objectives *because of their civilian function* requires taking a closer look, through this "new" prism, at the key IHL principles, namely distinction, precautions, military necessity, and humanity.

4.5.1 *The Principle of Distinction*

The present study has already delved extensively into the principle of distinction and the crucial role that it plays with respect to dual-use objects, especially since, as stressed on several occasions, "IHL doesn't 'tell us who or what the protected persons and objects are".[115] There is no need to further linger on the main elements of this principle,[116] whereas it is useful to focus more at length on the presumption of

[109] Blum 2010, p. 7.

[110] Melzer 2022, p. 17.

[111] Kalshoven and Zegveld 2011, p. 2.

[112] Ibid.

[113] Dinstein and Dahl 2020, p. 75.

[114] Ibid., p. 78.

[115] Dinstein 2004, p. 114.

[116] See Chap. 1, Sect. 1.3 and Chap. 3 in this book.

civilian status, which has been eloquently dubbed as the "doubt rule".[117] As already anticipated in Chap. 1 of this book,[118] the presumption of civilian status for targeting persons and certain objects is a corollary to the principle of distinction,[119] and it is enshrined in Article 50(1) and 52(3) of API, respectively. More in detail, whereas in relation to persons everyone *enjoys consideration* as civilians in cases of doubt,[120] the wording of Article 52(3) is less straightforward as *the presumption* only applies to objects ordinarily dedicated to civilian purposes, "such as a place of worship, a house or other dwelling or a school". Furthermore, the presumption only applies with respect to their qualification as military objectives "by virtue of use".[121] Qualification as a military objective by location and/or purpose does not trigger the Article 52(3) presumption.[122] This entails that the situation involves exclusively enemy forces "using for military ends" an object that is normally dedicated to civilian purposes.[123]

According to the predominant view on the issue, which has re-gained momentum in 2023 following the revision of the US Department of Defense (DoD) Law of War Manual,[124] it is important to differentiate between objects "ordinarily dedicated to civilian purposes" and the "remaining civilian objects" that are not military objectives by nature nor *prima facie* civilian objects.[125] Some authors have strongly asserted that "[c]ategories of objects *that are not ordinarily devoted solely* to civilian purposes, such as installations and means of transport as well as communication facilities, are not subject to the presumption".[126] Notably, the same existence of a presumption admits that that the distinction between civilian objects and military objectives is imprecise, leading to the paradoxical, and wrong conjecture that only some civilian objects are "definitely" civilian.[127] The ICRC study on customary IHL seems to partially echo this sentiment, by affirming that "the issue of how to classify an object in case of doubt is not entirely clear".[128]

Yet, it is important to highlight that the examples included in Article 52(3) of API are considered to be only illustrative. The objects that are listed "do not have any

---

117 Van Coller 2024, pp. 1–3.

118 See Chap. 1, Sect. 1.3.1 in this book.

119 This is the reading (correctly) embraced by the 2023 US DoD Law of War Manual which expresses the presumption as an aspect of the principle of distinction as opposed to a precaution (US DoD 2023).

120 According to Article 50(1) of API "[I]n case of doubt whether a person is a civilian, that person shall *be considered to be* a civilian". (Emphasis added).

121 Nasu and Watts 2023.

122 As stated in Article 52(3) in case of doubt as to whether an object, which is normally dedicated to civilian purposes, is being used to make an effective contribution to military action shall be presumed not to be so used.

123 Harvard Air and Missile Warfare Manual 2013, Rule 12(b) p. 92.

124 US DoD 2023, para 5.4.3.4. See Chap. 1, Sect. 1.3.1 in this book.

125 Kalshoven and Zegveld 2011, p. 105.

126 Nasu and Watts 2023.

127 Sutton 2021, p. 180.

128 Henckaerts and Doswald-Beck 2005, Rule 10, p. 35.

special status compared to other typically civilian buildings or installations".[129] Additional examples, mentioned in the Military Manuals of some States,[130] are commercial offices, shopping areas and facilities, and markets. The fact that the list is not exhaustive triggers several considerations. First, it gives leave to interpret the norm in a less restrictive way, allowing this author to argue in favour of a presumption of civilian status applicable to all those objects that play a civilian function and that, in some instances, are even essential for the survival of the civilian population. Second, States can obviously expand the list, by applying the presumption of civilian status to what they see as "objects ordinarily dedicated to civilian purposes". The wording of the provision, in fact, does not limit its scope to selected civilian objects, which would otherwise be singled out as "class A" objects, thus creating a misnomer within the IHL framework. Rather, the goal of the provision is to prevent belligerents from "arbitrarily and unilaterally declare as a military objective *any civilian object*".[131] To this end, a presumption of civilian status is both legally required, not only for State parties to API,[132] and operationally advisable in the context of attacks against persons and objects during armed conflict, contrary to what was stated in the previous versions of the US DoD Law of War Manual.[133]

Under API, the presumption applies exclusively "in case of doubt", meaning that it is triggered only when there are "mixed indications which create doubt" about the targetability of a given object.[134] The threshold of doubt or uncertainty that precludes the attack is far from settled, with countries like the United Kingdom limiting the scope of the presumption only to cases of "substantial doubt".[135] The commentary to the Harvard Air and Missile Warfare Manual sheds further light on the notion of doubt, by explaining that it is not "the existence of *any doubt* that precludes attack", but rather of a "reasonable doubt".[136] States are also free to embrace and implement a presumption "untethered from doubt".[137] This is the approach astonishingly adopted by the US, which went from refuting the presumption *tout court* to accepting its broadest and demanding formulation, according to which "[u]nder the principle of distinction, commanders and other decision-makers *must presume* that persons or objects are protected from being made the object of attack *unless the information available at the time indicates that the persons or objects are military objectives*".[138] Although this formulation—which has attracted strong reactions from both critics and enthusiastic commentators—discards the "doubt threshold", it

---

[129] Harvard Air and Missile Warfare Manual 2013, Rule 12(b) p. 92.

[130] See for instance para. 5.4.2 of the UK Military Manual.

[131] Sandoz et al. 1987, p. 638, para 2037 (emphasis added).

[132] Whether the presumption has attained customary status is no longer unsettled. See Hathaway et al. 2017; Goodman 2022.

[133] US DoD 1992, para 752. See Chap. 1, Sect. 1.3.1 in this book.

[134] Nasu and Watts 2023.

[135] Ibid.

[136] Harvard Air and Missile Warfare Manual 2013, Rule 12(b) p. 91.

[137] Nasu and Watts 2023.

[138] US DoD 2023, para 5.4.3.4.

still has to deal with the "standard of rebuttal", i.e. the quantum of information (not evidence)[139] needed to rebut the presumption.[140] It is generally agreed on that the status of the object believed to be used for military purposes need not be established "beyond reasonable doubt",[141] yet the burden remains undetermined, at least in absolute terms. As affirmed in the San Remo Manual on International Law Applicable to Armed Conflicts at Sea, the presumption "imposes an obligation on a party to the conflict to gather and assess relevant information before commencing an attack".[142] On the one hand it is true that, as stressed by Schmitt, this requirement simply restates the well-known obligation to identify the target as a military objective,[143] on the other hand it is undeniable that the presumptive civilian status is embedded in the existing legal framework and, without establishing the "quantum of information", its value is undermined. According to the 2023 DoD Law of War Manual commanders and other decision-makers must assess whether persons or objects are military objectives "in good faith".[144] Some authors note that identifying "good faith" as the rebuttal standard provides "an incomplete solution to the rebuttal equation" because it is normally associated with subjective judgment.[145] Corn, hence, argues that the commander must make a "reasonable" judgment, because, unlike good faith, "reasonableness is normally considered an objective term".[146] Although, as it will be discussed in the next chapter, reasonableness lies at the intersection of subjectivity and objectivity and it is a transversal but certainly not fixed standard,[147] it is still possible to conclude that "an attacker *must act reasonably* in deciding to attack such objects, specifically taking into account, among other factors, the fact that the intended target is normally one used for civilian purposes".[148]

The presumption of civilian status and its essential, but still controversial, elements so far have been the subject of a range of different interpretations. One that goes in the direction of strengthening the protection of dual-use objects, as defined in the present work,[149] considers that uncertainty about the nature of certain objects—including dual-use objects—will require that the object be treated as civilian until it is not possible to *reasonably assess* whether the use of that object makes an effective contribution to the military action.

[139] Corn 2023.

[140] Lawless 2023

[141] Harvard Air and Missile Warfare Manual 2013, Rule 12(b) p. 92.

[142] Doswald-Beck 1995, para 58.

[143] Schmitt 2023.

[144] US DoD 2023, para 5.4.3.2.

[145] Corn 2023.

[146] Ibid.

[147] See Chap. 5, Sect. 5.3 in this book.

[148] Harvard Air and Missile Warfare Manual 2013, Rule 12(b) p. 92. See also Henderson and Reece 2018.

[149] See Chap. 3, Sect. 3.4 in this book.

4.5.2 The Principle of Precautions

The principle of precautions, which is embedded both in treaty and customary law,[150] deals with the precautions that must be taken when planning, executing an attack as well as being on the receiving end of it. Therefore, it encompasses several distinct obligations that cover both the precautions that need to be undertaken by the attacker as well as those that must be implemented by the belligerent party subject to the attack.[151] With regard to the former, which are characterised by a sharper focus on the role of individuals, the content of the principle and the respective obligations will be introduced and discussed at length in the next chapter,[152] which focuses on the "reasonable military commander standard" and how it unfolds in the various phases of the targeting process and vis-à-vis each of the most prominent IHL principles. Concerning the latter, it is clear that the precautionary measures against the effects of attacks refer to those measures which every party must take in its own territory in favour of its nationals, or in territory under its control.[153] Rule 22 of the ICRC study on customary IHL articulates this obligation by stating that parties to the conflict must take "all feasible precautions" to protect the civilian population and civilian objects under their control against the effects of attacks.[154] Furthermore, each party to the conflict must, *to the maximum extent feasible*, avoid locating military objectives within or near densely populated areas and remove civilian persons and objects under its control from the vicinity of military objectives.[155]

As noted in the ICRC Commentary some of these measures have a preventive, rather than just precautionary, character. This pertains to the measures concerned with averting the construction of certain buildings in specific places or removing objectives from an area where such buildings are located, or otherwise separating the population and their homes from dangerous places.[156] As far as permanent or immovable objectives—such as military bases and installations—are concerned, parties should endeavour to locate them away from densely populated areas. This precaution, as stressed in the ICRC study on customary IHL, should already be taken into consideration in peacetime.[157] Although the rule "does not constitute a restriction on a State's military installations on its own territory",[158] some (limited) practice refers to the

[150] Henckaerts and Doswald-Beck 2005, Rules 15-24. See Arts. 57 and 58 of API, Article 13 of APII. See also ICTY (TC), *Prosecutor v Kupreskic et al.*, 14 January 2000, IT-95-16-T, para 46.

[151] The complementary relation between active and passive precautions indicates that an attacker is not prevented from attacking military objectives if the defender fails to take appropriate precautions or deliberately uses civilians to shield military operations. Ibid.

[152] See Chap. 5, Sect. 5.3.2 in this book.

[153] Sandoz et al. 1987, p. 692, para 2239.

[154] Henckaerts and Doswald-Beck 2005, Rule 22, p. 68.

[155] Ibid., Rule 23 and Rule 24.

[156] Sandoz et al. 1987, p. 692, para 2244.

[157] Henckaerts and Doswald-Beck 2005, Rule 23, p. 74.

[158] Several delegations raised this point during the discussion of Article 58 of API. See O.R. VI, pp. 234–235, CDDH/SR.42, Annex (Republic of Korea).

existence of a "duty to locate military bases and installations outside densely populated areas".[159] Rather surprisingly, the interpretation of this Rule enshrined in the ICRC Commentary ends with a cryptic phrase according to which "dual use installations, such as railway stations and airports, may even be located near or inside densely populated areas *on purpose*".[160] This statement reinforces the idea that the provision should not impose limits on State' sovereignty. At the same time, however, it contradicts the essence of the precautionary principle itself, whose respect is required also by the principles of distinction and proportionality.

Concerning movable military objectives, the 1987 ICRC Commentary laconically states that "care should be taken in particular during the conflict to avoid placing troops, equipment or transports in densely populated areas".[161] Authors like Quéguiner have contributed to shedding further light on this measure, by clarifying that in all their movements, it is preferable that military units avoid coming near densely populated areas.[162] Whenever they are unable to avoid this, then they must pass through the populated area as swiftly as possible and deploy in such a manner as to create the least possible risk to the civilian population and civilian objects.[163] In relation to civilian persons, a typical measure would be to evacuate areas close to military objectives, such as contact zones, military airports, and munitions factories.[164] In some instances the goal would be to move particularly vulnerable parts of the civilian population (such as children and expectant mothers) from affected areas. Clearly and in light of the vulnerabilities of certain categories of civilians, such measures must also take into account the potentially traumatic effects connected to an evacuation.[165] Therefore, the rule will apply only when it is materially impossible to guarantee the population safety by other means, and only until the danger has passed.[166] The Rule is also related to the prohibition on using human shields as in no event the belligerent party subject to an attack may use civilians to shield military objectives.[167]

The Commentary emphasises that "it is likely that governments are sufficiently concerned with sparing their own population and that they will therefore act in the best interests of that population".[168] In fact, the whole set of passive precautions rests on the idea that "it is in their own interest that States should take such measures".[169] Although this assumption is, logically, difficult to contradict, the reality is different

---

[159] Henckaerts and Doswald-Beck 2005, Rule 23, p. 73.

[160] Ibid., p. 74 (emphasis added).

[161] Sandoz et al. 1987, p. 692, para 2252.

[162] Quéguiner 2006, p. 818.

[163] Ibid.

[164] Harvard Air and Missile Warfare Manual 2013, Rule 43, p. 165.

[165] Quéguiner 2006, p. 818.

[166] Ibid.

[167] Harvard Air and Missile Warfare Manual 2013, Rule 45, pp. 168–170.

[168] Ibid., para 2253.

[169] Ibid., para 2244.

and State practice shows that the duty to take these precautions is worded and implemented in relative terms.[170] In particular, the precautionary measure to avoid locating military objectives within or near densely populated areas was met with so much resistance during the Diplomatic Conference that it cannot be considered to have expressed customary law at that time.[171] This is a rule that has significant implications for dual-use objects and that needs to be discussed in more detail. In addition to the Republic of Korea, several other States strongly objected to the obligation to endeavour to avoid the presence of military objectives within densely populated areas.[172] For example, the Swiss Confederation expressed its opposition in light of Switzerland's mountainous topography, which means that the civilian population is heavily concentrated in valleys, i.e. areas of vital economic and military importance where, in case of war, fighting would inevitably take place despite the density of civilian population and housing.[173]

Contrary to the majority of States, the US, which as is known has not experienced attacks on its mainland for two centuries before the 9/11 events, and has a relatively scarcely populated territory, "favours a rule putting the burden of the protection of the civilian population at least as much upon the belligerent controlling that population".[174] According to Sassòli and Quintin, States' vocal opposition to this precautionary measure represents a clear indication of the general agreement that the defender has "less responsibilities than the attacker".[175] Moreover, States have stressed that this duty imposes too heavy an economic burden to disperse States' "industrial, communications and transportation facilities from existing locations in densely populated areas",[176] thus assuming that those dual-use objects will be regarded as military objectives by the attacker. The present study, which stems from the urge to challenge the mainstream approach to dual-use objects and the many wrong assumptions that come with it, cannot agree on this conflation, nor does it support the position that the main responsibility to take precautionary measures is conferred solely upon the "attacker".[177] What this author shares, instead, is the view that, as Schmitt puts it, "there is no absolute prohibition on being in the vicinity of civilians and civilian objects or any absolute duty to remove them".[178] In the case of dual-use objects, which notably fulfil an important civilian function and therefore are usually located inside populated areas, claiming otherwise would first mean that the

[170] Quéguiner 2006, 820.

[171] Sassòli and Quintin 2014, p. 38.

[172] When becoming parties to API, various countries including Belgium, Italy, the Netherlands, and Algeria declared that the term "feasible" must be understood taking the available means or military considerations into account. Austria even made a formal reservation subjecting Article 58 to the "exigencies dictated by the defence of the national territory." Ibid., p. 37.

[173] Quéguiner 2006, 819.

[174] Sassòli and Quintin 2014, p. 37. See also US DoD 2023, para 5.14; Schmitt 2022c.

[175] Sassòli and Quintin 2014, p. 37.

[176] Ibid., p. 39.

[177] Ibid., p. 36.

[178] Schmitt 2022c.

mainstream approach to the issue is correct, and as discussed so far this is certainly not the case, and second, that the passive precautions not only risk imposing a restriction on how States organise their national defences, but it would even trespass on civilian authorities' decisions concerning, for example, the allocation of financial resources and the adoption of practical measures during peacetime.

4.5.3 The Principle of Proportionality

The principle of proportionality is consistently brought up when the topic of dual-use objects is addressed. Despite being a pillar of the IHL framework, "the application of the principle of proportionality is more easily stated than applied in practice".[179] In a nutshell the principle affirms that attacks on lawful targets only remain lawful if the incidental civilian casualties or damages are not excessive. Despite the long history of IHL treaties, API marks the first time that the customary international law principle of proportionality was codified in a multilateral legal instrument.[180] The rule relating to proportionality is mentioned three times in API, i.e. in Articles 51(5)(b) and 57(2)(a)(iii) and (b). These three provisions establish that a disproportionate attack is one "which may be expected to cause incidental loss of civilian life, injury to civilians, damage to civilian objects, or a combination thereof, which would be excessive in relation to the concrete and direct military advantage anticipated". When assessing the proportionality of an attack, Fenrick stresses that the two essential issues are collateral damage on one side and military advantage on the other,[181] both of them deserve to be duly analysed with respect to dual-use objects.

Collateral damage, i.e. the "civilian side" of the proportionality equation, encompasses the loss of civilian life, injury to civilians, and damage to civilian objects. Concerning the latter, i.e. harm to non-human things, the military commander has a duty to consider only the damage caused to civilian objects.[182] In other words, when a civilian object meets the test for being a military objective, then the civilian object itself, once it is subject to the attack, does not form part of the collateral damage assessment.[183] Reinforcing this aspect, Pomson argues that there is not enough States' support to claim that the damage to the civilian function of *what has become* a military objective, and therefore a lawful target, constitutes incidental harm for the purposes of a proportionality assessment. Other authors, including Gillard, agree on the fact that there does not appear to be "any legal basis for considering damage to

[179] Final Report to the Prosecutor by the Committee Established to Review the NATO Bombing Campaign against the Federal Republic of Yugoslavia, (13 June 2000), (hereinafter OTP Report) reprinted in (2000) ILM 39:1257, para 19.

[180] Henderson 2009, p. 181; Gardam 2004.

[181] Fenrick 1997, pp. 548–549.

[182] Pomson 2021. See also Cannizzaro 2000; Cannizzaro 2014, p 340.

[183] Henderson 2009, p. 207.

the dual-use object in proportionality assessments",[184] even when distinct parts of a single structure are being used for civilian and military functions.[185] This reasoning is perfectly in line with the mainstream approach to dual-use objects, which, as discussed above, oftentimes are even subject to an unlawful presumption of military status. However, for many commentators how to consider the harmful effects on the civilian function of key infrastructures and their impact on the civilian population is not a settled issue. Experts involved in the drafting of an ICRC report on proportionality departed from the predominant stance, by agreeing that the civilian function of a dual-use object must be considered in a proportionality analysis.[186] From that perspective, putting an end to or impairing the civilian use of essential infrastructure such as bridges, electricity-generating and distribution networks, and water treatment systems, "could render the attack unlawful, despite the fact that the object had become a military objective".[187] Two problems are triggered by this assumption. The first concerns the still scant acceptance of this approach by States. The ICRC report notably cites the US practice, expressed in several documents as follows:

> [i]f the attack is directed against dual-use objects that are legitimate military targets but also serve a legitimate civilian need (e.g., electrical power or telecommunications), then this factor must be carefully balanced against the military benefits when making a proportionality determination.[188]

Obviously, such a limited support is not enough to claim that there is an emerging norm, and therefore that there are developments *de lege ferenda*. Nonetheless, if the policy is adopted by a growing number of militaries, it could, indeed, contribute to advancing agreement. The second problem regards, as Lubell puts it, which harm shall be considered (e.g. is it the incidental harm to the civilians as a result of losing the infrastructure and can this be distinguished from the harm to the infrastructure itself?) and how much of it.[189] These are difficult questions that deal with the so-called "internal" dimension of proportionality,[190] i.e. the one that pertains to the incidental harm that derives directly from an attack against a dual-use object. The issue, as mentioned in the previous section, has been marginally discussed also in the *Prlić et al.* case, in which the ICTY grappled, albeit inconclusively, with the harm that the destruction of the Old Bridge in Mostar had caused to the civilian population.[191] As already recalled, in its decision the Trial Chamber included in the proportionality assessment the impact of the bridge's destruction on the Muslim

---

[184] Gillard 2018, p. 35.

[185] Pomson 2021. Schmitt, instead, notably suggests that, if the circumstances and the military capabilities of the attacker so allow, the aspect of the structure the enemy is using qualifies as a military objective, but its separate and distinct components that are not being used for military purposes retain their civilian character. Schmitt 2021; see Chap. 1, Sect. 1.2 in this book.

[186] ICRC 2016, p. 38.

[187] Ibid.

[188] See for instance US Joint publication 3-60, Joint Targeting, 31 January 2013, p. A-5.

[189] Lubell 2015, p. 85.

[190] ICRC 2016, p. 39.

[191] *Prlić et al.* TC Judgement, para 1584.

civilian population of Mostar, referring to both the psychological impact of the attack, which according to some authors went a "stretch too far for ordinary considerations of proportionality",[192] and the cultural and "symbolic" importance that the bridge had. The consideration of the Old Bridge's inherent cultural value represents a crucial, and controversial, aspect of the judgment inasmuch as the ICTY has departed from the common approach to proportionality, according to which the damage to the military objective itself should not be considered in the assessment, and, perhaps unwittingly, it opened the door for the inclusion of the "internal" dimension of proportionality in the proportionality calculus. As the judgment, and the following Appeals Chambers' decision, failed to engage in a substantive examination of proportionality, it is difficult to ascertain how much weight has been assigned to the civilian (and cultural) function of the target.

In spite of the limited attention devoted to this issue so far and the restrictive interpretation endorsed by the doctrine, the ICRC report provides some partial answers on how to include the intrinsic value of a dual-use object in the proportionality assessment, by describing the proportionality test as "a balance between the military advantage anticipated" (from the destruction of the military part of the object or from otherwise putting an end to the military use or function of this object) and the incidental harm deriving from destroying the civilian part of the object or otherwise ending its civilian use or function.[193] Such a balance, obviously, must be struck by the actors who are called to make the proportionality assessment in real life.

Nowadays, what seems to be widely accepted is the inclusion in the proportionality assessments of the so-called reverberating effects that stem from attacks against dual-use objects.[194] These reverberating ("indirect", "knock-on", "cascading", or "second- or third-tier") harm or effects that are reasonably expected to physically harm civilians or civilian objects, are uncontroversially considered "as long as the harm meets the criteria of causation and foreseeability".[195] This is also the position of the ICRC, which in its 2022 handbook on IHL, has clarified that

> When assessing the excessiveness of incidental harm, *the foreseeable second-and third-order effects of an attack must also be taken into account.* For example, attacks against dual-use infrastructure, such as electrical grids or telecommunication networks, may not only have the immediate effect of preventing the enemy from using that infrastructure for military purposes and exposing the civilian population to short-term shortages. They may well have a crippling effect on the medium- and long-term ability of the civilian authorities and medical services concerned, and of the general civilian population, to cope with the everyday consequences of the war.[196]

One point that remains controversial, or rather underexplored, concerns whether reverberating effects also cover mental harm and diseases caused by an attack.

[192] Moffett 2020, p. 245.

[193] Ibid.

[194] Henderson reports that prominent authors like Kalshoven in the past have expressed scepticism towards the possibility to include indirect effects on the proportionality calculus. See Henderson 2009, pp. 208–209.

[195] Gillard 2018, pp. 18–19; Robinson and Nohle 2016, p 107. See Chap. 5, Sect. 5.3.3 in this book.

[196] Melzer 2022, p. 102 (emphasis added).

Notably, the wording of Article 51(5)(b) AP I does not expressly circumscribe the relevant injury to physical injury. The ordinary meaning of the term "injury" today encompasses both physical and mental injury. The ICTY in the *Prlić et al.* case considered the psychological damage caused to civilians and the Appeals Chamber did not object, although it remains unclear if the Trial Chamber looked at the harm through the lenses of "internal proportionality" or of the reverberating effects. Gillard notes that, in light of the increasing medical understanding of the mental health problems caused to civilians by armed conflicts, such as post-traumatic stress disorder, there is no reason, in principle, to exclude mental harm from proportionality assessments.[197] The experts that contributed to the Tallinn Manual 2.0 also share this view, as they accept that it is "reasonable to extend the definition to serious illness and severe mental suffering that are tantamount to injury".[198] The ICRC report on proportionality, instead, claims that the interpretation of "injury" for IHL has not expanded to include mental harm in the proportionality assessment and several experts contested the practicality of properly assessing mental harm *ex ante* during armed conflicts.[199] State practice, as stressed by Gillard, is almost non-existent.[200] It is unclear whether this is because States do not consider that they are legally obliged to take into account mental harm in proportionality assessments or because of the practical challenges of identifying and quantifying the mental harm expected from an attack.[201] One of the arguments used by the detractors of the opportunity to assess incidental mental harm is that it would be too difficult to identify a causal link between one particular attack and mental harm, which, in armed conflicts, could be caused by general exposure to hostilities. However, in relation to dual-use objects, especially in light of the civilian function that they play, it is possible for the mental harm to be linked to a specific attack and not being merely hypothetical, like in the cases of the Old Bridge and of Russia's attacks against Ukraine's power facilities.

An additional aspect that deserves to be explored concerns the scope of the attack(s) and whether the cumulative effects of attacks should be weighed in the proportionality assessment. The controversial notion of "attack as a whole", which has already been discussed with respect to the principle of distinction,[202] is relevant also to proportionality. The mainstream approach to the issue is that one cannot always assess proportionality on a "bullet by bullet basis" or even on the basis of discrete military objectives.[203] Notably, the approach of assessing the proportionality of the whole of an attack is not just a legal concept, as it is almost unanimously supported by military practice. For the purposes of proportionality, States consider

197 Gillard 2018, p. 32.

198 Schmitt 2017, p. 417. See also Cohen and Zlotogorski 2021, pp. 78–79.

199 ICRC 2016, pp. 35–36.

200 Gillard 2018, p. 33.

201 Ibid. The author mentions that the effects on mental health of exposure to an attack are likely to vary significantly, both among individuals and also depending on the context of where the attack occurs.

202 See Chap. 3, Sect. 3.2.2 in this book.

203 Fenrick 1997, p. 548.

the military advantage anticipated from the attack as a whole and not only from isolated parts thereof.[204] Claiming otherwise would create a serious gap between military practice and IHL,[205] and this is certainly contrary to the scope of this work. While an attack may be considered "as a whole" when assessing military advantage, there are necessarily limits as to what constitutes the whole of the attack. Proportionality can never be appraised by looking at the "total amount of collateral damage at the end of an armed conflict" and then determining whether that collateral damage is excessive when compared against the goals of the armed conflict itself.[206] For example, the OTP report shockingly erred in claiming that the legal evaluation of "the proportionality of the attack should not be premised on a specific incident", but rather refer to "an overall assessment of the totality of civilian victims as against the goals of the military campaign".[207]

To better explain the extent to which the notion of "attack as a whole" could be stretched and within which limits, Doswald-Beck authoritatively affirms that proportionality assessments shall consider the military advantage anticipated within the context of a given tactical operation:

> such an operation may necessitate, for example, the destruction of six military objectives, one of which, being particularly difficult to get at, might involve far greater casualties than the other five. The attack of that one objective on its own might be of no great use, *but within the context of the operation as a whole, absolutely essential.*[208]

Authors have reflected on this issue, taking into consideration also the peculiarities of dual-use objects. Rowe, for example, provides the following illustrative example:

> It is, however, still possible to argue that only the destruction of all forms of certain types of dual-purpose object would make an effective contribution to military action and offer a definite military advantage. If there are, for instance, two bridges across a strategically significant river, the destruction of one only may give no military advantage; only the destruction of both would achieve this objective.[209]

This example triggers two additional considerations. First, if the military advantage expected from a single attack as defined in Article 49 of API is not dependent on or affected by other acts, then nothing prevents the act alone from being considered an "attack as a whole" for the purpose of proportionality assessments, even when it involves a dual-use target that belongs to a given category of objects, infrastructures, installations etc… If, on the other hand, a single attack is one component of a broader operation where other attacks contribute to achieving the military advantage anticipated, then the operation in its entirety, as stressed also by Doswald-Beck, should be considered the "attack as a whole".[210] Second, the civilian function of dual-use objects and the excessive damage to the civilian population that their damage

[204] Gillard 2018, p. 9.

[205] Henderson 2009, p. 201.

[206] Laursen 2002, p. 795.

[207] OTP Report, paras 51–52.

[208] Doswald-Beck 1989, p. 156.

[209] Rowe 2000, p. 152.

[210] Gillard 2018, pp. 9–10. See also Bothe et al. 2013, p. 329.

or destruction can cause, need to be duly taken into account in the proportionality assessment of a single attack or of an attack as a whole, interpreted, however, as a finite military operation.

As mentioned in Chap. 1 of this book,[211] Shue and Wippman have developed an interesting approach to enhance the protection of dual-use objects through the prism of the proportionality principle. Said approach connects the two key aspects of proportionality identified by Fenrick and discussed also in the present section.[212] In their view, which is in line with this study's effort to place increasing emphasis on the civilian function of dual-use objects, the adoption of a "compelling military advantage" standard in proportionality assessments (combined with the inclusion of indirect and cumulative effects of attacks against vital infrastructures) could contribute to strengthening the protection of civilians.[213] The challenge to ingrain the civilian function of dual-use objects in the so-called "proportionality calculus", however, does not end here and it is important to stress the essential role that is played by individual actors, who, as discussed in the next chapter, are ultimately called to determine whether the incidental harm expected to be caused by an attack would be excessive in relation to the concrete and direct military advantage anticipated.

4.5.4 The Principles of Military Necessity and Humanity

As famously stated by Schmitt the principle of military necessity "exists in equipoise with the principle of humanity, which seeks to limit the suffering and destruction incident to warfare".[214] The balance between military necessity and humanity represents the foundation of IHL,[215] and, as such, it could hardly be encapsulated in one specific provision; rather, it permeates the whole LOAC's architecture.[216] On the one hand, the existing framework recognises that, in order to overcome an adversary in wartime, it may be militarily necessary to cause death, injury and destruction, and to impose more severe security measures than would be permissible in peacetime. On the other hand, IHL also establishes very clearly that "military necessity does not give the belligerents *carte blanche* to wage unrestricted war".[217] The principle of humanity, imposes, *inter alia*, certain limits on the means and methods of warfare, and requires that those who have fallen into enemy hands be always treated humanely. The words used by Pictet to interpret the principle of humanity still resonate today,

[211] See Chap. 1, Sect. 1.2 in this book.

[212] Shue and Wippman 2002.

[213] Ibid., pp. 574–575.

[214] Schmitt 2010, p. 796.

[215] On the complementarity between these two concepts, which are sometimes, and wrongly, depicted as "polar opposites", see Beer 2016.

[216] Winter notably suggests framing military necessity and humanity as "pillars" of IHL, rather than principles *stricto sensu*. See Winter 2020.

[217] Melzer 2022, pp. 17–18; Draper 1973.

as they provide some examples of what applying this concept means. Therefore, humanity translates in preferring capture over wounding the enemy, wounding over killing, sparing non-combatants as much as possible, making captivity as endurable as feasible etc...[218]

However, the scope of the principle goes much further than this. As enshrined in the Martens Clause,[219] the principle of humanity deters the assumption that anything that is not explicitly prohibited by specific IHL rules is therefore permitted.[220] The Martens Clause demonstrates that IHL is excluded from any positivist assertion, as famously articulated in the *Lotus* case before the Permanent Court of International Justice (PCIJ),[221] to the effect that all which is not forbidden in international law is permitted. As a result of this, the lack of an express IHL rule on point does not necessarily justify an action based on military necessity; actions in warfare must equally reflect respect for humanity.[222] Over time, different and nuanced understandings of the concepts of military necessity and humanity have been advanced.[223] In particular, two approaches have emerged with regard to the legal effect of the principles of humanity and military necessity. The narrower one considers that while the two principles inform the entire body of IHL, they do not create obligations above and beyond specific rules of IHL. The broader view, instead, considers that these principles impose limits "beyond specific IHL rules".[224] The ICRC, endorsing the latter, further notes how the conjunction of both principles is particularly important in cases where the interpretation of the existing law is uncertain.[225] Mauri also stresses that military necessity and humanity as general principles can and should be resorted to when interpreting existing law because their combination "offers a theoretical framework that helps any interpreter reach a solution for an unregulated case".[226] Mauri, and the ICRC in its most recent publication on the subject,[227] had

[218] Pictet 1985, p. 62.

[219] The Martens Clause was formulated and introduced for the first time in the Preamble of the 1899 Hague Conventions on the Laws and Customs of War on Land. The Clause reads "Until a more complete code of the laws of war has been issued, the High Contracting Parties deem it expedient to declare that, in cases not included in the Regulations adopted by them, the inhabitants and the belligerents remain under the protection and the rule of the law of nations, as they result from the usages established among civilized peoples, from the laws of humanity and the dictates of public conscience." It is understood today as of general applicability, has acquired the status of a customary rule and has been adopted, either in whole or in part, by other IHL instruments, including the Geneva Conventions and their Additional Protocols. See Meron 2000.

[220] Ticehurst 1997, pp. 128–130.

[221] The so-called Lotus principle consecrates States' freedom to act unless explicitly prohibited by international law. PCIJ, *SS Lotus (France v. Turkey)*, Judgment, 7 September 1927, paras 16–18.

[222] Schmitt 2010, p. 800; Hayashi 2010; Hayashi 2020.

[223] For an overview of the main theoretical perspectives on the issue, see Mauri 2022, pp. 64–65.

[224] ICRC 2023, p. 1.

[225] Ibid., p. 2.

[226] Mauri 2022, p. 65.

[227] ICRC 2023.

specific domains in mind when discussing military necessity and humanity, respectively autonomous weapons systems and cyber operations during armed conflict. The conclusions reached, which reflect also the predominant doctrine, are relevant beyond the scope for which they were originally conceived. In the case of dual-use objects that are subject, as this study has shown, to an unsettled interpretation and application of the existing framework, turning to the essential balance between military necessity and humanitarian considerations can provide sensible input, also in light of the civilian function that dual-use objects play. Although exercising intentional force against civilians and civilian objects is clearly forbidden under the existing set of IHL norms, those in the military forces "who still believe that using excessive force against civilians is militarily desirable" are still able to "manipulate the rules to a limited extent but mainly within a specific niche",[228] i.e. dual-use objects. Whenever objects fulfil both civilian and military functions "over-enthusiastic soldiers might inflate their military profile at the expense of their civilian functions in order to legitimize their targeting".[229]

Authors have noted an increasing and worrying tendency to place emphasis on the "almost automatic validation of military necessity"[230] at the expense of humanity, and this, as discussed in the previous chapters, is especially true when it comes to attacks against dual-use objects. Effectively striking a balance between military necessity and humanity is not an impossible task to achieve, but it requires significant efforts from all the actors involved, e.g. the legislators and the interpreters, and even more from the military commanders, since the "determination of military necessity is, to a large extent, the commander's profession".[231] To this end, and as it will be discussed in detail in the next chapter, the determination of relative values must be that of the "reasonable military commander", a crucial standard that must be applied to all the key IHL principles.

4.6 Conclusion

The analysis carried out in the present chapter has shed light on several important aspects. The focus has been placed on the peculiar status of dual-use objects, which are objects that play a relevant, if not essential, civilian function. So far, this unique feature has been acknowledged but never properly discussed, neither in general/theoretical terms nor regarding its concrete implications.[232] The concept of "function" is not new to the IHL framework, in particular in relation to cultural property. The process of assessing the civilian function of a certain target and attributing to it some weight in a judicial forum, remains however, underexplored, with limited and

[228] Beer 2016, p. 823.

[229] Ibid.

[230] Ibid. See also Luban 2013.

[231] Bill 2009, p. 119.

[232] Hathaway et al. 2024, pp. 82–83.

not necessarily successful attempts carried out in the past. The *Prlić et al.* case before the ICTY and the EECC's award on the aerial bombardment of the Hirgigo power station provide two illustrative examples of the challenges that need to be faced in order to incorporate a meaningful reflection on the civilian function of a dual-use object in the legal reasoning of a court of law. The starting point, in this author's view, must be reconsidering and appraising the applicable framework through the prism of the civilian function that critical infrastructures, installations, systems etc… play. Therefore, after introducing and explaining the essence of dual-use objects' civilian function, this chapter has addressed what this recognition entails on a more practical level, that concerns the interpretation and the application of the existing IHL rules and principles.

First, the inquiry has delved into the rules that are most often associated with dual-use objects in armed conflict. Even though discussions on dual-use objects frequently include references to norms such as the rule governing destruction or seizure of property during hostilities, the prohibition on attacking, destroying, removing or rendering useless objects indispensable to the survival of the civilian population, the prohibition to spread terror amongst the civilian population, the attention devoted to unfolding the existing connection and explore its depth has been scant. Second, the analysis carried out has finally offered a reading of the key IHL principles that is compatible with the centrality of the civilian function played by dual-use objects. For each principle the study has identified and discussed one or more pivotal aspects that allows the lawmakers, the interpreters and the military commanders to operate in a more consistent and hopefully effective way. In particular, with regard to the latter category of actors, this chapter has paved the way for reclaiming the prominence of the reasonableness standard that will be discussed at length in the next chapter.

References

Beer Y (2016) Humanity Considerations Cannot Reduce War's Hazards Alone: Revitalizing the Concept of Military Necessity. European Journal of International Law 26(4): 801–828

Bill B J (2009) The Rendulic "Rule": Military Necessity, Commander's Knowledge, and Methods of Warfare. Yearbook of International Humanitarian Law 12: 119–155

Blum G (2010) The Laws of War and the "Lesser Evil". Yale Journal of International Law 35(1): 1–69

Bothe M, Partsch K J, Solf W A (1982) New Rules for Victims of Armed Conflicts Commentary on the Two 1977 Protocols Additional to the Geneva Conventions of 1949. Martinus Nijhoff Publishers, The Hague/Boston

Bothe M, Partsch K J, Solf W A (eds) (2013) New Rules for Victims of Armed Conflicts Commentary on the Two 1977 Protocols Additional to the Geneva Conventions of 1949, 2nd edn. Martinus Nijhoff, Leiden/Boston

Byron C (2011) International Humanitarian Law and Bombing Campaigns: Legitimate Military Objectives and Excessive Collateral Damage. In: Schmitt M, Arimatsu L, McCormack T (eds) Yearbook of International Humanitarian Law—2010. T.M.C. Asser Press, The Hague, pp 175–211

Cannizzaro E (2000) Il principio della proporzionalità nell'ordinamento internazionale. Giuffré, Milan

Cannizzaro E (2014) Proportionality in the Law of Armed Conflict. In: Gaeta P, Clapham A (eds) The Oxford Handbook of International Humanitarian Law. Oxford University Press, Oxford, pp 333–352

Capone F (2021) The International Criminal Law Aspects of the Protection of Global Commons: The Case of Cultural Heritage. In: Iovane M, Amoroso D, Palombino F M, Zarra G (eds) The Protection of General Interests in Contemporary International Law. Oxford University Press, Oxford, pp 211–238

Capone F (2022) Winter has Come: Can It Be Used as a 'Weapon of War' by Russia?, 15 December 2022. http://www.sidiblog.org/2022/12/15/winter-has-come-can-it-be-used-as-a-weapon-of-war-by-russia/. Accessed 19 August 2024

Capone F (2023) The Wave of Russian Attacks on Ukraine's Power Infrastructures: An Opportunity to Infuse Meaningfulness into the Notion of "Dual-use Objects"? European Papers 8(2): 741–754

Cassese A (1998) On the Current Trends towards Criminal Prosecution and Punishment of Breaches of International Humanitarian Law. European Journal of International Law 9: 2–17

Cohen A, Zlotogorski D (2021) Proportionality in International Humanitarian Law: Consequences, Precautions, and Procedures. Oxford University Press, New York

Corn G (2023) 2023 DoD Manual Revision—What's in a Presumption? https://lieber.westpoint.edu/whats-in-a-presumption/. Accessed 16 September 2024

Cotter M (2018) Military Necessity, Proportionality and Dual-Use Objects at the ICTY: A Close Reading of the Prlić et al. Proceedings on the Destruction of the Old Bridge of Mostar. Journal of Conflict & Security Law 1–23

Crawford J W (1997) The law of noncombatant immunity and the targeting of national electrical power systems. The Fletcher Forum of World Affairs 21(2): 101–119

D'Alessandra F, Gillett M (2019) The War Crime of Starvation in Non-International Armed Conflict. Journal of International Criminal Justice 17: 815–847

Darcy S (2014) Judges, Law and War: The Judicial Development of International Humanitarian Law. Cambridge University Press, Cambridge

Dinstein Y (2004) The Conduct of Hostilities under the Law of International Armed Conflict. Cambridge University Press, Cambridge

Dinstein Y (2010) The Conduct of Hostilities under the Law of International Armed Conflict, 2nd edn. Cambridge University Press, Cambridge

Dinstein Y, Dahl A W (2020) Oslo Manual on Select Topics of the Law of Armed Conflict. Springer, Cham

Doswald-Beck L (1989) The Value of the 1977 Geneva Protocols for the Protection of Civilians. In: Meyer M (ed) Armed Conflict and the New Law. British Institute for International and Comparative Law, London

Doswald-Beck L (1995) San Remo Manual on International Law Applicable to Armed Conflicts at Sea. Grotius Publications, Cambridge University Press, Cambridge

Draper G I A D (1973) Military Necessity and Humanitarian Imperatives. The Military Law and the Law of War Review 12(2): 129–151

Drazewska B (2021) Military Necessity in International Cultural Heritage Law. Brill Nijhoff, Leiden/Boston

Fenrick W J (1997) Attacking the Enemy Civilian as a Punishable Offense. Duke Journal of Comparative & International Law 7: 539–569

Fenrick W J (2004) The Prosecution of Unlawful Attack Cases before the ICTY. Yearbook of International Humanitarian Law 7: 153–189

Frulli M (2011) The Criminalization of Offences against Cultural Heritage in Times of Armed Conflict: The Quest for Consistency. European Journal of International Law 22(1): 203–217

Gardam J (2004) Necessity, Proportionality and the Use of Force by States. Cambridge University Press, Cambridge

Gasbarri L (2021) The Concept of an International Organization in International Law. Oxford University Press, Oxford

Gillard EC (2018) Proportionality in the Conduct of Hostilities: The Incidental Harm Side of the Assessment. Research paper, Chatham House. https://www.chathamhouse.org/sites/default/files/publications/research/2018-12-10-proportionality-conduct-hostilities-incidental-harm-gillard-final.pdf. Accessed 15 August 2024

Gioia A (2003) The Development of International Law Relating to the Protection of Cultural Property in the Event of Armed Conflict: The Second Protocol to the 1954 Hague Convention. Italian Yearbook of International Law 9: 25–57

Glanz J, Santora M, Robles P, Willis H, Leatherby L, Koettl C, Khavin D (2023) Why the Evidence Suggests Russia Blew Up the Kakhovka Dam. A dam in Ukraine was designed to withstand almost any attack imaginable — from the outside. The evidence suggests Russia blew it up from within. The New York Times 16 June 2023, https://www.nytimes.com/interactive/2023/06/16/world/europe/ukraine-kakhovka-dam-collapse.html. Accessed 14 August 2024

Goodman R (2022) Clear Error in the Defense Department's Law of War Manual: On Presumptions of Civilian Status, 9 February 2022. https://www.justsecurity.org/80147/clear-error-in-the-defense-departments-law-of-war-manual-on-presumptions-of-civilian-status/. Accessed 12 September 2024

Greenwood C (1993) Customary International Law and the First Geneva Protocol of 1977 in the Gulf Conflict. In: Rowe P (ed) The Gulf War 1990–91 in International and English Law. Routledge, London, pp 63–88

Harvard Air and Missile Warfare Manual (2013) Program on Humanitarian Policy and Conflict Research at Harvard University (HPCR), Manual on International Law Applicable to Air and Missile Warfare. Cambridge University Press, Cambridge

Hathaway O A, Khan A, Revkin M R (2024) The Dangerous Rise of Dual-Use Objects in War. Duke Law School Public Law & Legal Theory Series No. 2024-56. https://ssrn.com/abstract=4938707. Accessed 30 September 2024

Hathaway O A, Lederman M, Schmitt M N (2017) Two Lingering Concerns about the Forthcoming Law of War Manual Amendments, 30 November 2016. https://www.justsecurity.org/35025/lingering-concerns-forthcoming-law-war-manual-amendments/. Accessed 10 September 2024

Hayashi N (2010) Requirements of Military Necessity in International Humanitarian Law and International Criminal Law. Boston University International Law Journal 28(1): 40–140

Hayashi N (2020) Military Necessity. The Art, Morality and Law of War. Cambridge University Press, Cambridge

Henderson I (2009) The Contemporary Law of Targeting. Martinus Nijhoff Publishers, Leiden/Boston

Henderson I, Reece K (2018) Proportionality under International Humanitarian Law (IHL): The 'Reasonable Military Commander' Standard and Reverberating Effects. Vanderbilt Journal of Transnational Law 51(3): 835–855

Henckaerts J M (1999) New Rules for the Protection of Cultural Property in Armed Conflict. International Review of the Red Cross, 81(835): 593–620

Henckaerts J M, Doswald-Beck L (2005) Customary International Humanitarian Law, Volume I: Rules. Cambridge University Press, Cambridge/Geneva

Human Rights Council (2023) Report of the Independent International Commission of Inquiry on Ukraine of 15 March 2023, UN A/HRC/52/62

ICRC (2016) The Principle of Proportionality in the Rules Governing the Conduct of Hostilities under International Humanitarian Law. International Expert Meeting, 22–23 June 2016, Quebec. https://www.icrc.org/sites/default/files/document/file_list/4358_002_expert_meeting_report_web_1_0.pdf. Accessed 1 October 2024

ICRC (2023) The Principles of Humanity and Necessity. https://www.icrc.org/sites/default/files/wysiwyg/war-and-law/02_humanity_and_necessity-0.pdf. Accessed 24 September 2024

Johansen S R (2019) The Military Commander's Necessity: The Law of Armed Conflict and its Limits. Cambridge University Press, Cambridge

Kalshoven F, Zegveld L (2011) Constraints on the Waging of War, 4th edn. Cambridge University Press/ICRC, Cambridge/Geneva

Laursen A (2002) NATO, the War over Kosovo, and the ICTY Investigation. American University International Law Review 17(4): 765–814

Lawless R (2023) 2023 DoD Manual Revision – The Civilian Presumption's Durability, 8 September 2023. https://lieber.westpoint.edu/civilian-presumptions-durability/. Accessed 20 September 2024

Luban D (2013) Military Necessity and the Cultures of Military Law. Leiden Journal of International Law 20(2): 315–349

Lubell N (2015) Current Challenges with regard to the Notion of Military Objective – Legal and Operational Perspectives. In: Greppi E (ed) Conduct of Hostilities: the Practice, the Law and the Future. Franco Angeli, Milan, pp 79–85

Mauri D (2022) Autonomous Weapons Systems and the Protection of the Human Person: An International Law Analysis. Edward Elgar, Cheltenham

Melzer N (2009) Interpretive Guidance on the Notion of Direct Participation in Hostilities under International Humanitarian Law: Adopted by the Assembly of the International Committee of the Red Cross on 26 February 2009. International Review of the Red Cross 90(872): 991–1047

Melzer N (2022) International Humanitarian Law. A Comprehensive Introduction. International Committee of the Red Cross, Geneva

Meron T (2000) The Martens Clause, Principles of Humanity, and Dictates of Public Conscience. The American Journal of International Law 94(1): 78–89

Moffett L (2020) A Bridge Too Far? Attacks against Cultural Property used as Military Objectives as War Crimes: The Prlić et al. Case and the Mostar Bridge. International Criminal Law Review, 20(2): 214–250

Nasu H, Watts S (2023) 2023 DoD Manual Revision – The Civilian Presumption Misnomer, 1 August 2023. https://lieber.westpoint.edu/civilian-presumption-misnomer/

Petrovic J (2013) The Old Bridge of Mostar and Increasing Respect for Cultural Property in Armed Conflict. Martinus Nijhoff Publishers, Leiden/Boston

Pictet J (1985) Development and Principles of International Humanitarian Law. Martinus Nijhoff/ Henry Dunant Institute, Dordrecht/Geneva

Pomson O (2021) Proportionality and Civilian Use of a Military Objective, 24 June 2021. http://opiniojuris.org/2021/06/24/proportionality-and-civilian-use-of-a-military-objective/. Accessed 21 September 2024

Quéguiner J F (2006) Precautions under the Law Governing the Conduct of Hostilities. International Review of the Red Cross 88: 793–821

Robinson I, Nohle E (2016) Proportionality and Precautions in Attack: The Reverberating Effects of Using Explosive Weapons in Populated Areas. International Review of the Red Cross 98 (1): 107–145

Rowe P (2000) Kosovo 1999: The Air Campaign: Have the Provisions of Additional Protocol I Withstood the Test? International Review of the Red Cross 82: 147–174

Salvadego L (2016) Struttura e funzioni della necessità militare nel diritto internazionale. Giappichelli, Turin

Sandoz Y, Swinarski C, Zimmermann B (eds) (1987) Commentary on the Additional Protocols of 8 June 1977 to the Geneva Conventions of 12 August 1949. Martinus Nijhoff Publishers, Geneva

Sassòli M, Cameron L (2006) The Protection of Civilian Objects: Current State of the Law and Issues de lege ferenda. In: Ronzitti N, Venturini G (eds) The Law of Air Warfare: Contemporary Issues. Eleven International, Utrecht, pp 35–74

Sassòli M, Quintin A (2014) Active and Passive Precautions in Air and Missile Warfare. Israel Yearbook on Human Rights 44: 69–123

Schmitt M N (2006) Faultlines in the Law of Attack. In: Breau S, Jachec-Neale A (eds) Testing the Boundaries of International Humanitarian Law. British Institute of International and Comparative Law, London, pp 277–307

Schmitt M N (2010) Military Necessity and Humanity in International Humanitarian Law: Preserving the Delicate Balance. Virginia Journal of International Law 50(4): 795–838

Schmitt M N (ed) (2017) Tallinn Manual 2.0 on the International Law Applicable to Cyber Operations. Cambridge University Press, Cambridge

Schmitt M N (2021) Targeting Dual-Use Structures: An Alternative Interpretation, 28 June 2021. https://lieber.westpoint.edu/targeting-dual-use-structures-alternative/. Accessed 21 September 2024

Schmitt M N (2022a) Ukraine-Symposium—Attacking Power Infrastructure under International Humanitarian Law, 20 October 2022. https://lieber.westpoint.edu/attacking-power-infrastructure-under-international-humanitarian-law/. Accessed 19 August 2024

Schmitt M N (2022b) Ukraine Symposium—Further Thoughts on Russia's Campaign against Ukraine's Power Infrastructure, 25 November 2022. https://lieber.westpoint.edu/further-thoughts-russias-campaign-against-ukraines-power-infrastructure/. Accessed 19 August 2024

Schmitt M N (2022c) Ukraine Symposium—Amnesty International's Allegations of Ukrainian IHL Violations, 8 August 2022. https://lieber.westpoint.edu/amnesty-allegations-ukrainian-ihl-violations/

Schmitt M N (2023) 2023 DoD Manual Revision—Handling Uncertainty in the Law of Attack 2 August 2023. https://lieber.westpoint.edu/handling-uncertainty-in-law-of-attack/. Accessed 14 September 2024

Shue H, Wippman D (2002) Limiting Attacks on Dual-Use Facilities Performing Indispensable Civilian Functions. Cornell International Law Journal 35(3): 553–579

Sutton R (2021) The Humanitarian Civilian: How the Idea of Distinction Circulates Within and Beyond International Humanitarian Law. Oxford University Press, Oxford

Thynne K (2021) Better a War Criminal or a Terrorist? A Comparative Study of War Crimes and Counterterrorism Legislation. International Review of the Red Cross 103 (916–917): 237–266

Ticehurst R (1997) The Martens Clause and the Laws of Armed Conflict. International Review of the Red Cross 317: 125–134

Tignino M, Kebebew T, Pellaton C (2023) International Law and Accountability for the Nova Kakhovka Dam Disaster. https://lieber.westpoint.edu/international-law-accountability-nova-kakhovka-dam-disaster/. Accessed 14 August 2024

UN Security Council (2021) Resolution 2573 (2021), UN Doc. S/RES/2573 (2021)

US DoD (2023) Law of War Manual (June 2015, updated July 2023). https://media.defense.gov/12692023/Jul/31/2003271432/-1/-1/0/DOD-LAW-OF-WAR-MANUAL-JUNE-2015-UPDATED-JULY%202023.PDF. Accessed 4 September 2024

Van Coller A (2024) Redefining Doubt in Cases of Uncertainty: An Analysis of the 2023 US DoD Law of War Manual Revision to the Presumption of Civilian Status in Armed Conflict. Journal of International Humanitarian Action 9(3): 1–15

Van Schaack B (2016) Evaluating Proportionality and Long-Term Civilian Harm under the Laws of War https://www.justsecurity.org/32577/evaluating-proportionality-long-term-civilian-harm-law-war/. Accessed 17 August 2024

Venturini G (2011) Necessity in the Law of Armed Conflict and in International Criminal Law. In: Dekker I F, Hey E (eds) Netherlands Yearbook of International Law 41: 45–78

Venturini G (2017) International Law and Intentional Destruction of Cultural Heritage. In: Pinton S, Zagato L (eds) Cultural Heritage. Scenarios 2015–2017. Edizioni Ca' Foscari, Venice, pp 103–118

Winter E (2020) Pillars not Principles: The Status of Humanity and Military Necessity in the Law of Armed Conflict. Journal of Conflict and Security Law 25 (1): 1–31

Chapter 5
The Centrality of the "Reasonable Military Commander Standard" in the Paradigm Shift

Contents

Abstract Under the IHL framework, the reasonableness standard is traditionally resorted to in the determination of the possible excessiveness of the expected incidental harm with the concrete and direct military advantage anticipated, i.e. during the proportionality assessment. The analysis carried out in the present chapter aims at challenging this narrow view, by arguing that this standard is a transversal one that could, and should, inform the application of all the other IHL principles, i.e. distinction, precautions, military necessity, and humanity (or unnecessary suffering), both during military actions in general and in the specific case of attacks against dual-use objects. As the standard is far from well-settled, this chapter will first provide the reader with a thorough overview of the theoretical underpinnings of reasonableness, and then it will discuss it in combination with each of the key IHL principles. The goal is to define the contours of the "reasonable military commander standard" in a more precise way and detail how it unfolds in the process of targeting dual-use objects. The findings of this chapter ultimately show that there is a sliding scale in the application of the reasonable standard that potentially allows both the actors and those who review the actions undertaken to operate with greater certainty.

Keywords Reasonableness standard · Reasonable military commander · IHL principles · ICTY · Israeli Supreme Court

F. Capone, *Dual-use Objects under International Humanitarian Law: Towards a Paradigm Shift*, https://doi.org/10.1007/978-94-6265-679-6_5

5.1 Introducing the Reasonable Military Commander Standard

Under the IHL framework, the reasonableness standard is traditionally resorted to in the determination of the possible excessiveness of the expected incidental harm with the concrete and direct military advantage anticipated, i.e. during the proportionality assessment.[1] It is hereby argued that this standard is a transversal one that could, and should, inform the application of all the other IHL principles, i.e. distinction, precautions, military necessity, and humanity (or unnecessary suffering), both during military actions in general and in the specific case of attacks against dual-use objects. Notably, the Goldstone Report drafted to appraise the legality of Operation Cast Lead, the 2008 Israeli incursion into Gaza,[2] contains several references to the relevance of the reasonableness standard.[3] Much of the criticism of the findings of the Goldstone Report focused on an improper methodology utilised to "assess the reasonableness of Israeli target selection and engagement",[4] however the issue has never been sufficiently addressed, nor has the doctrine ever worried about possible ramifications of the standard beyond proportionality. Albeit rarely studied and very often overlooked, the reasonableness standard has a pivotal role to play within the IHL framework and deserves to be duly analysed. This chapter will explore the central role played by military commanders, and more in general by those responsible for deciding upon, planning or executing attacks, before, during, and after the qualification of a dual-use object as a legitimate military target. This author believes that the "reasonable military commander standard",[5] must be better, more broadly and more in depth framed and assessed, considering its prominence in guiding all belligerents. As the standard is far from a well-settled concept, this chapter will discuss it first adopting a broader perspective and later in combination with each of the key IHL principles analysed in the previous chapter. The goal is to define this concept's contours in a more precise way and detail how the standard unfolds in the process of targeting dual-use objects.

5.2 Shedding Light on Reasonableness as a Legal Concept

Before diving into the relevance of the reasonableness standard in the LOAC context, it is worth sketching its breadth and scope as a legal concept in general. The difficulties associated with pinning down the notion of reasonableness and applying it in practical settings are not easy to overcome. From a theoretical point of view, the first challenge

[1] Gillard 2018, pp. 21–23.

[2] See Chap. 3, Sect. 3.3.2 in this book.

[3] Corn 2012, p. 497.

[4] Blank 2010, pp. 298–299.

[5] ICTY (TC), *Prosecutor v. Galić*, Judgment and Opinion, 5 December 2003, IT-98-29-T, paras 57–58 (*Prosecutor v. Galić* TC Judgment); ICTY (TC), *Prosecutor v Prlić*, Judgment 9 May 2013, IT-04-74, paras 1583–1584. See also ICRC 2016, pp. 59–60.

stems from defining what reasonableness means as a legal concept, and, even before that, what reasonableness means in general terms. The question is not a trivial one and it has attracted the (moderate) attention of authors like Kant, Rawls, von Wright, Habermas, and Alexy;[6] without, however, paving the way for a uniform approach to the matter.

The motivation behind the lack of more consistent and greater efforts towards understanding reasonableness, is that, as Artosi explains, "reasonableness is not a philosopher's term".[7] Indeed, even on the handful of occasions on which the concept of "reasonableness" is taken up, there is hardly more than a partial characterisation that can be found of its traits. What, then, does it mean to be "reasonable"? The "reasonable person", who rarely appears on the philosophical scene, is depicted as "a great moral character" displaying in every circumstance many "amiable and respectable virtues".[8] Nowhere in philosophical literature is it possible to find such clear-cut definitions of reasonableness as for other concepts that are described as its "twin". As is well known, reasonableness bears a very close relationship with "rationality",[9] but whereas rationality is "goal-oriented", reasonableness, by contrast, is "value-oriented".[10]

As noted by Rawls, reasonableness draws on moral considerations, among others, and cannot be reduced to "correctness of reasoning" or to "instrumental rationality".[11] As von Wright eloquently puts it "the reasonable, is, of course, also rational, but the 'merely rational' is not always reasonable".[12] Though reasonableness needs to be characterised with reference to rationality, it is to be distinguished from the latter.[13] Whereas rationality evokes the idea of a type of decision-making that maximises the utility of an individual, without necessarily taking into account the interests of others, reasonableness includes a sense of justice, the idea of taking into account not only one's own interests but also the legitimate interests of others.[14] Reasonableness implies that "different reasonable assessments of the importance of values and of the appropriateness of means are possible".[15] Such reasonable assessments also cover non-optimal determinations, which may nonetheless remain appropriate or adequate. Indeed, reasonableness leaves room for differences of opinion, for antagonist views of what is needed in given circumstances. Influenced by common sense, reasonableness seeks, in all domains, what is "adequate and may vary over time and across different communities".[16] This infers that, in order for a determination to be reasonable with

[6] Kant 1996; Rawls 1993; von Wright 1993; Habermas 1996; Alexy 1989.
[7] Artosi 2009, p. 69.
[8] Ibid., pp. 69–71.
[9] Alexy 2009, p. 3.
[10] Von Wright 1993, p. 173.
[11] Rawls 1993, p. 48.
[12] Von Wright 1993, p. 173.
[13] Sartor 2009, p. 20.
[14] Barak 2005, p. 199.
[15] Alexy 2009, p. 3.
[16] Perelman 1979, pp. 118–119.

regard to a certain context, culture or form of life, it must also be consonant, or at least not completely dissonant, with the ideas prevailing in that context and in particular, with the norms that are practised in that context.[17]

So, why is there a need for actors that are reasonable rather than just rational? The reason for "resort[ing] to the requirement of reasonableness is the existence of a plurality of factors requiring [evaluation] in respect of their relevance to a common focus of concern".[18] Therefore, reasonableness can be conceived as a concept that comes into play whenever we need to look for a "practical equilibrium",[19] in an attempt to bring into balance different normative possibilities, measures, and arguments in relation to different circumstances. The idea of reasonableness requires, first, that all factors that might be relevant in answering a practical question be considered and, second, that they be assembled in a correct relation to each other. In this way, balancing is identified as the essence of reasonableness. Balancing would, indeed, be "unreasonable" if it were completely subjective, for being reasonable presupposes objectivity at least to a certain degree, that is, it precludes being completely subjective.[20]

Given its inherent complexity, reasonableness is regarded as a transversal legal concept, with widespread ethical and political connotations.[21] Various explicit or implicit values connected to reasonableness are pervasive in public law and private law, constitutional law and international law, and across common law, civil law, and mixed legal systems. It has to be noted that while "reasonableness" is often associated with the common law tradition,[22] it also has deep roots in civil law.[23] Roman law sources referred to the concept of "reasonableness" under different variations, be it *ratio naturalis*, *ratio civilis*, *ratio humanus*, *ratio strictus* or simply *rationabilis* ("reasonableness").[24] A few studies have focused on reasonableness as an element of good faith and the rule of law, but have failed to fully address the growing presence of reasonableness in international law in general, as well as its connection with other normative standards, for example proportionality.[25] Notwithstanding the limited consideration, legal philosophers have stressed the importance of reasonableness in law,[26] and at the same time, practitioners, in particular judges and lawyers, have used reasonableness to fill *lacunae* in existing positive law.[27] Yet, and in spite

[17] Sartor 2009, p. 21.

[18] MacCormick 2005, p. 173.

[19] Alexy 2009, p. 13.

[20] Ibid., pp. 8–12.

[21] Corten and Kolb 2021.

[22] Craig 2013, p. 131.

[23] Garrido-Muñoz 2017, pp. 461–463.

[24] Luchetti et al. 2010, pp. 55–62.

[25] Cannizzaro 2000, pp. 166–202; Vadi 2018, p. 130.

[26] Craig 2013; Young 2014.

[27] Sartor 2009; Corten and Kolb 2021.

of its pervasiveness, reasonableness in international legal studies is a concept that has received scant attention so far.[28]

It would be interesting to further explore the reasons why the multifaceted and multilayered nature of reasonableness, which at the very least doubles as both a theoretical concept and as a legal standard that can be applied in practical contexts, so far has not been the object of extensive, nor comprehensive analysis.[29] The detractors of this legal concept, as summarised by Vadi, have raised three main criticisms against reasonableness: (1) vagueness; (2) complexity; and (3) ambivalence.[30] The first criticism tackles reasonableness' vagueness. In light of it, it has been noted that the distinction between what is reasonable and what is not, can be "subjective, arbitrary and ultimately indefensible".[31] In the absence of strict parameters, State authorities are left unbound, as the reasonableness criterion does not articulate a clear-cut methodology, nor does it provide a well-structured analytical framework. Authors have noted how reasonableness is an essentially complex and contested concept,[32] a quality the specifics of which have been understood in a number of different and, at times, competing ways; for instance when reasonableness constitutes a practical guide for state behaviour,[33] serving as both an instrument to preserve the margin of appreciation of States and a tool for courts to curb the exercise of discretionary power.[34] At the same time, the application of reasonableness has been deemed to be extremely challenging, also in light of its ambivalence, to the point where it has been dubbed as "one of the most intangible notions" in the jurisprudence of the ICJ, and probably of any judicial body.[35] Nonetheless, the ICJ has mentioned the notion frequently. So far the Court has referred to reasonableness with respect to its own procedural law in the *Armed Activities in the Territory of the Congo* case.[36] Moreover, the ICJ has invoked "reasonableness" in relation to treaty interpretation, maritime delimitation, compensation issues, and the review of State discretionary powers.[37] Looking more closely at the ICJ case law, in the widely scrutinised *Barcelona Traction* case the Court famously held that "in the field of diplomatic protection as in all other fields of international law, it is necessary that the law be *applied reasonably*".[38]

---

[28] Salmon 1982; Corten 1999; Ortino 2005; Bongiovanni et al. 2009; Craig 2013; Young 2014; Vadi 2018; Corten and Kolb 2021.

[29] Salmon 1982; Corten 1999.

[30] Vadi 2018, pp. 147–151.

[31] Henckels 2015, p. 123.

[32] Young 2014, p. 2.

[33] Contiades and Fotiadou 2012, p. 678.

[34] Tully 2015, p. 551.

[35] Garrido-Muñoz 2017, p. 457.

[36] ICJ, *Armed Activities in the Territory of the Congo* (Democratic Republic of the Congo v. Uganda), Order of 29 November 2001, ICJ Reports 660, paras 48–49.

[37] Garrido-Muñoz 2017, p. 458.

[38] ICJ, *Barcelona Traction* (Belgium v. Spain), Judgment of 5 February 1970, ICJ Reports 3, 48, para 93 (emphasis added).

In the case *Concerning Elettronica Sicula S.p.A.* (ELSI), dealing with a dispute arising out of the requisition by the Government of Italy of the plant owned by two US corporations, the ICJ declared that if an act of a public authority is "unreasonable or arbitrary under municipal law", this does not necessarily mean that such act is also arbitrary under international law.[39] In the *Gabcikovo-Nagymaros* case, the Court invoked the customary law formula that every riparian state of an international watercourse has a right to an "equitable and reasonable share" of the natural resources of the river.[40] More recently in the *Whaling in the Antarctic* case the ICJ concluded that the design and implementation of Japan's whaling programme "was not reasonable in relation to achieving its stated objectives".[41] The judgement is remarkable because for the first time, "reasonableness", qualified by the ICJ as "objective reasonableness", has been critical in adjudicating a high-profile case dealing with the review of State discretionary powers in the implementation of a treaty. The Court, by positing a test of "objective reasonableness" as the applicable standard of review, has attracted significant criticism, with Tully in particular commenting that for the Court to employ this standard of review "would subvert its judicial function, exceed authority and take it beyond its expertise".[42] Other scholars have instead argued that, while being inherently vague, reasonableness gives a justifiable degree of discretion to judges, "enabling them to make difficult adjudicatory choices without departing from the legal framework under consideration".[43]

Notwithstanding the ICJ's reliance on the reasonableness standard on several occasions, scant efforts have been made to contribute to making reasonableness a less volatile concept. The lack of thorough consideration is surprising given the recurrence of reasonableness in different fields of international law as well as the many functions that it plays. Corten and Kolb single out the different functions of reasonableness as i) a tool to enhance flexibility in the application of legal rules, ii) a gap filler in the body of applicable law, iii) a standard for actions of some organs of the States and iv) a standard of evaluation for the review of the exercise of powers by States.[44] The following examples, which of course do not claim to be exhaustive, will hopefully provide some additional insight on how these functions unfold in different domains of international law.

Starting with human rights law, it is certainly possible to affirm that the notion of reasonableness is central to both civil, political, and cultural rights as well as economic, social, and cultural rights. In relation to the former set of human rights, reasonableness is mainly used as a standard for actions of some organs of the State.

---

[39] ICJ, *Concerning Elettronica Sicula SpA* (ELSI) (United States v. Italy) Judgment of 20 July 1989, ICJ Reports 76, para 124.

[40] ICJ, *Gabcikovo-Nagymaros* (Hungary v. Slovakia), Judgment of 25 September 1997, ICJ Reports 7, 53, para 75.

[41] ICJ, *Whaling in the Antarctic* case (Australia v Japan, New Zealand intervening), Judgment of 31 March 2014, ICJ Reports 226, paras 67–68.

[42] Tully 2015, p. 546.

[43] Garrido-Muñoz 2017, p. 459.

[44] Corten and Kolb 2021.

For instance, Article 9 (3) of the International Covenant on Civil and Political Rights (ICCPR) requires that "[a]nyone arrested or detained on a criminal charge' be tried 'within a *reasonable* time".[45] With regard to the latter, reasonableness has been predominantly employed as a standard of evaluation. The Optional Protocol (OP) to the International Covenant on Economic, Social and Cultural Rights (IESCR)[46] is the first complaint mechanism of a core human rights treaty to specify a standard of review to be used in the assessment of alleged States' violations,[47] providing for a "reasonableness test" in Article 8(4). According to Liebenberg the major advantage of the "reasonableness model of review" in the context of human rights claims is that it acknowledges that "a variety of policy options are available to States in fulfilling these rights".[48] There is no single correct, optimal solution to the contextual diversity and complexity of economic, social and cultural rights, but at the same time the open-textured nature of reasonableness as a review standard allows adjudicatory bodies to develop flexible criteria or factors, on a case-by-case basis, that trigger heightened scrutiny of the State's justifications for violations of "minimum core obligations".[49] Domestic courts have also relied on various notions of minimum levels of social rights to adjudicate cases. Prominent examples include the right to an *Existenzminimum* based on human dignity and the social State principle by the German Federal Constitutional Court, and the *mínimo vital* doctrine of the Colombian Constitutional Court.[50]

In the law of the sea, reasonableness is often cited and used in a wide array of contexts. Several provisions of the United Nations Convention on the Law of the Sea (UNCLOS)[51] make explicit reference to reasonableness. For example, Article 60(4) of UNCLOS speaks of "reasonable safety zones" around artificial islands, installations, and structures in the State's exclusive economic zone. Article 79(2) talks about States' right "to take reasonable measures for the exploration of the continental shelf"; whilst Article 98(1)(b) mentions the actions that can be "reasonably expected" of the master of a ship required to rescue persons in distress. Moreover, the International Tribunal for the Law of the Sea (ITLOS) has not shied away from the principle of reasonableness, for instance when assessing the enforcement measures implemented by the coastal State in its exclusive economic zone under Article 73 of the Convention, which, at para 2, states that "arrested vessels and their crews shall be promptly released upon the posting of *reasonable bond* or other security".[52]

[45] International Covenant on Civil and Political Rights, opened for signature 16 December 1966, 999 UNTS 171, entered into force 23 March 1976 (ICCPR).

[46] International Covenant on Economic, Social and Cultural Rights, opened for signature 16 December 1966, 993 UNTS 3, entered into force 3 January 1976 (ICESCR).

[47] Griffey 2011.

[48] Liebenberg 2020, pp. 51–55.

[49] Messineo 2012; Magi 2021.

[50] Liebenberg 2023.

[51] United Nations Convention on the Law of the Sea, opened for signature on 10 December 1982, 1833 UNTS 397, entered into force on 16 November 1994 (UNCLOS).

[52] Ikeshima 2009; Jianjun 2020.

Reasonableness plays a prominent role also in investment treaty law and arbitration law.[53] Reasonableness appears in the text of investment treaties under different provisions. For example, many international investment agreements (IIAs) prohibit the adoption of "unreasonable or discriminatory measures", affecting foreign investors and/or their investments.[54] Other IIAs require State parties to bestow "equitable and reasonable treatment" to foreign investors and/or their investments, or link reasonableness to full protection and security. Thus, arbitral tribunals have relied on the concept of reasonableness extensively. Such use in investor–state arbitration reflects what Vadi describes as a "triadic structure of reasonableness" in this field.[55] First, arbitrators have used the reasonableness test to assess the legitimacy of State conduct and the legitimate expectations of foreign investors. Second, arbitral tribunals have also referred to the need for reasonable interpretation of the relevant investment treaty provisions. Finally, reasonableness has also been invoked regarding procedural matters, for example to determine whether the arbitration claim amounted to an abuse of rights.

So far IHL represents one of the areas of international law in which the concept of reasonableness has been subject to less scrutiny, at least until very recently. This is, however, in contrast with the growing awareness towards every element that contributes to the "humanisation of IHL", which has been registered in the past two decades.[56] In particular, it is undeniable that the recognition of the convergence between IHL and human rights law,[57] as well as the affirmation of international criminal law (ICL),[58] have greatly contributed to shaping a new understanding of the law of armed conflict. This progress has opened the doors to new developments, also with respect to the role of individuals, broadening the focus from accountability to the wider spectrum of capabilities of the decision makers, which, indeed, covers also the standard of reasonableness.

5.3 Reasonableness as a Transversal Standard Under International Humanitarian Law

Reasonableness under the IHL framework has been employed as a standard for action of military commanders in the proportionality assessment and as a standard of evaluation for the review of the decisions made in this context. As already mentioned, the role of the individual actor/decision maker/executor has become increasingly relevant to assess the application of IHL rules. Most recently this central position has been revamped, without exploring its full potential, in the discussion concerning Russia's

[53] See Vadi 2018; Palombino 2018, pp. 91–92; Corten and Kolb 2021.

[54] Vadi 2018, pp. 151–152.

[55] Ibid., p. 153.

[56] Meron 2000.

[57] Greppi 1996, p. 473; Pedrazzi 2012, p. 79.

[58] Cassese 1998, pp. 2–4; Greppi 2012, pp. 10–14; Droege and Giorgou 2022, pp. 1818–1820.

attacks against Ukraine electrical infrastructures since October 2022.[59] Commenting on the events in Ukraine, experts have suggested that the Russian military commanders who are planning the attacks against power infrastructures "appear to be either ignoring IHL altogether or fairly incompetent".[60] As is well known, the attacks have been labelled as violations of IHL, and in particular of the principles of precautions and proportionality, two of the pillars of international humanitarian law. Obviously, the attacks' abidance with the principle of distinction has also been called into question due to Russia's swift qualification of all electrical infrastructures as military objectives. More in general, the standard of reasonableness may, and shall, be applied to all key IHL principles. However, it is still debatable if the same degree of reasonableness is expected by all of them, or if there is a "sliding scale" which allows differentiation regarding the level required based on the specific aim that needs to be fulfilled. The next sub-sections seek to provide an answer to this question, in view of dual-use objects' peculiarities. To this end, the analysis will identify and discuss the different nuances of the reasonableness standard that have emerged from the existing norms, the case law of the judicial bodies that have dealt with the issue so far, in particular the ICTY and the Israeli Supreme Court, and the relevant scholarship. When the research does not result in a more precise qualification of the standard, it is argued that the one applicable is that of "a reasonably well-informed person in the circumstances of the actual [original decision-maker]".[61]

5.3.1 *Reasonableness and the Principle of Distinction*

With regard to the principle of distinction, which lies at the heart of this study and has been the object of a thorough analysis in the previous chapters,[62] it is by now well established that as far as dual-use objects are concerned—such as civilian means of transportation and communication which can be used for military purposes—practice considers that the classification of these objects depends, in the final analysis, on the application of the definition of military objectives. International law does not currently identify the level of certainty required to lawfully attack an object. Therefore, someone needs to make a value judgment that will lead to the decision to target, or not, a given object. As already clarified, the process of targeting involves all of LOAC's core principles—precautions, proportionality, and military necessity, unnecessary suffering/humanity—and first and foremost distinction.[63] As explained by Corn the targeting process is "made in a myriad of contexts, sometimes involving split-second decisions by soldiers at the proverbial 'tip of the spear', sometimes

[59] Capone 2023.

[60] Schmitt 2022.

[61] Henderson and Reece 2018, p. 842.

[62] See especially Chap. 1, Sect. 1.3 and Chap. 3 in this book.

[63] See Chap. 2, Sect. 2.1 in this book. See also Solis 2010, p. 519.

involving complex and deliberate processes at high levels of command, and sometimes involving summarized processes at those same levels of command to address time-sensitive targeting requirements".[64] Adhering to the IHL framework, the decision to attack must be based first on the judgment that the object of the attack—a person, place, or thing—qualifies as a lawful military objective, i.e. that the principle of distinction is correctly applied and duly respected.

In general terms it is possible to affirm that the person who identifies that target may be any soldier or commander.[65] He or she may be on the ground and involved in a current combat operation, or he or she may be an Air Force officer who is planning an attack and identifies potential targets that support the operation. When States are parties to a coalition, as it happened with the 1991 Gulf War and with the NATO bombing campaign against the FRY,[66] States will always retain power over their own contingents. This national "interference" is not limited to issues of prosecution and disciplinary actions, but it also covers core activities of combat operations, for example the decision on whether to strike or not a certain objective. Often referred to as the "red card holder" procedure, it entails that the use of military assets remains subject to national approval in relation to combat missions.[67] As explained by De Cock, the final responsibility to engage national air assets to strike military targets rests with the national "red card holder" and this has an impact on the decision-making process and on the coalition commanders. To provide a significant example, LTG M. Short reports that during NATO's Operation Allied Force "[...] target decisions were taken out of our hands. Target decisions were made by the president of the United States, the prime minister of Great Britain, the president of France, and the president of Germany, and targets were just issued to me".[68]

Regardless of who is the decision-maker and/or the actual "targeter" in each scenario, it is important to stress that the principle of distinction binds all the parties to an armed conflict, be it an IAC or a NIAC, and everyone in their ranks. Military Manuals make clear that "a soldier cannot fight without knowing exactly who is a combatant and who is not",[69] and, equally, that "commanders shall at all times distinguish between the civilian population and combatants".[70] Practitioners are usually adamant that it cannot be expected that armed conflict will be reduced to the point where a commander (or a soldier) can act only when he or she is 100 per cent certain in all cases about the nature of an object.[71] Whereas this is, to some extent

[64] Corn 2012, p. 438.

[65] Henderson 2009, p. 164.

[66] See Chap. 2, Sects. 2.4 and 2.5 in this book.

[67] De Cock 2016, p. 254.

[68] Short 2002, p. 25.

[69] Cameroon, Droit des conflits armés et droit international humanitaire, Manuel de l'instructeur en vigueur dans les forces de défense, Ministère de la Défense, Présidence de la République, Etat-major des Armées, 2006, p. 21.

[70] Canada, The Law of Armed Conflict at the Operational and Tactical Level, Office of the Judge Advocate General, 1999, p. 4-1, para 4.

[71] Henderson 2009, p. 164.

at least, understandable although far from endearing, the standard of reasonableness can play a prominent role to limit the amount of discretion on the part of the combatants engaged in this determination. The claim that "[t]he degree of doubt necessary to preclude an attack is that which would cause *a reasonable attacker in the same or similar circumstances* to abstain from ordering or executing an attack",[72] is simply untenable as it circularly refers to the same standard without qualifying it. The 1987 ICRC Commentary contains a reference to the importance of the subjective assessment in relation to the application of the principle of distinction. The Commentary, however, does not shed much light on the issue, as it affirms that

> […] the text adopted by the Diplomatic Conference largely *relies on the judgment of soldiers who will have to apply these provisions*. It is true that there are clear-cut situations where there is no possibility of doubt, but there are also borderline cases where the responsible authorities could hesitate. In such circumstances *the general aim of the Protocol should be borne in mind, i.e., the protection of the civilian population*. In any case an essential step forward has been taken in that belligerents *can no longer arbitrarily and unilaterally declare as a military objective any civilian object*, as happened all too often in the past.[73]

The ICRC Commentary further details the level of information required for deciding upon the target identification, by affirming that

> […] the identification of the objective, particularly when it is located at a great distance, should be carried out *with great care*. Admittedly, those who plan or decide upon such an attack will base their decision on information given them, and they cannot be expected to have personal knowledge of the objective to be attacked and of its exact nature. However, this does not detract from their responsibility, and in case of doubt, even if there is only slight doubt, they must call for additional information […].[74]

Albeit not resolutive, the Commentary's contribution is still relevant to the extent to which it expressly ties the subjective threshold to the aim of protecting the civilian population. A crucial step in the direction of adding more substance to the reasonableness standard in the application of the principle of distinction, comes once again from the ICTY's case law. In its findings in the *Galić* case the ICTY provides some clarity on the matter, by stating that

> [i]n case of doubt as to whether an object which is normally dedicated to civilian purposes is being used to make an effective contribution to military action, it shall be presumed not to be so used. The Trial Chamber understands that such an object shall not be attacked *when it is not reasonable to believe,* in the circumstances of the person contemplating the attack, including the information available to the latter, that *the object is being used* to make an effective contribution to military action.[75]

This often-quoted extract of the judgment, which has already been discussed in other sections of this work,[76] explains that a commander is required to come

[72] Schmitt 2008, pp. 56–57 (emphasis added).

[73] Sandoz et al. 1987, p. 638, para 2037.

[74] Ibid., para 2195.

[75] *Prosecutor v. Galić* TC Judgment, para 51.

[76] See Chap. 1, Sect. 1.3.3 in this book.

to a "reasonable belief" about whether the object meets the criteria for being a military objective. Notably, both the ICTY and the working definition of dual-use objects provided for in this work exclude that objects that play a civilian function, as discussed in the previous chapter,[77] could be transformed into military objectives by applying the purpose criterion.[78] This view is based on the necessity to make the definition of military objectives compatible with all the relevant rules and principles of IHL, as explained in Chap. 3 of this book. Therefore, the approach authoritatively brought forward by the International Law Association Study Group (ILA-SG) in 2017 is, respectfully, rejected as a reasonable commander cannot conclude that a specific object, currently used by the civilian population will, in the future, be used for contributing to the enemy's military action.[79] Notwithstanding the caveats added by the ILA-SG, i.e. that the information must refer to a specific object (and not a class of objects) and each object must individually fulfil the definition of military objective to become a lawful target,[80] this author considers the purpose criterion, even if understood in the restrictive meaning of "intended future use" of an object,[81] as too vague to justify both the loss of protection of the civilian objective *per se* and the potential (direct and indirect) damage to the civilian population. Furthermore, and as already discussed elsewhere in this book,[82] the applicability of the "purpose" criterion is also expunged from the "doubt rule", i.e. the presumption of civilian status enshrined in Article 52(3) of API. In the revised US Department of Defense (DoD) Law of War Manual the presumption of civilian status is presented as "the starting point for the commander or other decision-maker" for the proposed attack.[83] The decision-maker thus bears a legal responsibility to "assess whether persons or objects are military objectives", and, based on the presumption, a person or object may not be attacked "unless the available information evaluated in good faith indicates" lawful targetability.[84] The Manual goes on to explain that an assessment of targetability must rest upon "an honest and genuine belief" that the proposed target is a military objective.[85] The HPCR Manual on International Law Applicable to Air and Missile Warfare also provides that

> "[I]n case of doubt as to whether an object which is ordinarily dedicated to civilian purposes is being used for military purposes, it may only be attacked if, based on all the information

[77] See Chap. 4, Sect. 4.2 in this book.

[78] See Chap. 3, Sect. 3.4 in this book.

[79] International Law Association Study Group on the Conduct of Hostilities in the 21st Century, Final Report presented at the 77th ILA Conference in Johannesburg, South Africa (ILA-SG Report), p. 8, https://www.ila-hq.org/en_GB/documents/ila-final-report-25-june-2017 (accessed 1 September 2024).

[80] Ibid.

[81] See Chap. 1, Sect. 1.3.2 in this book.

[82] Ibid.; see also Chap. 4, Sect. 4.5.1 in this book.

[83] US DoD 2023.

[84] Ibid., para 5.4.3.4.

[85] Ibid., para 5.4.3.2.

> reasonably available to the commander at the time, *there are reasonable grounds to believe* that it has become and remains a military objective".[86]

Like many other such judgments under IHL, any rebuttal of the presumption of civilian status must be based on the attacker's reasonable assessment based on the information available at the time.[87] As stated also in the commentary to the HPCR Manual, the status of the object believed to be used for military purposes need not be established beyond reasonable doubt.[88] Rather a "reasonable conclusion to the effect that an object is being so used" will suffice.[89] Nonetheless, it is not enough to ascertain whether a commander or soldier considered all the feasible information in support of his decision, but instead the assessment should be made on both the *quantum* and *quality* of the information upon which the decision was taken. Corn explains that this entails a good faith commitment to gather "*as much information* related to potential targets as possible and *to assess that information as thoroughly as possible* given the conditions of combat".[90] Hence, the standard of "reasonable belief" calls for the verification of the two prongs of the military objectives test based on information that satisfies both the quantitative criterion, i.e. as much as possible, and the qualitative one, as thoroughly assessed as possible.

The qualification of the reasonableness standard applicable to the principle of distinction is hence developed by the ICTY in a passage dedicated to dual-use objects and is also enshrined in the US DoD Manual. Furthermore, in the maritime environment—where enemy and neutral merchant vessels may be targeted if they make an effective contribution to the enemy's military effort by their purpose or use and if targeting them yields a definite military advantage—[91] both the San Remo Manual on International Law Applicable to Armed Conflicts at Sea and the 2023 Newport Manual on the Law of Naval Warfare state that before targeting a neutral vessel the attacker must first have "a reasonable belief" that it is carrying contraband or attempting to breach a blockade.[92] The validity of this standard in the context of the principle of distinction is widely supported also by the doctrine, with authors like Haque claiming that "states should embrace this dictum as legally valid, thereby incorporating the *reasonable belief threshold* into customary international law".[93]

86 Harvard Air and Missile Warfare Manual 2013, Rule 12(b) p. 91.

87 Blank 2018, p. 333.

88 Harvard Air and Missile Warfare Manual 2013, Rule 12(b) p. 92.

89 Ibid.

90 Corn 2012, p. 496 (emphasis added).

91 See Doswald-Beck 1995, para 40.

92 Ibid., para 67(a); Kraska and Pedrozo 2023, p. 176. See also Schmitt and Widmar 2016, p. 133.

93 Haque 2017, p. 134 (emphasis added).

5.3.2 Reasonableness and the Principle of Precautions

As already discussed in the previous chapter, Article 57 of API enshrines the key elements of the so-called "active" precautions, or "precautions in attacks". As the 1976 US Air Force Pamphlet correctly states, "[p]recautionary measures are not a substitute for the general immunity of the civilian population, but an attempt to give effect to the immunity of civilians and the requirements of military necessity".[94] The principle of precautions in attacks comprises different components, with the goal to operationalise most weapons law and targeting law rules.[95] A wide array of precautionary rules can be identified both in treaty and customary IHL.[96] First, Article 57(1) requires belligerents to exercise "constant care" in the conduct of military operations to spare the civilian population, civilians, and civilian objects.[97] Unsurprisingly, no definition is provided of the term "constant care". However, it is commonly understood as a "general and continuous obligation" to respect the civilian population.[98] In other words, the provision enshrines an obligation for commanders and others involved in military operations to "always bear in mind that civilians and civilian objects may be harmed as a result of the operations",[99] and, therefore, to take "all feasible precautions to avoid, and in any event to minimize, incidental loss of civilian life, injury to civilians and damage to civilian objects".[100] As a second rule, it is required that the parties involved in a IAC or NIAC "do everything feasible"[101] to verify that selected targets fit in the category of military objectives,[102] and abstain from indiscriminate attacks.[103] Third, the rule enshrined in para 2(a)(2) of Article 57 and echoed in the ICRC study on customary IHL imposes the choice of means and methods of warfare with a view to minimising or avoiding collateral damage.[104] Fourth, precautionary rules require parties to a conflict to both refrain from attacking and suspend or cancel attacks when it becomes evident that these cannot be conducted anymore in a way that is consistent with the rules on distinction and proportionality.[105] Fifth, belligerents are required to refrain from deciding to launch any attack which may be expected to violate the principle of proportionality.[106] Sixth, when attacks are expected to affect the civilian population, and unless circumstances do not make it impossible, parties are obliged to give "effective advance warning" on the purpose

[94] Cited in Sassòli and Quintin 2014, p. 72.
[95] Mauri 2022, p. 155.
[96] Henckaerts and Doswald-Beck 2005, Rules 15–21.
[97] Article 57(1) of API.
[98] Neuman 2018, p. 76.
[99] Ibid., p. 77.
[100] Ibid., Rule 15, p. 51.
[101] Ibid., Rule 15, p. 54.
[102] Article 57(2)(a)(i) of API.
[103] Article 57(2)(a)(i) of API.
[104] Article 57(2)(a)(ii) of API; Henckaerts and Doswald-Beck 2005, Rule 17, p. 56.
[105] Article 57(2)(b) of API. Henckaerts and Doswald-Beck 2005, Rule 19, p. 60.
[106] Article 57(2)(a)(iii) of API; Henckaerts and Doswald-Beck 2005, Rule 18, p. 58.

of limiting civilians' exposure to avoidable harm.[107] Seventh, according to Article 57(3) of API "when a choice is possible between several military objectives for obtaining a similar military advantage, the objective to be selected shall be that the attack on which may be expected to cause the least danger to civilian lives and to civilian objects".

Finally, but this last precautionary rule is binding only for States parties to API as it has not attained the status of a customary IHL norm, "in the conduct of military operations at sea or in the air, each Party to the conflict shall [...] take *all reasonable precautions* to avoid losses of civilian lives and damage to civilian objects".[108] As reported in the 1987 ICRC Commentary, this provision is concerned with the risk that military operations at sea or in the air may endanger the civilian population and civilian objects,[109] referring to the effects of hostilities between adverse fleets and/or adverse military aircraft. Notably, the Commentary affirms that the term "reasonable precautions" is "slightly different from and a little less far-reaching than the expression 'take all feasible precautions'", used in para 2 of Article 57. Unfortunately, the Commentary fails to better address this "tenuous" nuance, and this provision has been generally overlooked by the doctrine as it appears merely to reaffirm the rules that exist to protect civilians in such situations. As noted by Mauri and other authors,[110] it is clear that the notion of "feasibility" plays a particularly crucial role in determining the scope and breadth of all the rules on precautions, a reading that is authoritatively affirmed by the ICRC study on customary IHL.[111] Even though the notion of feasibility has not been defined, it has been interpreted by many States as being limited to "those precautions which are *practicable or practically possible*, taking into account all circumstances ruling at the time, including humanitarian and military considerations".[112] Albeit some authors equate it to reasonableness,[113] it is argued here that the two concepts are separated, with feasibility exercising a supporting role to the degree to which it contributes to flashing out some of the elements of the reasonableness standard in the various contexts in which it is applied. More in detail, and in light of the combination of objective and subjective elements that characterises the reasonableness standard,[114] in this author's view feasibility is crucial to the former, for instance in the process of gathering and verifying information, whereas the latter necessarily requires a value judgment that belongs to the subjective sphere, allowing the reasonable actor to make "reasonable use of the information available".[115]

Feasibility, hence, pertains to all aspects of the precautions in attack requirements, and has a bearing in setting the adequate standard of reasonableness for each of them,

---

[107] Article 57(2)(c) of API.

[108] See Article 57(4) of API.

[109] Sandoz et al. 1987, p. 686, para 2230.

[110] Mauri 2022, p. 155; Schmitt 2006, pp. 301–303; Thurnher 2018.

[111] Henckaerts and Doswald-Beck 2005, Rules 15–21.

[112] Ibid., Rule 15, p. 54 (emphasis added).

[113] Mauri 2022, pp. 154–155.

[114] Cannizzaro 2014, p. 340.

[115] *Prosecutor v. Galić* TC Judgment, para 58.

starting with the verification of the targets. Considering the relevance of the rules on precautions for the protection of dual-use objects, and despite the lesser attention devoted to them in comparison with the principle of distinction and proportionality, the next sub-sections will offer a thorough reading of each measure in light of the reasonable standard required of military commanders. The analysis will not cover the rule of precaution that imposes the obligation to refrain from deciding to launch disproportionate attacks. The reason is that, in this author's view, the same standard of reasonableness that finds application in the proportionality assessment should be employed also in this context.[116] Said standard, as will be explained in more detail, should also consider the reasonably foreseeable reverberating effects of an attack.

5.3.2.1 Verifying the Objectives to Be Attacked

As mentioned above, the law fails to establish the level of certainty required to identify a military target and to "verify" its legitimacy at the later stage.[117] As stated in the previous section, regarding the principle of distinction, the jurisprudence of the ICTY has identified the threshold of "reasonable belief" as the applicable standard. In the context of precautions in attacks, it is required that those who plan or decide upon an attack to do everything feasible to subsequently verify that the objectives to be attacked are still "neither civilians nor civilian objects and are not subject to special protection but are military objectives within the meaning of para 2 of Article 52 and that it is not prohibited by the provisions of this Protocol to attack them."[118]

As far as the subjects that shall make the determination is concerned, at the Diplomatic Conference leading to the adoption of the Additional Protocols several States, including Switzerland, Austria, and the UK, expressed concerns that the obligations imposed by Article 57(2) on "those who plan or decide upon an attack" apply only to "commanding officers at the battalion or group level and above".[119] However, the 1987 ICRC Commentary departs from this view, by stating that "the high command of an army has the duty to instruct personnel adequately so that the latter, even if of low rank, can act correctly in the situations envisaged".[120] Commanders and the military staff officers, which often include military legal advisors who advise them, instinctively focus "on the facts and circumstances available at the time these decisions are made to frame their judgments as to the legality of engaging proposed targets".[121]

On a more substantial level, the ICRC study on customary IHL clarifies that the principle of distinction "inherently requires respect" for the precautionary rule

[116] Robinson and Nohle 2016, pp. 118–119; Gillard 2018.

[117] Ibid., p. 109.

[118] Article 57(2)(a)(i) of API. See also Article 13(1) APII, Rule 15 of the ICRC study on customary IHL.

[119] Ibid., p. 54.

[120] Sandoz et al. 1987, p. 680, para 2197.

[121] Ibid.

concerning the verification of targets,[122] hence it is logical to assume that the same standard of reasonableness should find application. It is thus argued here that the "reasonable belief standard", which is employed in the phase of contemplating an attack, remains valid also when said attack is conducted and the attacker must verify if the target remains legitimate.

5.3.2.2 Choosing the Means and Methods of Attack

Concerning the precautionary rule that deals with the choice of means and methods of attack, as reported in the ICRC study the examples of the application of this rule include "considerations about the timing of attacks, avoiding combat in populated areas, the selection of means of warfare proportionate to the target, the use of precision weapons and target selection".[123] There are several means and methods which might be relevant in this regard. The first is the gathering of information concerning the target or the collateral damage anticipated, to which the considerations made above find application. In addition, when executing an attack, the timing of the attack might be critical in saving civilian lives.[124] For example, when attacking a bridge it is arguably correct to affirm that there is a precautionary requirement to attack when civilians are not expected to be crossing it (most likely during night time), or in case of attacks against a factory, a precautionary requirement is to attack when the factory is not operating (if this is feasible), in order to save the lives of the civilians workers. As for "weaponeering",[125] a commander needs to determine which weapon to use and in what way to seek to achieve a specific level of damage to a given target. Compliance with this obligation will of course depend on the context, but it will require an appraisal of the foreseeable effects of the available weapon systems, in view of their technical characteristics and the expected circumstances of their use. This should also encompass a reflection on the way in which the technical features of each weapon can be manipulated, to minimise the foreseeable direct and indirect effects on civilians, "including the type and size of the warhead, the type of fuse, the delivery system, the distance from which the weapon is launched, as well as the angle and the timing of the attack".[126] As an example, Schmitt and Widmar report that carbon filament bombs can be used to interrupt electricity "with far less collateral damage than regular bombs, while cyber operations are especially useful in avoiding collateral damage".[127] Shedding further light on the issue, Rogers, quoting the British Defence Doctrine, affirms that

> If there is a choice of weapons or methods of attack available, *a commander should select* those which are most likely to avoid, or at least minimize, incidental civilian casualties or

---

[122] Henckaerts and Doswald-Beck 2005, Rule 15, p. 53.

[123] Henckaerts and Doswald-Beck 2005, Rule 17, p. 58.

[124] Neuman 2018, p. 80.

[125] Ibid.

[126] Robinson and Nohle 2016, p. 139.

[127] Schmitt and Widmar 2014, p. 402; see also Pascucci 2017.

> damage [...] there may be occasions when a commander will have to accept a higher level of risk to his own forces in order to avoid or reduce collateral damage to the enemy's civil population.[128]

A significant example concerning the modality of employment of weapons is that of the cluster munitions by aircraft flying above 15,000 feet by NATO aircraft during the bombing campaign in Kosovo. Commenting on this, Benvenuti notes that the height (or range) from which certain weapons are employed will affect their accuracy as "[t]his is an altitude which makes it difficult to select accurately military objectives in the targeted area, and to control properly the trajectory of the projectiles, in conformity with the principle of distinction".[129] Lacking more precise input on the standard required to fulfil this legal obligation, it is safe to assume that in this case the precautionary rule demands that the military commanders and soldiers exercise "reasonable care" when implementing precautions that deal with weapon choice and how the weapon is employed.

5.3.2.3 Cancelling or Suspending an Attack

A further precautionary obligation requires parties to a conflict to do everything feasible to cancel or suspend an attack if it becomes apparent that the target is not a military objective or that the attack may be expected to violate proportionality. Upon ratification of API, the United Kingdom stated that this obligation only applied to "those who have the authority and practical possibility to cancel or suspend the attack".[130] The doctrine has not reached a unanimous stance on the matter. Fenrick for example is of the view that the personnel who are required to take action to cancel or suspend an attack under article 57(2)(b) API are those who are "higher in the chain of command and, possibly, those subordinates with a sufficient knowledge of all aspects of the attack to determine that excessive incidental obligation as imposed upon anyone who has effective control over the attack".[131] He further affirms that not every member of the armed forces "may have the authority to cancel or suspend an attack or sufficient information available" to assess properly whether an attack should be cancelled or suspended.[132] Henderson, and the present author as well, on the other hand support a broader reading of the subjective element of the rule, by stating that this obligation is imposed upon anyone who has "effective control over the attack".[133] This might be the person conducting the attack, for instance the pilot of the aircraft, or it might be a commander who can issue orders to the person conducting the attack. While APII does not include an explicit reference to this rule, more recent treaty law applicable in NIACs does so, i.e. Article 7 of the Second

---

[128] Rogers 2000, p. 178 (emphasis added).

[129] Benvenuti 2001, p. 513.

[130] Henckaerts and Doswald-Beck 2005, Rule 19, p. 60.

[131] Fenrick 1982, p. 109.

[132] Ibid.

[133] Henderson 2009, pp. 235–237.

Protocol to the Hague Convention for the Protection of Cultural Property,[134] as well as other treaties applicable to non-international armed conflicts.[135] Disregard for this rule would lead to an attack in violation of the principles of distinction and/or of proportionality and would be illegal on that basis.[136]

A well-known example of an attack which should have been cancelled based on this precautionary rule is the deadly attack against the Leskovac railway bridge, which led to the destruction of a passenger train that was crossing it, as discussed in Chap. 2.[137] The incident was addressed also in the report submitted by the ad hoc committee (Review Committee) set up by the Prosecutor of ICTY to ascertain whether war crimes had been committed during the NATO bombing campaign.[138] In the OTP Report the facts are described as follows:

> On 12 April 1999, a NATO aircraft launched two laser guided bombs at the Leskovac railway bridge over the Grdelica gorge and Juzna Morava river, in eastern Serbia. A 5- carriage passenger train [...] was crossing the bridge at the time and was struck by both missiles. The various reports made of this incident concur that [...] at least ten people were killed in this incident and at least 15 individuals were injured. The designated target was the railway bridge, which was claimed to be part of a re-supply route being used for Serb forces in Kosovo. After launching the first bomb, the person controlling the weapon, at the last instant before impact, sighted movement on the bridge. The controller was unable to dump the bomb at that stage and it hit the train, the impact of the bomb cutting the second of the passenger coaches in half. Realising the bridge was still intact, the controller picked a second aim point on the bridge at the opposite end from where the train had come and launched the second bomb. In the meantime the train had slid forward as a result of the original impact and parts of the train were also hit by the second bomb.[139]

As summarised by Ronzitti, the question to pose is "whether the pilot had the obligation to stop the attack when he became aware that the train"[140] (i.e. a civilian object) was crossing the bridge (swiftly labelled as a military objective). On this point the Committee admits that it "has divided views concerning the attack with the second bomb in relation to whether there was *an element of recklessness* in the conduct of the pilot or WSO [Weapons System Officer]".[141] This notwithstanding, the Committee concluded that the incidents should not be investigated,[142] and thus it provided no insight into the responsibility of the pilot and whether he violated the relevant IHL rules, including the precautionary obligation to cancel or suspend

---

[134] See Second Protocol to the Hague Convention of 1954 for the Protection of Cultural Property in the Event of Armed Conflict (Second Protocol to the 1954 Hague Convention), open for signature 26 March 1999, 38 ILM 76, entered into force 9 March 2004.

[135] Henckaerts and Doswald-Beck 2005, Rule 19, p. 61.

[136] Ibid.

[137] See Chap. 2, Sect. 2.5.2 in this book.

[138] Final Report to the Prosecutor by the Committee Established to Review the NATO Bombing Campaign against the Federal Republic of Yugoslavia, (13 June 2000), (hereinafter OTP Report) reprinted in (2000) ILM 39:1257.

[139] Ibid., para 58.

[140] Ronzitti 2000, p. 1025.

[141] OTP Report, paras 61–62.

[142] Ibid.

an attack. Henderson notes that the rule requires that the attack be cancelled or suspended if "contrary to *expectations and the assessments* made during the planning phase, it becomes apparent that the object is not a military objective, the object is subject to special protection from attack, or the expected collateral damage will be excessive".[143] The standard to apply also in this context is that of "reasonable care", which should be exercised as an overarching standard of precaution in all phases of executing an attack.

5.3.2.4 Giving Effective Advance Warning of Attacks

Parties to an armed conflict, whatever its nature, are also required to give advance warning if an attack may affect the civilian population, unless circumstances do not permit.[144] As reported in the 1987 ICRC Commentary, Article 26 of the 1907 Hague Regulations already required that the officer in command of an attacking force should, "before commencing a bombardment, except in cases of assault, do all in his power to warn the authorities".[145] *In primis,* the rule establishes that if there is no expected harm to civilians or civilian objects, then an attacker does not need to provide a warning.[146] Second, the rule allows for derogation, for instance advance warning that would result in a loss of operational surprise or increase of risk to friendly forces is not required.[147] As an example, Schmitt and Widmar report that in the case of the 2006 airstrike against al-Qaeda's leader Abu Musab al-Zarqawi, providing a warning to nearby civilians would have alerted him to flee.[148] Therefore, the elements that need to be evaluated by the attacker for each attack include the effectiveness of the warning, the determination of whether the attack may affect civilians and civilian objects and the extent to which the circumstances may dispense from the requirement of issuing an effective warning.[149] The attacker hence, has a complex assessment to make in order to fulfil this precautionary measure, which, as noted by Henderson can be even described as "one aspect of compliance" with the principles of distinction and proportionality,[150] and arguably with the other precautionary rules as well. In fact, the issuing of a warning does not relieve an attacker neither of the obligations with respect to the principle of distinction and the conduct of hostilities, nor of the obligation to take other precautions to protect civilians from harm.[151] Given the peculiar status of the precautionary rule that requires belligerents to issue effective warning and the impossibility to separate it from other principles and rules it is not possible to

[143] Henderson 2009, p. 235 (emphasis added).
[144] See Chap. 4, Sect. 4.3.2 in this book.
[145] Sandoz et al. 1987, p. 686, para 2222.
[146] Thurnher 2018, p. 111.
[147] Henckaerts and Doswald-Beck 2005, Rule 20, p. 64.
[148] Schmitt and Widmar 2016, p. 140.
[149] Henderson 2009, p. 187.
[150] Ibid., pp. 188–189.
[151] Henckaerts and Doswald-Beck 2005, Rule 20, p. 65.

determine a specific standard of reasonableness to be employed, but it could be safely assumed that the general standard of "reasonable care" finds application.

5.3.2.5 Making a Choice Between Several Military Objectives

Rule 21 of the ICRC customary IHL database contains a very important norm according to which "when a choice is possible between several military objectives for obtaining a similar military advantage, the objective to be selected must be that the attack on which may be expected to cause the least danger to civilian lives and to civilian objects".[152] The provision fully echoes para 3 of Article 57, thus extending its reach to States that are not parties to API as well to belligerents involved in NIACs. As noted by Henderson, the occasions where the norm might be applicable are "where the goal of the attack is distinct", and "more than one target is readily available to achieve that distinct goal".[153] He stresses that, for example, if an attack is carried out with the goal to disrupt electricity distribution, then an attack on either the power generation station or the distribution network might be equally as effective in achieving that goal.[154] The application of this precautionary rule would require the person in charge of the attack to make an assessment of the military advantage stemming from targeting each of the possible targets and weigh it against the danger that can be caused to civilian lives and to civilian objects. In other words, the measure entails a value judgment resulting in the identification of the "lesser of two evils" based on the expected collateral damage, that covers loss of civilian life, injury to civilians, and damage to civilian objects.

Whereas traditionally the value assigned to material damage has been regarded as very low,[155] authors have increasingly pointed out that "very deleterious consequences *may result for civilians from material damage caused by an attack*".[156] This view results from the recognition of the different value that civilian objects hold, arguably in light of the function that they play,[157] and the direct and indirect effects that stem from their damage or destruction.[158] How is a commander expected to select which object shall be attacked then? The answer, in this author's view, is that the assessment that needs to be made to fulfil this precautionary requirement is the same that is expected of a military commander in the context of the principle of proportionality. Therefore, the next sub-section will shed light on the reasonableness standard that needs to be applied when relevant actors are called on to make a

[152] Ibid., Rule 21, p. 61.

[153] Henderson 2009, p. 189.

[154] Ibid.

[155] For example, the OTP Report explicitly states that the Committee "focused primarily on incidents in which civilian deaths were alleged and/or confirmed". OTP Report, para 13.

[156] Benvenuti 2001, p. 508 (emphasis added).

[157] See Chap. 4, Sect. 4.2 in this book.

[158] Henderson 2009, pp. 192–193.

decision that requests an appraisal of the military advantage expected vis-à-vis the foreseeable collateral damage.

5.3.3 Reasonableness and the Principle of Proportionality

As is well known the principle of proportionality protects civilians and civilian objects against expected incidental harm from an attack that is excessive to the military advantage anticipated from the attack. In case of an attack against a dual-use object, the destruction of the civilian part of this object, or more generally, the fact that the attack puts an end to its use by civilians, as well as the reverberating effects of such damage forms part of the incidental damage that must be considered under the proportionality principle.[159] Proportionality in attack is accepted as a norm of customary international law applicable in both IACs and NIACs and the "test" for proportionality has been codified in Additional Protocol I.[160]

The relevant provisions of API prohibit attacks that "may be expected to cause incidental loss of civilian life, injury to civilians, damage to civilian objects, or a combination thereof, which would be excessive in relation to the concrete and direct military advantage anticipated".[161] Embedded within the broader prohibition against indiscriminate attacks ex Article 51(5)(b), the proportionality rule forbids any attack against an otherwise lawful military objective, but only when the attacker anticipates that the civilian casualties and/or destruction to civilian property will be excessive in relation to the concrete and direct military advantage anticipated from the attack.[162] Instead, Article 57 enshrines a proportionality rule within the scope of precautionary measures to prevent or reduce civilian casualties during an attack.[163]

Experts agree on the fact that the decision as to whether the incidental harm would be excessive cannot result from the application of a mechanical formula but remains a "value judgment" to be made adopting the "reasonable commander standard".[164] Notably, the codified principle of proportionality in Additional Protocol I does not refer to a "reasonable military commander" at all. The obligation to comply with the principle of proportionality lies with both "those who plan or decide upon an attack", and those who execute an attack.[165] Whilst in the case of Article 57 the relevant

[159] Gisel 2015, p. 123.

[160] Henderson and Reece 2018, p. 836.

[161] The principle of proportionality in attack is codified in Article 51(5)(b) of Additional Protocol I, and repeated in Article 57. While Additional Protocol II does not contain an explicit reference to the principle of proportionality in attack, it has been argued that it is inherent in the principle of humanity which was explicitly made applicable to the Protocol in its preamble and that, as a result, the principle of proportionality cannot be ignored in the application of the Protocol. See Henckaerts and Doswald-Beck 2005, Rule 14, pp. 46–48.

[162] Sandoz et al. 1987, p. 685, para 2216.

[163] Corn 2019, p. 330.

[164] Gillard 2018, pp. 47–48.

[165] Henderson and Reece 2018, p. 840.

provisions apply to "those who plan or decide upon an attack",[166] the 1987 ICRC Commentary explains that the rule is primarily directed at the individual executing an attack.[167]

As noted by Corn, even the best efforts to enhance implementation of the proportionality rule have been unable to eradicate the "inevitable uncertainty that still exists as to when, where, and how the rule limits the lawful use of combat power".[168] In his words, "this uncertainty is a consequence of a rule that is laden with ostensibly objective elements that, in reality, are inherently subjective in nature".[169] Authors agree on the claim that the "quantification" of the military value of a target in terms of collateral damage does not require surgical precision.[170] Rather, the "test is one of reasonableness", and the actor is the "reasonable military commander".[171] As noted by Henderson and Reece,[172] it would seem that the term "reasonable military commander" owes its genesis to the Final Report to the Prosecutor by the Committee Established to Review the NATO Bombing Campaign Against the Federal Republic of Yugoslavia.[173] In the OTP Report, some key questions were asked concerning how to assess proportionality, namely:

(a) What are the relative values to be assigned to the military advantage gained and the injury to non-combatants and or the damage to civilian objects?
(b) What do you include or exclude in totaling your sums?
(c) What is the standard of measurement in time or space? and
(d) To what extent is a military commander obligated to expose his own forces to danger in order to limit civilian casualties or damage to civilian objects?[174]

The Committee did pose the right questions, but it provided only a vague answer, according to which "it may be necessary to resolve them on a case-by-case basis, and the answers may differ depending on the background and values of the decision maker".[175] Furthermore, the Committee stressed that "it is unlikely that military commanders with different doctrinal backgrounds and differing degrees of combat experience or national military histories would always agree in close cases. It is suggested that the determination of relative values must be that of the 'reasonable

---

[166] Article 57(2)(iii)(b) of API.

[167] "The rule set out here, relating to the cancellation or suspension of attacks, applies not only to those planning or deciding upon attacks, but also and primarily, to those executing them". Sandoz et al. 1987, p. 685, para 2197.

[168] Corn 2019, p. 332.

[169] Ibid.

[170] Schmitt and Thurnher 2013, p. 256.

[171] Rogers 2012, p. 151.

[172] Henderson and Reece 2018, pp. 840–841.

[173] See Chap. 2, Sect. 2.5 in this book. Final Report to the Prosecutor by the Committee Established to Review the NATO Bombing Campaign against the Federal Republic of Yugoslavia, (13 June 2000), (hereinafter OTP Report) reprinted in (2000) ILM 39:1257.

[174] Ibid., p. 19, para 49.

[175] Ibid., para 50.

military commander'".[176] The practical application of the OTP's statement in the concrete scenario triggered extensive criticism and did not offer useful insights. Benvenuti, for example, notes how "in the Committee's view, the requirement for the legitimacy of the attack is no longer the objectivity of the reasonable military commander as one would expect: it is sufficient that the objects attacked are perceived to be legitimate by the attacking belligerent in order to exclude responsibility".[177]

To objectivise a standard that risks being too volatile, the ICTY once again provided some guidance in its jurisprudence. A few caveats, however, are needed. As the court that has considered the issue most frequently under international criminal law,[178] various chambers have addressed the rule of proportionality, contributing to outlining the rule and recognising its customary status. However, since serious violations of the rule were treated by the ICTY as underlying evidence of "unlawful attacks", namely attacks directed against civilians or civilian objects, only a few decisions considered whether the rule itself was violated in a particular case. In some instances, the judges decided whether an attack was "disproportionate" or "excessive" but did not motivate their conclusion. Only in a few cases proportionality was discussed in detail, and even though the trial chambers in those cases concluded that "the expected incidental harm was excessive", the attacks in question were not actually directed at a military objective and therefore proportionality should not have been assessed at all.[179] Moreover, some cases were overturned on appeal, with the ICTY Appeals Chamber either expressly stating that the trial chamber's analysis of proportionality was flawed or failing to deal with proportionality *tout court*, as it happened in the already discussed *Prlić et al.* case.[180] Notwithstanding these intrinsic limits to its case law, in the well-known *Galić* case the ICTY further developed the concept of the reasonable commander standard, by holding that

> [o]ne type of indiscriminate attack violates the principle of proportionality [...] The basic obligation to spare civilians and civilian objects as much as possible must guide the attacking party when considering the proportionality of an attack. In determining whether an attack was proportionate it is necessary to examine *whether a reasonably well-informed person in the circumstances of the actual perpetrator, making reasonable use of the information available to him or her*, could have expected excessive civilian casualties to result from the attack.[181]

In the literature, and in the very few applications before domestic courts, this approach has been refined by replacing the notion of reasonable "person" with that of reasonable "commander", which appeared in the OTP Report.[182] Besides the terminology, it is important to reiterate that the ICTY in the *Galić* case was not called upon to actually decide on an issue concerning the proportionality of an attack. Instead,

---

[176] Ibid.

[177] Benvenuti 2001, p. 518. See Chap. 2, Sect. 2.5.2 in this book.

[178] Gillard 2018, p. 23.

[179] Ibid.

[180] *Prlić et al.* Appeal Judgement para 411.

[181] *Prosecutor v. Galić*, TC Judgment, para 58 (emphasis added).

[182] Henderson and Reece 2018, p. 842.

the Tribunal was setting out a general principle that has been later implemented only in a handful of cases. The most scrutinised and discussed are the ones brought before the Supreme Court of Israel, sitting as the High Court, which, at least in two occasions,[183] made reference to the "reasonable military commander".[184] The case law of the Israeli Supreme Court is undoubtedly relevant, however the judgments did not provide additional insight into the concept *per se.*[185] Rather, they contributed to crystallising the applicability of the reasonable military commander standard in proportionality assessments and clarified that the decisions of military commanders are justiciable and it is the court's job to determine the law and authoritatively interpret it.

The doctrine has provided a more significant input. First, it is worth noting that there is a widespread agreement that proportionality must be assessed from the perspective of the "reasonable commander". Kalshoven and Zegveld, for instance, indicate that the relevant standard is "that of a normally alert attacker who is reasonably well-informed and who, moreover, makes reasonable use of the available information".[186] However, the authors also affirm that the assessment is "not entirely left to the subjective judgment of the attacker".[187] As authoritatively emphasised by Cannizzaro, the standard of the reasonable commander "on the one hand tends to locate the assessment of proportionality with the subjective situation of the agent, but on the other hand seems to require an objective degree of diligence".[188] Shedding additional light on the balance between subjectivity and objectivity, Cannizzaro further stresses that:

> [p]roportionality does not require the agent simply to be prudent and charitable. It requires his or her actions to be based o*n a careful apprehension of facts and on an objective balance of interests*. This character would be illusory if the agent were allowed to conduct the assessment *on the basis of his subjective situation.*[189]

It would be illogical, and contrary to the key IHL tenets, if the standard of safety of civilians would be "dependent upon the degree of experience or the degree of training of the military personnel".[190] At the same time, however, while the average "reasonable person" on the street might not be required to foresee that destroying electricity facilities would cut off the civilian fresh water supply, the reasonable

---

[183] Ibid., pp. 843–844; Gillard 2018, p. 24, para 88.

[184] See HCJ 2056/04 *Beit Sourik Vill. Council v. Gov't of Israel,* 58(5) PD 817, (2004) (Beit Sourik), para 46; HCJ 769/02 *Pub. Comm. against Torture in Israel v. Gov't of Israel* 62(1) PD 507 (2006) (Isr.), reprinted in 46 I.L.M. 375, para 57.

[185] Criticizing the decision in the *Beit Sourik* case, Koskenniemi complains that "[i]f people were able to agree on what is reasonable or proportionate, no courts, or law, would ever be needed". In his view, talking about proportionality "tests" invokes "pretensions of science that lawyers cannot possibly deliver on". Koskenniemi 2008, p. 22.

[186] Kalshoven and Zegveld 2011, p. 113.

[187] Ibid., p. 115.

[188] Cannizzaro 2014, p. 340.

[189] Ibid.

[190] Ibid., p. 341.

military commander, who should be aware of "the interconnectedness of infrastructure",[191] would be expected to foresee this consequence. Similarly, if the attacker knows that a civilian infrastructure has been partially damaged, it must be *foreseeable*, to him or her, that any further incidental damage caused by an attack will increase the reverberating effects on civilians. For example, if he or she is aware that a water treatment plant is functioning at only 50 per cent of its capacity due to the damage caused by a previous attack, the reverberating effects on civilians caused by further incidental damage to the plant will be more significant than if the treatment plant was fully functioning. This is particularly true if cumulative attacks take place in a short window of time, as it is expected that the attacker is cognizant of the extent of past incidental loss of life, injury and damage.[192]

As claimed by Robinson and Nohle, and regardless of the level of expertise and training of the attacker, the rules on proportionality and on the relevant precautionary measures in attack require that reverberating effects are taken into consideration for all attacks.[193] While the operational context might influence the extent to which a commander is expected to proactively obtain information to assess the estimation of incidental damage, a commander may never ignore reasonably available information, including such information that renders the reverberating effects of an attack reasonably foreseeable.[194] Fulfilling this obligation entails the application of a specific standard, which the authors identify as that of "reasonable foreseeability". This means that the incidental harm to be considered is

> that harm which would not occur *but for* the attack but excluding harm that results from the conduct of another actor and is not due to the physical effects of the attack; and which was reasonably foreseeable at the time the attack was planned or launched, on the basis of information that the attacker had or could reasonably have been expected to have in the circumstances.[195]

Robinson and Nohle go on to explain that this standard means that commanders are "put on notice regarding reverberating effects" that may be viewed as "reasonably and objectively foreseeable".[196] This view is also shared by authors like Henderson and Reece, who, albeit noting that there is still "insufficient state practice and case law to provide a confident view of what the law says about this situation",[197] conclude that indirect effects do need to be considered. The reverberating effects are based on certain elements that it would be unreasonable to ignore, encompassing "past practice and empirical research, lessons learned and publicly available information, including information about the reverberating effects of using explosive weapons in populated areas".[198] This approach clearly bears significant relevance in the proportionality

[191] Sassòli and Cameron 2006, p. 6.
[192] Robinson and Nohle 2016, pp. 124–125.
[193] Ibid., pp. 118–119.
[194] Robinson and Nohle 2016, p. 145.
[195] Gillard 2018, pp. 18–19.
[196] Robinson and Nohle 2016, pp. 144–145.
[197] Henderson and Reece 2018, p. 855.
[198] Robinson and Nohle 2016, pp. 144–145.

assessment of attacks launched against dual-use objects. Its implementation also requires the attacker to obtain information regarding "the location and nature of essential infrastructure" and, as affirmed by Robinson and Nohle and reiterated by Gillard, to ensure that relevant technical experts are involved in assessing the expected incidental harm of an attack.[199]

In addition to foreseeability, Gillard stresses that the applicable standard of reasonableness when carrying out the proportionality test, must also cover the "likelihood of the incidental harm".[200] In other words, when conducting proportionality assessments, not only must belligerents determine whether incidental harm and its reverberating effects are foreseeable, they must also assess *how likely* it is that they will actually occur.[201] Neither the notions of "foreseeability" or "reasonable foreseeability", imply a "particular degree of certainty that the incidental harm in question will actually occur".[202] Still, the problem is relevant and it is legitimate to ask, if an essential civilian infrastructure is damaged or destroyed, what is the degree of likelihood of the consequent disruption in essential services and subsequent effects on the lives and well-being of the civilian population? Albeit it is not possible to quantify it in exact terms, the "more likely than not" test, that some authors consider adequate,[203] is not correct as it restricts too much the meaning of the "expected" harm mentioned in Article 51(5)(b) of API. What "expected" entails is the harm that is "likely to occur" rather than "more likely than not".[204] Therefore, an attack against a water installation is *likely* to cause civilians dying of thirst, targeting an electrical power station is *likely* to cut off a nearby hospital's power supply and so on. Surely, it is not easy to predict what the threat and/or damage to the civilian population will be, based on the information reasonably available to the commander at the time the attack was ordered, but this is exactly why the reasonableness standard applied to the principles of precautions and proportionality must cover the reasonably foreseeable reverberating effects of an attack as well as the likelihood of the incidental harm.

[199] Ibid. See also Gillard 2018, pp. 16–18.

[200] Gillard 2018, p. 17.

[201] Ibid.

[202] Ibid., p. 26.

[203] See Christopher Greenwood, Observations dated 13 November 2003 circulated by the United Kingdom Delegation to the CCW Group of Governmental Experts, 17–24 November 2003, cited in Boothby 2009, p. 28.

[204] Robinson and Nohle 2016, p. 118.

5.3.4 The Role of the Standard of Reasonableness in Striking a Balance between Military Necessity and Humanitarian Considerations

A well-established opinion in the international legal literature maintains that LOAC as a whole represents a compromise between the opposed principles of necessity and humanity.[205] In contemporary LOAC, examples of rules incorporating military necessity as a general principle restraining belligerents' freedom in warfare abound, including the definition of legitimate military objects,[206] which manifestly conveys the principle of military necessity in its wider meaning.[207] The current definition of military necessity, as reported by Venturini, describes it as "the principle whereby a belligerent has the right to apply any measures which are required to bring about the successful conclusion of a military operation and which are not forbidden by the laws of war".[208] As already stressed,[209] the principle of necessity neither conflicts with nor opposes the principle of humanity: on the contrary, it ensures that humanitarian values are duly taken into account during the conduct of hostilities.[210] It follows that necessity and humanity may be seen as two aspects of the same principle,[211] which obviously finds application also in the targeting process.

Lacking more clear legal standards, several leading States, scholars, and practitioners embrace what Haque describes as a "balancing approach",[212] according to which the required level of certainty in the targeting process varies with the balance of military and humanitarian considerations. As the balance tips in favour of humanitarian considerations, the required level of certainty rises. As the balance tips in favour of military considerations, the required level of certainty falls.[213] Along the same lines, Henderson writes that "the level of verification required to reduce doubt, and the degree of acceptable doubt, will vary depending upon the likely adverse consequences of a wrong decision",[214] while Schmitt affirms that "the greater the military advantage, the more doubt will be justified".[215]

---

[205] Venturini 2011, p. 48.

[206] However, it is worth explaining that military necessity does not coincide with military advantage: while the latter is a specific notion strictly connected to each particular situation of warfare, the former represents the ratio underlying the positive content of the rule as a norm of customary international law. Ibid.

[207] Ibid.

[208] Ibid., p. 50. See also Dinstein 2010, p. 6.

[209] See Chap. 4, Sect. 4.3.3 in this book.

[210] Gardam 2004, p. 7.

[211] Venturini 2011, p. 50; Hayashi 2020, pp. 51–60.

[212] Haque 2017, p. 110.

[213] Ibid.

[214] Henderson 2009, p. 164.

[215] Schmitt 2006, p. 304.

However, to date, proponents of the balancing approach have not offered significant insight on how to weigh military considerations against humanitarian considerations or how to derive the required level of certainty from the resulting balance.[216] As Rogers further notes"[h]umanitarian considerations would require a pilot to get close to the target to identify it properly; military considerations would require the pilot to fly at a safe height to be at reduced risk from anti-aircraft fire. This is a conflict that cannot be resolved easily."[217] Prior to delving into the issue of how to achieve the balance and what role reasonableness is expected to play, it is worth specifying who oversees this crucial task. As noted by Beer, "the determination of military necessity is, to a large extent, the commanders' profession".[218] To cite a few examples, only the commanders of forces in the field are authorised to make use of the buildings, material, and stores of fixed medical establishment in case of urgent military necessity.[219] Likewise, when fighting occurs on a war-ship, its sick-bays and their equipment may be used for other purposes if militarily necessary only by the commander into whose power they have fallen.[220] In other words, military necessity does not function as a justification for brutality but, rather, it pushes the commanders to do their job competently, "using their brains and professional skills when exercising force".[221]

In this light, it is not surprising that the German nineteenth-century doctrine of *Kriegsraison geht vor Kriegsmanier*, roughly translated as "necessity in war overrules the manner of warfare",[222] never gained traction as it is utterly incompatible with international law. This emerged very clearly from the war crimes trials that took place in the aftermath of WWII, and which definitely put to rest the argument that extreme necessity could deprive the laws of war of their binding force.[223] The Nuremberg trials rejected the claims brought by German generals that necessity justified actions such as reprisal killings of civilians during occupation.[224] However, the United States Military Tribunal at Nuremberg in the *Hostages* case accepted the defence of military

216 Haque 2017, p. 111.

217 Rogers 2000, p. 175.

218 Beer 2018, p. 66.

219 Article 33 of the Geneva Convention for the Amelioration of the Condition of the Wounded and Sick in Armed Forces in the Field (Geneva Convention I, or GCI) opened for signature 12 August 1949, 75 UNTS 31, entered into force 21 October 1950.

220 Article 28 of the Geneva Convention for the Amelioration of the Condition of Wounded, Sick and Shipwrecked Members of Armed Forces at Sea (Geneva Convention II or GCII) opened for signature 12 August 1949, 75 UNTS 85, entered into force 21 October 1950. See Hayashi 2010, pp. 100–101.

221 Beer 2018, p. 66.

222 Schmitt 2010, p. 797.

223 Johansen 2019, pp. 122–124.

224 Trial of Heinz Eck and Four Others (The Peleus Trial), ibid., Vol. I (1947); Trial of Hans Albin Rauter, ibid., Vol. XIV (1949) p. 106; Trial of Gunther Thiele and Georg Steinert, Law Reports of Trials of War Criminals, London HMSO 1947–1949, Vol. III (1948) p. 59. See Venturini 2011, pp. 65–66.

necessity raised by the German General Lothar Rendulić,[225] who had engaged in "scorched earth" tactics in the Norwegian province of Finmark,[226] during the retreat of the army commanded by him and found that

> [military necessity] permits the destruction of life of armed enemies and other persons whose destruction is incidentally unavoidable by the armed conflicts of the war [...] but it does not permit the killing of innocent inhabitants for purposes of revenge or the satisfaction of a lust to kill. The destruction of property to be lawful must be imperatively demanded by the necessities of war [...] Military necessity or expediency do not justify a violation of positive rules.[227]

This famous passage goes on by stating that "[d]estruction as an end in itself is a violation of international law".[228] The judges, moreover, affirmed that "there must be some reasonable connection between the destruction of property and the overcoming of the enemy forces".[229] As momentous as the passage in the *Hostages* case is, it shall be noted that ultimately the judges concluded that "military necessity permits a belligerent, subject to the laws of war, *to apply any amount and kind of force to compel the complete submission of the enemy with the least possible expenditure of time, life, and money*".[230] This confirms that the so-called *Hostages* formulation remains "overwhelmingly slanted in favour of militaries, and grants them enormous latitude".[231] Military necessity in the Tribunal's view includes "any lawful act that saves a dollar or a day in the pursuit of military victory". Ultimately, however, these are claims of military convenience, not military necessity.[232] Therefore, although the case law of the Nuremberg Trials confirmed that "carte blanche deviation from established legal norms based on military necessity is impermissible",[233] and that the balancing of necessity and humanity is reflected in the entire body of IHL, the *Hostages* formula makes "only a half-break from the doctrine of *Kriegsraison*".[234] Furthermore, also emerging from the post WWII case law, there is the realisation that what is "necessary" to achieve the defeat of the enemy with a "minimum expenditure of time, life and physical resources" involves "a complex assessment that is likely

---

[225] For a thorough appraisal of the law and facts underlying his trial, see Hayashi and Lingaas 2024.

[226] The evidence adduced at trial showed that military necessity did not, in fact, exist. The tribunal ruled however that Rendulic "genuinely perceived danger of an enemy attack, under the circumstances prevailing at the time, should not be second-guessed simply because the full facts as they had become subsequently available contradicted or otherwise under- mined his original perception about the danger". See Hayashi 2010, p. 95.

[227] *United States v. List* (The Hostage Case), Case No. 7 (19 February 1948), reprinted in 11 Trials of War Criminals before the Nuremberg Military Tribunals under Control Council Law No.10, paras 1253–1256.

[228] Ibid.

[229] Ibid.

[230] Ibid., para 1253.

[231] Luban 2013, pp. 341–342.

[232] Ibid.

[233] Schmitt 2010, p. 798.

[234] Luban 2013, p. 343.

to be strongly influenced by subjective perceptions",[235] especially when determined with respect to individual operations against specific targets. This input, however, has not been developed beyond acknowledging the crucial role of the commanders and the "great deal of latitude" accorded to them under such circumstances, when called to make and implement quick decisions.[236] Luban sharply notes that "under the *Hostages* formulation, an air force can use non-precision-guided bombs rather than more discriminating precision-guided munitions merely because they are cheaper, or merely because commanders do not want to wait for a shipment of PGMs to arrive, and describe the choice as military necessity".[237] This approach, obviously, has devastating implications also in interpreting treaty-based protections of civilians against the incidental damage stemming from attacks against dual-use objects.

The more recent case law departs from this view and provides a different reading of military necessity and of the standard that commanders must apply when striking a balance with humanitarian considerations. The ICTY, although it never discussed the requirements of military necessity at any length, has not shied away from making factual determinations about the existence or absence of military necessity in the context of specific incidents.[238] These factual determinations have been made mainly, but not exclusively, in connection with two crime categories: (i) large-scale property destruction, of which the absence of military necessity appears as an element; and (ii) forcible displacement of persons.[239] Without lingering on the attempt to provide an extensive overview of the Tribunal's case law on the matter,[240] it is worth recalling the main findings of the ICTY. For example, in *Kordic* the Appeals Chamber clarified that "the prohibition against attacking civilians and civilian objects may not be derogated from because of military necessity",[241] and in another crucial passage pointed at discriminatory attacks as "attacks which could not be justified by military necessity".[242] In the *Gotovina* decision, the Trial Chamber found that the *Hrvataska Vojska* (the Croatian army) paid little or no regard to the risk of civilian casualties and injuries and damage to civilian objects when firing artillery at a military target.[243]

As noted by Luban, for military lawyers it is outrageous that judges dare to "second-guess a field commander's risk–benefit assessment on such a fact-intensive and situation-sensitive decision".[244] Reversing Gotovina's conviction, the Appeals

---

[235] Melzer 2006; Melzer 2008, p. 291.

[236] *United States v. Wilhelm von Leeb, et al.* (The High Command Case), Case No. 12 (27–28 October 1948) Law Reports of Trials of War Criminals, Vol. XII (1949) pp. 86–89.

[237] Luban 2013, p. 343.

[238] Hayashi 2010, pp. 101–103.

[239] Ibid.

[240] See Venturini 2011, pp. 66–69; Salvadego 2016, pp. 221–232.

[241] ICTY (AC), *Prosecutor v Dario Kordić and Mario Čerkez*, Judgment, 17 December 2004, IT-95-14/2-A, para 54.

[242] Ibid., para 485.

[243] ICTY (TC), *Prosecutor v. Gotovina*, Judgement, 15 April 2011, IT-06-90-T, para 1910.

[244] Luban 2013, p. 327.

Chamber partly agreed with this view, complaining that the Trial Chamber's assessment was not based on a concrete appraisal of comparative military advantage, and did not make any findings on resulting damages or casualties.[245] The Appeals Chamber found that the Trial Chamber's analysis rested on faulty assumptions about the accuracy of artillery fire, and ultimately reversed the decision on that ground. Luban stresses that, had the assumptions been justified, the Appeals Chamber might have sustained the Trial Chamber's verdict; "there is no hint in its opinion that it would defer to commanders in a fog-of-war case".[246]

A further step away from the *Hostages* formula and in the same direction of the ICTY has been made by the Israeli Supreme Court, which, in the already cited *Beit Sourik* case, carried out an analysis of the separation barrier that Israel constructed during the second Intifada and found that under IHL, civilian property could be seized (with compensation paid) "[t]o the extent that construction of the fence is a military necessity".[247] The Court deferred to the military commander's judgement that alternative routes proposed by the plaintiffs offered less security than the Jebel Muktam route. If the judges applied the *Hostages* formulation, that would have been enough to demonstrate military necessity. Instead, the Court rejected the Jebel Muktam route's argument because "the security advantage reaped from the route as determined by the military commander, in comparison to the [. . .] route [proposed by the plaintiffs], does not stand in any reasonable proportion to the injury to the local inhabitants caused by this route".[248] In its reasoning the Court analyses necessity claims in three steps.[249] As a first one, it asked whether the chosen military tactic bears a rational relationship to its goal. Second, it questioned whether that goal might be attained by an alternative that inflicts less damage on civilians. Third, the Israeli Supreme Court weighed the gains to the military against the injury to civilians in marginal terms "the...act is tested vis-à-vis an alternate act, whose benefit will be somewhat smaller than that of the former one."[250] Hence, "the original […] act is disproportionate[...] if a certain reduction in the advantage gained by the original act – by employing alternate means, for example – ensures a substantial reduction in the injury caused by the administrative act".[251] Therefore, the Court's conclusion was that, compared to the alternatives suggested by the petitioners, the route chosen by the commander was "disproportionately injurious".[252]

The approach brought forward by both the ICTY, and the Israeli Supreme Court marks a significant departure from the *Hostages* formula, which subordinates necessity to law, but *within* the limits of law it permits the commander to discount

[245] ICTY (AC), *Prosecutor v. Gotovina*, Judgement, 16 November 2012, IT-06-90-A, para 82.

[246] Luban 2013, p. 327.

[247] *Beit Sourik*, para 32.

[248] Ibid., para 41.

[249] Luban 2013, pp. 344–345.

[250] *Beit Sourik*, para 41.

[251] Ibid.

[252] Hayashi 2010, p. 79.

civilian interests completely.[253] Instead, the reading of military necessity upheld by these judicial bodies requires the commander to take civilian interests into account. Although these findings are of obvious relevance, they do not distinguish explicitly between the flexibility in the norm and the threshold of reasonableness on the part of the commander that is required when determining the content of military necessity. The question of necessity in fact relies upon whether it was reasonable for the commander to assess the facts as a situation of necessity.[254] Lacking a more precise qualification, the standard applicable to striking a balance between the principles of military necessity and humanity remains that of the reasonable commander.[255]

5.4 Conclusion

The analysis carried out in this chapter dealt with a topic that is central to the paradigm shift that this work aims to trigger in relation to dual-use objects. Additionally, it has provided this author with a unique opportunity to address a concept that remains largely underexplored, despite its unquestionable relevance and potentialities. Reasonableness to this date preserves its unscathed reputation as one of the least discussed legal concepts in the international legal domain and beyond. The first part of the chapter sought to fill this gap, by offering a thorough overview of the existing scholarship on the matter, on the purpose of making the reader acquainted with the wide spectrum of issues that this concept has triggered so far. Despite the scattered attention devoted to reasonableness as a legal notion, over the years there has been an increasing tendency to resort to it both as a standard of action for different categories of agents and as a standard of review by several judicial bodies, including the ICJ. This has obviously resulted in a growing doctrinal interest towards this concept, which, however, has never succeeded in shedding light on all its nuances.

As discussed in the previous (sub-)sections, reasonableness as a standard holds a prominent position also within the IHL framework. Contrary to the general view—as there is no doubt that one of the key elements of the rule of proportionality has been framed as a requirement of reasonableness—this standard has a much bigger role to play in relation to all the other IHL principles. In fact, the reasonableness standard can effectively inform the decision-making process of the relevant actors involved in the various phases of an attack. Hence, reasonableness can be the touchstone for determining the appropriate application of specific targeting rules and for assessing the lawfulness of action after the fact. Each of the key IHL principles requires commanders and individual soldiers to make decisions in good faith based on the information available to them at the time of the attack, however, as the present chapter has showed, there is a sliding scale in the application of the reasonable standard that allows both the actors and those who review the actions undertaken to

[253] Luban 2013, p. 347.

[254] Johansen 2019, p. 353.

[255] See Sect. 5.3 above.

operate with greater certainty.[256] Therefore the standard represents a fundamental measure for guiding commanders and soldiers in the implementation of and compliance with the law, as well as for judging responsibility for potential violations of the law after the fact.

The findings enshrined in this chapter, in particular the calibration of the reasonableness standard under the IHL framework, are important since reasonableness can be regarded as a transversal concept across the whole spectrum of the law of targeting.[257] As discussed in the previous sections the analysis carried out led to an identification of the threshold of reasonableness expected from the relevant actors in the application of the key IHL principles. Thus, the standard ranges from the "reasonable care", recognised as the baseline for the precautionary measures that must be implemented in attack, to the "reasonable foreseeability" attached to the principle of proportionality. Engaging in this exercise has certainly been enriching from a theoretical perspective, but it is possible to argue that its practical implications are equally important. Said implications include the possibility for the judicial bodies to implement a more uniform approach, the opportunity to design specific training for the military forces and the adoption of Rules of Engagement (RoE) that can, and should, take into due account the centrality of the reasonableness standard and, hopefully, its sliding scale.

References

Alexy R (1989) A Theory of Legal Argumentation. Clarendon, Oxford

Alexy R (2009) The Reasonableness of the Law. In: Bongiovanni G, Sartor G, Valentini C (eds) Reasonableness and Law. Springer, Cham, pp 3–15

Artosi A (2009) Reasonableness, Common Sense, and Science. In: Bongiovanni G, Sartor G, Valentini C (eds) Reasonableness and Law. Springer, Cham, pp 69–81

Barak A (2005) Purposive Interpretation in Law. Princeton University Press, Princeton

Beer Y (2018) Military Professionalism and Humanitarian Law: The Struggle to Reduce the Hazards of War. Oxford University Press, Oxford

Benvenuti P (2001) The ICTY Prosecutor and the Review of the NATO Bombing Campaign against the Federal Republic of Yugoslavia. European Journal of International Law 12(3): 503–529

Blank L R (2010) Finding Facts but Missing the Law: The Goldstone Report, Gaza and Lawfare. Case Western Reserve Journal of International Law 43(1): 279–302

Blank L (2018) New Technologies and the Interplay between Certainty and Reasonableness. In: Williams W S, Ford C M (eds) Complex Battlespaces: The Law of Armed Conflict and the Dynamics of Modern Warfare. Oxford University Press, Oxford, pp 317–344

Bongiovanni G, Sartor G, Valentini C (eds) (2009) Reasonableness and Law. Springer, Cham

Boothby W (2009) Weapons and the Law of Armed Conflict. Oxford University Press, Oxford

Cannizzaro E (2000) Il principio della proporzionalità nell'ordinamento internazionale. Giuffré, Milan

Cannizzaro E (2014) Proportionality in the Law of Armed Conflict. In: Gaeta P, Clapham A (eds) The Oxford Handbook of International Humanitarian Law. Oxford University Press, Oxford, pp 333–352

[256] Blank 2018, p. 321.

[257] Ibid., p. 324.

Capone F (2023) The Wave of Russian Attacks on Ukraine's Power Infrastructures: An Opportunity to Infuse Meaningfulness into the Notion of "Dual-use Objects"? European Papers 8(2): 741–754
Cassese A (1998) On the Current Trends towards Criminal Prosecution and Punishment of Breaches of International Humanitarian Law. European Journal of International Law 9: 2–17
Contiades X, Fotiadou A (2012) Social Rights in the Age of Proportionality: Global Economic Crisis and Constitutional Litigation. International Journal of Constitutional Law 10(3): 660–686
Corn G S (2012) Targeting, Command Judgment, and a Proposed Quantum of Information Component. Brooklyn Law Review 77(2): 437–498
Corn G S (2019) Attack Decision-Making: Context, Reasonableness, and the Duty to Obey. In: Alcala R T P, Talbot Jensen E (eds) The Impact of Emerging Technologies on the Law of Armed Conflict, The Lieber Studies Series. Oxford University Press, New York, pp 325–374
Corten O (1999) The Notion of "Reasonable" in International Law: Legal Discourse, Reason and Contradictions. International and Comparative Law Quarterly 48: 613–625
Corten O, Kolb R (2021) Reasonableness in International Law. In: Peters A (ed) Max Planck Institute for Comparative Public Law and International Law. Oxford University Press, Oxford
Craig P (2013) The Nature of Reasonableness Review. Current Legal Problems 66: 131–167
De Cock C (2016) Targeting in Coalition Operations. In: Ducheine P A L, Schmitt M N, Osinga F P B (eds) Targeting: The Challenges of Modern Warfare. T.M.C. Asser Press, The Hague, pp 231–260
Dinstein Y (2010) The Conduct of Hostilities under the Law of International Armed Conflict, 2nd edn. Cambridge University Press, Cambridge
Doswald-Beck L (1995) San Remo Manual on International Law applicable to Armed Conflicts at Sea. Grotius Publications. Cambridge University Press, Cambridge
Droege C, Giorgou E (2022) How International Humanitarian Law Develops. International Review of the Red Cross 104(920–921): 1798–1839
Fenrick W J (1982) The Rule of Proportionality and Protocol I in Conventional Warfare. Military L. Rev. 98: 91–127
Gardam J (2004) Necessity, Proportionality and the Use of Force by States. Cambridge University Press, Cambridge
Garrido-Muñoz A (2017) Managing Uncertainty: The International Court of Justice, "Objective Reasonableness" and the Judicial Function. Leiden Journal of International Law 30: 457–474
Gillard EC (2018) Proportionality in the Conduct of Hostilities: The Incidental Harm Side of the Assessment. Research paper, Chatham House. https://www.chathamhouse.org/sites/default/files/publications/research/2018-12-10-proportionality-conduct-hostilities-incidental-harm-gillard-final.pdf. Accessed 15 August 2024
Gisel L (2015) Relevant Incidental Harm for the Proportionality Principle, Urban Warfare, Proceedings of the 16th Bruges Colloquium, 15–16 October 2015. https://www.coleurope.eu/sites/default/files/uploads/page/collegium_46_1.pdf. Accessed 31 August 2024
Greppi E (1996) Diritto internazionale umanitario dei conflitti armati e diritti umani: profili di una convergenza. La Comunità Internazionale LI (3): 473–498
Greppi E (2012) I crimini dell'individuo nel diritto internazionale. UTET, Turin
Griffey B (2011) The Reasonableness Test: Assessing Violations of State Obligations under the Optional Protocol to the International Covenant on Economic, Social and Cultural Rights. Human Rights Law Review 11(2): 275–327
Habermas J (1996) Between Facts and Norms (Rehg W (transl)). MIT Press, Cambridge, Mass
Harvard Air and Missile Warfare Manual (2013) Program on Humanitarian Policy and Conflict Research at Harvard University (HPCR), Manual on International Law Applicable to Air and Missile Warfare. Cambridge University Press, Cambridge
Haque A A (2017) Law and Morality at War. Oxford University Press, Oxford
Hayashi N (2010) Requirements of Military Necessity in International Humanitarian Law and International Criminal Law. Boston University International Law Journal 28(1): 40–140
Hayashi N (2020) Military Necessity. The Art, Morality and Law of War. Cambridge University Press, Cambridge

Hayashi N, Lingaas C (2024) Honest Errors in Combat Decision-Making: State of Our Knowledge 75 Years after the Hostage Case. In: Hayashi N, Lingaas C (eds) Honest Errors? Combat Decision-Making 75 Years After the Hostage Case. T.M.C. Asser Press, The Hague, pp 3–21

Henckaerts J M, Doswald-Beck L (2005) Customary International Humanitarian Law, Volume I: Rules. Cambridge University Press, Cambridge/Geneva

Henckels C (2015) Proportionality and Deference in Investor–State Arbitration: Balancing Investment Protection and Regulatory Autonomy. Cambridge University Press, Cambridge

Henderson I (2009) The Contemporary Law of Targeting. Martinus Nijhoff Publishers, Leiden/Boston

Henderson I, Reece K (2018) Proportionality Under International Humanitarian Law (IHL): The ‘Reasonable Military Commander’ Standard and Reverberating Effects. Vanderbilt Journal of Transnational Law 51(3): 835–855

Ikeshima T (2009) The ‘Reasonableness’ of Unreasonable Arguments in Prompt Release Cases in the ITLOS. Waseda Global Forum 6: 107–128

Jianjun G (2020) The Exhaustion of Local Remedies Rule in the Settlement of Maritime Disputes: A Study of the Practice of the UNCLOS Tribunals. Chinese Journal of International Law 19: 425–458

Johansen S R (2019) The Military Commander’s Necessity: The Law of Armed Conflict and its Limits. Cambridge University Press, Cambridge

Kalshoven F, Zegveld L (2011) Constraints on the Waging of War, 4th edn. Cambridge University Press/ICRC, Cambridge/Geneva

Kant I (1996) Groundwork of the Metaphysics of Morals. In: Gregor M J (ed) Practical Philosophy. Cambridge University Press, Cambridge, pp 37–107

Koskenniemi M (2008) Occupied Zone—A Zone of Reasonableness? Israel Law Review 41(1): 13–40

Kraska J, Pedrozo R (2023) Newport Manual on the Law of Naval Warfare. International Law Studies 101: 1–251

Liebenberg S (2020) Between Sovereignty and Accountability: The Emerging Jurisprudence of the United Nations Committee on Economic, Social and Cultural Rights under the Optional Protocol. Human Rights Quarterly 42(1): 48–84

Liebenberg S (2023) Reasonableness Review. In: Young K, Langford M (eds) Oxford Handbook of Economic and Social Rights. Oxford University Press, Oxford

Luban D (2013) Military Necessity and the Cultures of Military Law. Leiden Journal of International Law 20(2): 315–349

Luchetti G, Petrucci A, Pontoriero I (2010) Fondamenti romanistici del diritto europeo. Le obbligazioni e i contratti dalle radici romane al Draft Common Frame of Reference. Pàtron Editore, Bologna

MacCormick N (2005) Rhetoric and the rule of law. A theory of legal reasoning. Oxford University Press, Oxford

Magi L (2021) Adattamento “a rovescio” e obblighi a realizzazione progressiva: una (possibile) lettura. SIDI Blog, 5 luglio 2021. http://www.sidiblog.org/2021/07/05/adattamento-a-rovescio-e-obblighi-a-realizzazione-progressiva-una-possibile-lettura/. Accessed 18 August 2024

Mauri D (2022) Autonomous Weapons Systems and the Protection of the Human Person: An International Law Analysis. Edward Elgar, Cheltenham

Melzer N (2006) Targeted Killing or Less Harmful Means? - Israel’s High Court Judgment on Targeted Killing and the Restrictive Function of Military Necessity. Yearbook of International Humanitarian Law 9: 87–113

Melzer N (2008) Targeted Killing in International Law. Oxford University Press, Oxford

Meron T (2000) The Humanization of Humanitarian Law. The American Journal of International Law 94(2): 239–278

Messineo D (2012) La garanzia del «contenuto essenziale» dei diritti fondamentali. Dalla tutela della dignità umana ai livelli essenziali delle prestazioni. Giappichelli, Turin

Neuman N (2018) Considering the principle of precautions. In: Pocar F (ed) The Additional Protocols 40 Years Later: New Conflicts, New Actors, New Perspectives 40th Round Table on Current Issues of International Humanitarian Law (Sanremo, 7th-9th September 2017). FrancoAngeli, Milan, pp 74–84

Ortino F (2005) From "Non-discrimination" to "Reasonableness": A Paradigm Shift in International Economic Law? NYU Jean Monnet Working Paper 01/05. https://papers.ssrn.com/sol3/papers.cfm?abstract_id=922524. Accessed 15 August 2024

Palombino F M (2018) Fair and Equitable Treatment and the Fabric of General Principles. T.M.C. Asser Press, The Hague

Pascucci P (2017) Distinction and Proportionality in Cyber War: Virtual Problems with a Real Solution. Minnesota Journal of International Law 257: 419–460

Pedrazzi M (2012) La protezione del diritto alla vita tra diritto internazionale umanitario e tutela internazionale dei diritti umani. In: Di Stefano A, Speranza R (eds) La tutela dei diritti umani e il diritto internazionale. Editoriale Scientifica, Naples, pp 79–92

Perelman C (1979) The Rational and the Reasonable. In: Perelman C (ed) The New Rhetoric and the Humanities: Essays on Rhetoric and Its Applications. Springer, Heidelberg, pp 117–23

Rawls J (1993) Political Liberalism. Columbia University Press, New York

Robinson I, Nohle E (2016) Proportionality and precautions in attack: The reverberating effects of using explosive weapons in populated areas. International Review of the Red Cross 98 (1): 107–145

Rogers A P V (2000) Zero-casualty Warfare. International Review of the Red Cross 82: 165–181

Rogers A P V (2012) Law on the Battlefield, 3rd edn. Manchester University Press, Manchester/New York

Ronzitti N (2000) Is the *non liquet* of the Final Report by the Committee Established to Review the NATO Bombing Campaign Against the Federal Republic of Yugoslavia Acceptable? International Review of the Red Cross 840: 1017–1027

Salmon J (1982) Le concept de raisonnable en droit international public. In: Reuter P (ed) Mélanges offerts à Paul Reuter. Le droit international: unité et diversité. Pedone, Paris 447–478

Salvadego L (2016) Struttura e funzioni della necessità militare nel diritto internazionale. Giappichelli, Turin

Sandoz Y, Swinarski C, Zimmermann B (eds) (1987) Commentary on the Additional Protocols of 8 June 1977 to the Geneva Conventions of 12 August 1949. Martinus Nijhoff Publishers, Geneva

Sartor G (2009) A Sufficientist Approach to Reasonableness in Legal Decision-Making and Judicial Review. In: Bongiovanni G, Sartor G, Valentini C (eds) Reasonableness and Law. Springer, Cham, pp 17–68

Sassòli M, Cameron L (2006) The Protection of Civilian Objects: Current State of the Law and Issues de lege ferenda. In: Ronzitti N, Venturini G (eds) The Law of Air Warfare: Contemporary Issues. Eleven International, Utrecht, pp 35–74

Sassòli M, Quintin A (2014) Active and Passive Precautions in Air and Missile Warfare 44: 69–123

Schmitt M N (2006) Faultlines in the Law of Attack. In: Breau S, Jachec-Neale A (eds) Testing the Boundaries of International Humanitarian Law. British Institute of International and Comparative Law, London, pp 277–307

Schmitt M N (2008) Human Shields in International Humanitarian Law. Israel Yearbook on Human Rights Law 38: 17–59

Schmitt M N (2010) Military Necessity and Humanity in International Humanitarian Law: Preserving the Delicate Balance. Virginia Journal of International Law 50(4): 795–838

Schmitt M N (2022) Ukraine Symposium - Further Thoughts on Russia's Campaign against Ukraine's Power Infrastructure, 25 November 2022. https://lieber.westpoint.edu/further-thoughts-russias-campaign-against-ukraines-power-infrastructure/. Accessed 19 August 2024

Schmitt M N, Thurnher J S (2013) 'Out of the Loop': Autonomous Weapon Systems and the Law of Armed Conflict. Harvard National Security Journal (4): 231–282

Schmitt M N, Widmar E W (2014) "On Target": Precision and Balance in the Contemporary Law of Targeting. Journal of National Security Law & Policy 7: 379–409

Schmitt M N, Widmar E (2016) The Law of Targeting. In: Ducheine P A L, Schmitt M N, Osinga F P B (eds) Targeting: The Challenges of Modern Warfare. T.M.C. Asser Press, The Hague, pp 121–146

Short M (2002) Operation Allied Force from the perspective of the NATO Air Commander. In: Wall AE (ed) Legal and ethical lessons of NATO's Kosovo campaign. United States Naval War College International Law Studies 78:19–26

Solis G D (2010) The Law of Armed Conflict: International Humanitarian Law in War. Cambridge University Press, Cambridge

Thurnher J S (2018) Feasible Precautions in Attack and Autonomous Weapons. In: Heintschel von Heineg W, Frau R, Singer T (eds) Dehumanization of Warfare. Springer, Cham, pp 99–117

Tully S (2015) "Objective Reasonableness" as a Standard for International Judicial Review. Journal of International Dispute Settlement 6: 546–567

US DoD (2023) Law of War Manual (June 2015, updated July 2023). https://media.defense.gov/2023/Jul/31/2003271432/-1/-1/0/DOD-LAW-OF-WAR-MANUAL-JUNE-2015-UPDATED-JULY%202023.PDF. Accessed 4 September 2024

Vadi V (2018) Proportionality, Reasonableness and Standards of Review in International Investment Law and Arbitration. Edward Elgar, Cheltenham, Glos

Venturini G (2011) Necessity in the Law of Armed Conflict and in International Criminal Law. In: Dekker I F, Hey E (eds) Netherlands Yearbook of International Law 41: 45–78

Von Wright G H (1993) Images of Science and Forms of Rationality. In: von Wright GH (ed) The Tree of Knowledge and Other Essays. Brill, Leiden, pp 172–192

Young S P (ed) (2014) Reasonableness in Liberal Political Philosophy. Routledge, Abingdon

Chapter 6
Concluding Remarks: Reconciling Dual-Use Objects with the Key Tenets of International Humanitarian Law

Contents

Abstract The present chapter aims at providing some concluding remarks on the analysis carried out in this work. First, the chapter will summarise the main findings of the book and further clarify some of the key issues that this inquiry has addressed, including the definition of dual-use objects, the need to reconcile this notion with the IHL framework in force and the two pillars of the proposed new paradigm. Second, this chapter will introduce some preliminary considerations on the potential application of the new paradigm to the ever-expanding field of new weapons and technologies. Without claiming to bring a significant contribution to the ongoing debate on autonomous weapons systems (AWS) and the militarisation of artificial intelligence (AI), this chapter stresses that the book's findings bear some relevance also in this domain.

Keywords Military objectives · ICTY · Reasonable military commander standard · Autonomous weapons systems · Artificial intelligence

6.1 Introduction

This book aimed at stimulating a thorough reflection on dual-use objects under international humanitarian law (IHL). As explained in the present study, dual-use objects are nowadays part of the IHL lexicon. This statement is correct even though the term "dual-use objects" does not refer to a legal concept and does not appear in any legal treaties or norms. The challenge to deal with something that is recognisable, but still volatile, that is acquiring increasing relevance, but is still looked at with suspicious, is an experience that many researchers can relate to. Yet, the journey that led to the finalisation of this book has been incredibly rewarding. The impetus for

F. Capone, *Dual-use Objects under International Humanitarian Law: Towards a Paradigm Shift*, https://doi.org/10.1007/978-94-6265-679-6_6

tackling such an underexplored and complex issue stems from the awareness that the armed conflicts fought in different regions of the world since the two world wars have become more and more lethal, impacting larger portion of the civilian population and inflicting short-and long-term damages that, in most cases, have proven impossible to reverse. Not learning from the mistakes made in the past seems to be a fixed feature of human nature. Still, this author finds it difficult to grapple with the idea that belligerents consistently fail to limit the harm caused to innocent children, women and men, despite the technological progress and the widespread awareness of the existing IHL rules. Clearly, the goal of this study could not be to rectify the many problems originating in modern warfare, nor to provide an exhaustive overview of all the factors that shaped the current global scenario. Rather, the more "modest" ambition of this work was to shed light on the mainstream approach to dual-use objects, according to which it is "normal" for civilian objects that can have also military uses to become legitimate targets,[1] and openly challenge it by proposing a paradigm shift.

As the first part of this book has demonstrated, the road that led to what has become the predominant, and rarely questioned, position towards dual-use objects in armed conflict is filled with contradictions. On the one hand the post-WWII period witnessed the crystallisation of humanitarian concerns and their transposition into a new set of norms to regulate armed conflicts, also of a non-international character; on the other hand, several different factors, in part analysed in Chap. 2 of this book, contributed to blurring the lines between military objectives and civilian objects, thus eroding the principle of distinction, i.e. the cornerstone of the entire IHL framework. However, as noted also by other authors, the rise of targeting dual-use objects has come to put pressure on all core principles of international humanitarian law, not only on the principle of distinction.[2] This is a crucial aspect, highlighted to the maximum extent possible also in the present work, as the mainstream approach to dual-use objects does not only represent a threat to the principles of distinction and proportionality, with the latter being increasingly considered by the current scholarship,[3] but to the IHL apparatus as a whole. Therefore, "reconciling" the notion of dual-use objects with the IHL framework has been the main task undertaken by this book. To achieve this goal, the analysis carried out in the first part of the study ended with a "working" definition of dual-use objects that aims at departing from the traditional understanding of the term and, thus, at separating in a sharper way dual-use objects from military objectives. According to this definition, which considers all the issues raised in the first three chapters of the book and in particular the challenges deriving from the interpretation and application of the definition of military objectives enshrined in Article 52(2) of API, dual-use objects under IHL are:

> objects, items, infrastructures, systems that fulfil a civilian function. Dual-use objects may become military objectives only when the following two cumulative criteria are satisfied in the circumstances ruling at the time: a) their *location* (when the dual-use object is situated

[1] Dinstein 2004, pp. 94–97; Sassòli and Cameron 2006, p. 66; Hathaway et al. 2024, p. 6.

[2] Hathaway et al. 2024, p. 11.

[3] Shue and Wippman 2002, pp. 573–577; Gillard 2018, pp. 34–35.

inside a specific area that is lawfully designated as a military objective), and/or their *use* makes an *effective and direct contribution* to military action and b) a *definite military advantage* derives from the total or partial destruction, capture or neutralisation of *every dual-use object* that is attacked.[4]

The definition clearly sets some boundaries that counter the ever-increasing reach of the mainstream approach to dual-use objects. In the first place the definition highlights the importance of the civilian function that dual-use objects fulfil and that needs to be considered in relation to several relevant rules as well as to the key IHL principles, as discussed in Chap. 4. On multiple occasions, pertinent rules, such as the prohibitions of starvation and of acts aimed at spreading terror among the civilian population, have been invoked in relation to attacks against dual-use objects.[5] However, the centrality of the civilian function of dual-use objects so far has not emerged in a convincing and consistent way. As this analysis has demonstrated the claim that dual-use objects are set apart from military objectives in light of the civilian function that they fulfil carries practical consequences. It entails that the relevant rules, and more in general the key IHL tenets, must be interpreted and applied giving due consideration to this unique feature.

Furthermore, the definition stresses how dual-use objects, which should not be regarded as military objectives by nature, might become lawful targets only and for the time in which two cumulative conditions are met. First, a dual-use object is transformed into a military objective due to its location, a criterion that must be interpreted in its narrowest sense, and/or use; but not because of its purpose, which is a volatile concept, prone to abuses and manifestly unable to strengthen the protection of items, systems and installations essential for the survival of the civilian population. Second, the conversion occurs if a definite military advantage derives from the total or partial destruction, capture or neutralisation of the dual-use object, which, by its location and/or use, makes an *effective and direct contribution* to military action. Deviating from the dominant view, which recognises to various degrees the interconnection between the two elements of the "effective contribution" and the "definite military advantage",[6] the definition provided in this book requires that there must exist a direct link, and not simply a "proximate nexus",[7] between the expected military advantage stemming from an attack and the contribution to the military action. Otherwise, a dual-use object should not be turned into a target. Furthermore, the definition seeks to clarify that, for the purpose of applying the principle of distinction in an effective way, the military advantage must be assessed

[4] See Chap. 3, Sect. 3.4 in this book.

[5] Schmitt 2022.

[6] See Chap. 3, Sect. 3.2.1 in this book.

[7] International Law Association Study Group on the Conduct of Hostilities in the 21st Century, Final Report presented at the 77th ILA Conference in Johannesburg, South Africa (ILA-SG Report), p. 6, https://www.ila-hq.org/en_GB/documents/ila-final-report-25-june-2017 (accessed 19 November 2024). See Chap. 3, Sect. 3.2.1 in this book.

for each individual attack and not for attacks against multiple targets, even if they belong to the same category.[8]

Ultimately, the definition restricts, but does not seek to rule out, the process of transforming a dual-use objects into a military objective. The reason for not pursuing a more radical approach is quite simple: placing dual-use objects that play a civilian function on "no-strike" lists is not an option that States seem incline to embrace. As noted by Gillard, "[b]elligerents should be encouraged to adopt such policies, both to facilitate the implementation of relevant rules of IHL and to reduce the adverse effects on the civilian population, even beyond the requirements of law".[9] Nonetheless, and especially given the current global scenario, a more realistic and tenable solution is needed and the combined effort of providing a working definition of dual-use objects and promoting a paradigm shift goes exactly in that direction.

In relation to the paradigm shift proposed as a result of the analysis carried out in the first part of this book, a few additional considerations are needed. As mentioned, the new approach described in Chap. 4 and Chap. 5 of the present work rests on two pillars. One is represented by the recognition of the central role ascribed to the civilian function performed by dual-use objects. Electrical power systems, industrial plants, oil refining, distribution and storage facilities, broadcasting stations, traffic infrastructures, water systems and installations, play a crucial role for the civilian population, both in times of peace and in situations of armed conflict. The obvious consequence stemming from realising the importance of those objects should be to spare them to the maximum extent possible and actively learn from previous experiences.[10] As proven by the current armed conflicts, developing such an argument is more urgent than ever. However, the argument needs not only to be appealing, but also "raisable" in a court of law. As discussed in Chap. 4, the intuition of the ICTY's Trial Chamber in the *Prlić et al. case* remained an intuition and was not further elaborated on in the Appeals Chamber's decision. When the Trial Chamber's judges, reflecting on the situation of the Muslim residents affected by the destruction of the bridge, stated that they were left "in virtually total isolation, making it impossible for them to get food and medical supplies resulting in a serious deterioration of the humanitarian situation for the population living there",[11] they opened a door, which unfortunately was rapidly shut. In this author's view, the claim that "some of the worst suffering by civilians in wars taking place today has happened as a result of targeting dual-use objects"[12] must be supported by a strong legal reasoning. Thus, placing the civilian function of dual-use objects at the heart of the legal analysis while revisiting the pertinent IHL rules and the key IHL principles is an essential piece of the puzzle.

---

[8] See Chap. 3, Sect. 3.2.2 in this book.

[9] Gillard 2018, p. 36.

[10] In Chap. 2, two examples were discussed, the First Gulf War and the NATO bombing campaign against the Former Yugoslavia. See Chap. 2, Sects. 2.4 and 2.5 in this book.

[11] ICTY (TC), *Prosecutor v Prlić*, Judgment 9 May 2013, IT-04-74 (*Prlić et al.* TC Judgement), para 1583.

[12] Hathaway et al. 2024, p. 9.

The second pillar of the novel paradigm is the application of the "reasonable military commander standard" to the principles of distinction, precautions, proportionality, military necessity and humanity. One of the most controversial and less explored notions in the legal domain, reasonableness doubles as a theoretical concept and as a standard.[13] In its latter form it guides the actions of State's actors and provides a standard of evaluation for the review of the decisions made. It is, therefore, useful also in judicial settings and increasingly resorted to in legal disputes concerning a growing number of fields. International humanitarian law is no exception. References to the reasonable military commander standard as a tool to assess compliance with the principle of proportionality go back to the Final Report to the Prosecutor by the Committee Established to Review the NATO Bombing Campaign Against the Federal Republic of Yugoslavia.[14] The ICTY has relied on the standard of the reasonable military commander on different occasions,[15] and the Israeli Supreme Court has followed in the ICTY's footsteps in some landmark decisions.[16] However, and as already stressed, the attempts to frame the reasonable military commander standard as a reliable instrument to ascertain the correct application of a given rule, so far has been limited to the principle of proportionality. The inquiry carried out in this work, instead, has shown that the reasonableness standard is a transversal one, that can, and should, be applied to all the IHL key principles. In addition to arguing in favour of this finding and discussing the rationale for such a choice, the present analysis has identified a sliding scale in the application of the reasonable standard.

In other words, the goal of Chap. 5 was not only to stress the utility of the reasonable military commander standard beyond the assessment of proportionality, but also to establish, based on the current practice, the existing doctrine and the relevant case law, the different gradation of reasonableness that are required in the application of the various principles. In targeting a dual-use object, in fact, considerations should be made with respect to the nature of the object, the measures to adopt to avoid, and in any event to minimise, harm to civilians and civilian objects, the extent of the acceptable level of collateral damage, and the balancing of necessity and humanity. When decisions are taken and attacks are launched and carried out, persons, not abstract entities, are in charge. Establishing in clear terms what is expected and required of them can certainly contribute to enhancing the protection of civilians and civilian objects; even more so if States agree to implement the standard of reasonableness in a uniform and coherent way. Furthermore, and this is certainly an aspect that deserves to be thoroughly addressed in a follow-up inquiry, these conclusions have

---

[13] See Chap. 5, Sect. 5.2 in this book.

[14] Final Report to the Prosecutor by the Committee Established to Review the NATO Bombing Campaign against the Federal Republic of Yugoslavia, (13 June 2000), (hereinafter OTP Report) reprinted in (2000) ILM 39:1257. Henderson and Reece 2018, pp. 840–841. See Chap. 5, Sect. 5.3.3 in this book.

[15] See Chap. 5, Sect. 5.3.3 in this book.

[16] See HCJ 2056/04 *Beit Sourik Vill. Council v. Gov't of Israel,* 58(5) PD 817, (2004) (Beit Sourik), para 46; HCJ 769/02 *Pub. Comm. against Torture in Israel v. Gov't of Israel* 62(1) PD 507 (2006) (Isr.), reprinted in 46 I.L.M. 375, para 57.

implications that transcends the IHL framework and bear significant relevance for the international criminal law domain.

In addition to summarising and further clarifying the main issues discussed in this work, the present chapter aims at outlining the ramifications of the book's findings, focussing in particular on one aspect, namely the new paradigm' significance with respect to new weapons and technologies. The discussion, which could certainly benefit from an extensive analysis, can only be introduced in this context. Nonetheless, in this author's view it is useful to shed light on some crucial points and offer a (limited) contribution to the ongoing debate.

6.2 Some Preliminary Considerations on the New Paradigm's Application to New Weapons and Technologies

The present work did not aim at stirring the discussion on dual-use objects towards the expanding field of new technologies in warfare and the increasing impact that cyber-operations,[17] as well as the use of Artificial Intelligence (AI),[18] have on the conduct of hostilities, and ultimately on the protection of civilians affected by armed conflict. However, it is important to introduce some preliminary considerations with respect to the application of the new paradigm to those novel humanitarian and legal challenges.

As noted by Blank, cyber operations, unmanned aerial vehicles, autonomous weapons systems (AWS), nanotechnologies, and new technologies, including AI based decision support systems (DSS)[19] and machine learning, have sparked an extensive discourse on the application of IHL rules.[20] Each of those new weapons and technologies triggers unique questions for human understanding, often exacerbated by the fact that "the technology is out of sight or out of reach of human senses, making actual concrete understanding of how it works challenging and elusive".[21] In particular, it is undeniable that both AI and autonomy are increasingly playing a significant role in the military domain.[22] Considering two of the current armed

[17] Schmitt 2019.

[18] Krupiy 2024.

[19] ICRC and Geneva Academy 2024, pp. 2–7.

[20] Blank 2018, p. 317.

[21] Ibid. See also Jain 2022; Mauri 2022; Amoroso 2020.

[22] "AI" and "autonomy" are deeply interconnected concepts. On the one hand AI denotes a class of computer programmes, on the other hand autonomy refers to how independently from human operators they can act. However, it is important to note that not all autonomous weapons and cyber capabilities incorporate AI and machine learning. Conversely, not all military robotic systems using AI and machine learning are autonomous weapons, and not all AI and machine learning-enabled cyber capabilities could automatically search for vulnerabilities to exploit or defend against cyber-attacks or automatically launching counter-attacks. See Pacholska 2023, p. 3; ICRC 2021, pp. 466–467.

conflicts, it is certainly possible to infer that AI and autonomy are in fact already being used by States in the conduct of hostilities. In the war on Gaza, Israel is deploying different types of AI-based systems,[23] including an AI-based targeting creation platform, "Lavender", which produces targeting recommendations "through the rapid and automatic extraction of intelligence".[24] In the Russian-Ukrainian conflict, AI is used from both sides for intelligence gathering, automated target recognition, and enabling weapons systems with different degrees of autonomy.[25]

Despite the absence of a comprehensive global governance framework for military artificial intelligence and the strong sense of uncertainty worldwide,[26] there are two fundamental points that provide at least some level of assurance. The first point is that international law still finds application in this domain. Voicing an ever growing and widespread concern, the UN General Assembly has recently approved a draft resolution on the emergence of new technological applications in warfare.[27] The draft resolution does not make any significant steps forward as it gives a mandate to the UN Secretary-General to seek the views of Member States and observer States on the matter, with a specific focus on areas other than lethal autonomous weapons systems, and to submit a substantive report summarising those views and cataloguing existing and emerging normative proposals to the General Assembly. However, one passage of the text is particularly relevant as it affirms that international law, including the UN Charter, IHL and international human rights law, applies to matters that "occur throughout all stages of the life cycle of artificial intelligence, including systems enabled by artificial intelligence, in the military domain".[28] This statement, which might seem trivial, is actually very important as it officially counters the narrative

---

[23] The Israel Defense Forces (IDF) employs AI applications in its: (1) Proactive Forecasting, Threat Alert, and Defensive Systems; and (2) Intelligence Analysis, Targeting, and Munitions. See Mimran and Dahan 2024.

[24] Mckernan and Davies (2024) "The Machine Did It Coldly": Israel Used AI to Identify 37,000 Hamas Targets, https://www.theguardian.com/world/2024/apr/03/israel-gaza-ai-database-hamas-airstrikes?_hsenc=p2ANqtz-_WLcXND6VhkalVDMCpPd29X-ctlR5GdLUe6SHFzPgwXL3xOApNJmMss1R0zqcUcWbDAg0T (accessed 4 September 2024). Notably, Israel has openly discussed its use of AI-tools on the battlefield.

[25] See Bennett 2023.

[26] In 2017, an open-ended Group of Governmental Experts (GGE) on Emerging Technologies in the Area of Lethal Autonomous Weapons Systems (LAWS) was created to discuss the legal, ethical, political, military and technical implications deriving from the development and use of LAWS. The GGE, which meets annually, remains to this day the main forum for debating AWS. It is open to all the 126 High Contracting Parties of the Convention on Certain Conventional Weapon (CCW), as well as to other States, international organisations, civil society and academia. Diplomatic efforts to govern military AI are also intensifying. In 2023, a summit on Responsible Artificial Intelligence in the Military Domain (REAIM), was hosted by the Netherlands in collaboration with South Korea. On the summit's final day, the US launched its "Political Declaration on Responsible Military Use of Artificial Intelligence and Autonomy". The Declaration, currently endorsed by 57 States, aims at paving the way for the establishment of a normative framework to address the use of these capabilities in the military domain. See US DoD 2023.

[27] UN General Assembly 2024.

[28] Ibid., para 1.

according to which those tools and systems "are not regulated by international law".[29] In particular with regard to the IHL framework it is useful to recall the central position taken by the provision enshrined in Article 36 of API, which states that

> In the study, development, acquisition or adoption of a new weapon, means or method of warfare, a High Contracting Party is under an obligation to determine whether its employment would, in some or all circumstances, be prohibited by this Protocol or by any other rule of international law applicable to the High Contracting Party.

While the issue of whether this provision corresponds to customary IHL still remains unsettled, currently API counts 174 signatory parties, rendering "the obligation to conduct legal review of new weapons spread almost worldwide".[30] This norm has been extensively commented upon,[31] so there is no need to further linger on its crucial role as a device for addressing the challenges posed by new technologies. Rather, what is worth noting is that States are already provided with a set of binding norms and with a "compass" to navigate the waters of new technologies.[32] This consideration does not wish to undermine the many appeals made to adopt a new international regulatory framework to address the concerns around the use of AWS and the "weaponisation" of AI,[33] particularly in the context of armed conflict, but only to highlight that these much needed developments will not take place in a legal vacuum. Therefore, all the issues addressed in the present book in relation to dual-use objects and their status under the IHL framework should remain valid and applicable, regardless of the military weapons and technologies deployed.

The second point to be raised concerns the "human-centric" approach toward new technologies of warfare.[34] In relation to AWS the debate has been heavily influenced by the no longer "emerging" notion of meaningful human control (MHC),[35] which roughly refers to the need to retain human presence in the targeting process.[36] As is well known, the introduction of the notion of MHC in the debate on AWS stemmed from two main considerations. First, it is ethically and legally questionable to allow the machines to apply force, especially if potentially lethal, "without any human control whatsoever". Second, and perhaps this represents the most challenging aspect enshrined in the concept, not every manifestation of human control would be "normatively satisfactory, since a human simply pressing a 'fire' button in response to indications from a computer […] is not sufficient to be considered 'human control' in a substantive sense".[37] MHC has been described as an "approach", rather than a

---

[29] Mimran and Dahan 2024.

[30] Mauri 2022, p. 136.

[31] Daoust et al. 2002, p. 345; McClelland 2003, p. 397; McFarland 2020, pp. 70–72.

[32] Mauri 2022, p. 137.

[33] Dresp-Langley 2023, pp. 2–4.

[34] ICRC 2021, p.

[35] The concept of MHC was used for the first time by a UK-based NGO, called "Article 36", in a paper reflecting on the UK's policy on AWS. See Article 36 2013, pp. 3–4.

[36] Crootof 2016, p. 53; Santoni de Sio and van den Hoven 2018, pp. 3–4; Amoroso and Tamburrini 2021, p. 23.

[37] Abbink et al. 2024, p. 4.

solution,[38] to cope with ethical and legal implications of autonomy, and more in detail with the role that human agents should maintain in increasingly automated systems.[39] The notion has become central to broader discussions on AI,[40] and although it is still contended who should retain control, in which phases, and to which degree,[41] it remains one of the rare elements which all actors involved seem to agree upon.[42] Furthermore, in the current debate on AI uses the accent is increasingly placed not only on the exercise of MHC but also on the necessity to preserve "human judgement in military decision-making".[43] This aspect is particularly relevant for this book's purposes. As discussed in the previous chapters of this work, many key IHL rules require the application of evaluative decisions and value judgements, taken on the basis of the "reasonable military commander standard", such as the presumption of civilian status in case of "doubt", the selection of the precautionary measures to implement during an attack, or the assessment of proportionality, which requires the attacker to determine what constitutes "excessive" collateral damage in relation to anticipated concrete and direct military advantage.

It has been argued,[44] and it is hard to disagree, that AI DSS are not suitable to proceed with such evaluative legal judgements, also because they would not able to explain how they have reached them.[45] At the same time, however, experts are increasingly noting how AI as a tool can be helpful in the intelligence gathering phase,[46] or even assist with an analysis of the degree to which the conduct of a particular military operation, say an attack against a dual-use object that play an important civilian function, deviated from how a "reasonable" commander would have planned it.[47] This is not to downplay the many, and legitimate, issues that have been raised to warn about the use of AI in armed conflict, including the increased speed and scale of target production through military AI,[48] but rather to stress the importance of taking on board the findings of this book to promote, and not inhibit,[49] the reasonableness of targeting decisions, especially when they concern dual-use objects.

---

[38] Ibid., p. 5.

[39] Ibid.

[40] Beck and Burri 2024, p. 106.

[41] Boutin and Woodcock 2024, pp. 182–183.

[42] Mauri 2022, p. 37.

[43] ICRC and Geneva Academy 2024, p. 5; ICRC 2021, pp. 474–477.

[44] ICRC and Geneva Academy 2024, p. 15.

[45] On the so-called "black-box" phenomenon, see Bathaee 2018.

[46] Mimran and Dahan 2024.

[47] Krupiy 2024.

[48] Renic and Schwarz 2023; Bo and Dorsey 2024.

[49] Klonowska 2024.

References

Abbink D, Amoroso D, Cavalcante Siebert L, van den Hoven J, Mecacci G, Santoni de Sio F (2024) Introduction to meaningful human control of artificially intelligent systems. In: Mecacci G, Amoroso D, Cavalcante Siebert L, Abbink D, van den Hoven J, Santoni de Sio F (eds) Research Handbook on Meaningful Human Control of Artificial Intelligence Systems. Edward Elgar, Cheltenham, pp 1–11

Amoroso D (2020) Autonomous Weapons Systems and International Law: A Study on Human-Machine Interactions in Ethically and Legally Sensitive Domains. Edizioni Scientifiche Italiane, Naples

Amoroso D, Tamburrini G (2021) The Human Control Over Autonomous Robotic Systems: What Ethical and Legal Lessons for Judicial Uses of AI? In: Kramer X, Biard A, Hoevenaars J, Themeli E (eds) New Pathways to Civil Justice in Europe. Challenges of Access to Justice. Springer, Cham, pp 23–42

Article 36 (2013) Killer Robots: UK Government Policy on Fully Autonomous Weapons, http://www.article36.org/wp-content/uploads/2013/04/Policy_Paper1.pdf. Accessed 20 November 2024

Bathaee Y (2018) The Artificial Intelligence Black Box and the Failure of Intent and Causation. Harvard Journal of Law & Technology 31(2): 890–938

Beck J, Burri T (2024) From "Human Control" in International Law to "Human Oversight" in the New EU Act on Artificial Intelligence. In: Mecacci G, Amoroso D, Cavalcante Siebert L, Abbink D, van den Hoven J, Santoni de Sio F (eds) Research Handbook on Meaningful Human Control of Artificial Intelligence Systems. Edward Elgar, Cheltenham, pp 104–130

Bennett S (2023) Roles and Implications of AI in the Russian-Ukrainian Conflict, 20 July 2023, https://www.cnas.org/publications/commentary/roles-and-implications-of-ai-in-the-russian-ukrainian-conflict. Accessed 18 November 2024

Blank L (2018) New Technologies and the Interplay between Certainty and Reasonableness. In: Williams W S, Ford C M (eds) Complex Battlespaces: The Law of Armed Conflict and the Dynamics of Modern Warfare. Oxford University Press, Oxford, pp 317–344

Bo M, Dorsey J (2024) Symposium on Military AI and the Law of Armed Conflict: The 'Need' for Speed – The Cost of Unregulated AI Decision-Support Systems to Civilians, 4 April 2024, https://opiniojuris.org/2024/04/04/symposium-on-military-ai-and-the-law-of-armed-conflict-the-need-for-speed-the-cost-of-unregulated-ai-decision-support-systems-to-civilians/. Accessed 21 November 2024

Boutin B, Woodcock T (2024) Aspects of Realizing (Meaningful) Human Control: A Legal Perspective. In: Geiß R, Lahmann H (eds) Research Handbook on Warfare and Artificial Intelligence. Edward Elgar, Cheltenham, pp 179–196

Crootof R (2016) A Meaningful Floor for Meaningful Human Control. Temple International and Comparative Law Journal 30(1): 53–62

Daoust I, Coupland R, Ishoey R (2002) New Wars, New Weapons? The Obligation of States to Assess the Legality of Means and Methods of Warfare. International Review of the Red Cross 84: 345–326

Dinstein Y (2004) The Conduct of Hostilities under the Law of International Armed Conflict. Cambridge University Press, Cambridge

Dresp-Langley B (2023) The Weaponization of Artificial Intelligence: What the Public Needs to Be Aware of. Front. Artif. Intell. 6: 1–5

Gillard EC (2018) Proportionality in the Conduct of Hostilities: The Incidental Harm Side of the Assessment. Research paper, Chatham House. https://www.chathamhouse.org/sites/default/files/publications/research/2018-12-10-proportionality-conduct-hostilities-incidental-harm-gillard-final.pdf. Accessed 15 November 2024

Hathaway O A, Khan A, Revkin M R (2024) The Dangerous Rise of Dual-Use Objects in War. Duke Law School Public Law & Legal Theory Series No. 2024-56. https://ssrn.com/abstract=4938707. Accessed 30 October 2024

Henderson I, Reece K (2018) Proportionality Under International Humanitarian Law (IHL): The 'Reasonable Military Commander' Standard and Reverberating Effects. Vanderbilt Journal of Transnational Law 51(3): 835–855

ICRC (2021) Artificial Intelligence and Machine Learning in Armed Conflict: A Human-Centred Approach. International Review of the Red Cross 102(913): 463–479

ICRC, Geneva Academy (2024) Expert Consultation Report on AI and Related Technologies in Military Decision-Making on the Use of Force in Armed Conflicts, Geneva Academy/ICRC, Geneva. https://www.geneva-academy.ch/joomlatools-files/docman-files/Artificial%20Intelligence%20And%20Related%20Technologies%20In%20Military%20Decision-Making.pdf. Accessed 17 November 2024

Jain A G (2022) International Law and the Regulation of Autonomous Military Capabilities. European Journal of International Law 33(4): 1093–1124

Klonowska K (2024) Designing for Reasonableness: The Algorithmic Mediation of Reasonableness in targeting Decision, 23 February 2024, https://lieber.westpoint.edu/designing-reasonableness-algorithmic-mediation-reasonableness-targeting-decisions/. Accessed 22 November 2024

Krupiy T (2024) What Role Artificial Intelligence Could Play in Evaluating the Compliance of Military Operations with International Humanitarian Law: The Case Study of the Conduct of Hostilities in Ukraine, 23 February 2024, https://www.ejiltalk.org/what-role-artificial-intelligence-could-play-in-evaluating-the-compliance-of-military-operations-with-international-humanitarian-law-the-case-study-of-the-conduct-of-hostilities-in-ukraine/. Accessed 18 November 2024

Mauri D (2022) Autonomous Weapons Systems and the Protection of the Human Person: An International Law Analysis. Edward Elgar, Cheltenham

McClelland J (2003) The Review of Weapons in Accordance with Article 36 of Additional Protocol I. International Review of the Red Cross 85: 397–415

McFarland T (2020) Autonomous Weapon Systems and the Law of Armed Conflict: Compatibility with International Humanitarian Law. Cambridge University Press, Cambridge

Mimran A, Dahan G (2024) Artificial Intelligence in the Battlefield: A Perspective from Israel, 20 April 2024, https://opiniojuris.org/2024/04/20/artificial-intelligence-in-the-battlefield-a-perspective-from-israel/. Accessed 18 November 2024

Pacholska M (2023) Many Hands in the Black Box: Artificial Intelligence and the Responsibility of International Organizations. T.M.C. Asser Institute for International & European Law, Asser Research 2023-04, https://ssrn.com/abstract=4501072. Accessed 20 November 2024

Renic N C, Schwarz E (2023) Inhuman-in-the-loop: AI-targeting and the Erosion of Moral Restraint, 19 December 2023, https://opiniojuris.org/2023/12/19/inhuman-in-the-loop-ai-targeting-and-the-erosion-of-moral-restraint/. Accessed 21 November 2024

Santoni de Sio F, van den Hoven J (2018) Meaningful Human Control over Autonomous Systems. A Philosophical Account. Frontiers in Robotics and AI 5: 1–14

Sassòli M, Cameron L (2006) The Protection of Civilian Objects: Current State of the Law and Issues de lege ferenda. In: Ronzitti N, Venturini G (eds) The Law of Air Warfare: Contemporary Issues. Eleven International, Utrecht, pp 35–74

Schmitt M N (2019) Wired warfare 3.0: Protecting the civilian population during cyber operations. International Review of the Red Cross 101(910): 333–355

Schmitt M N (2022) Ukraine-Symposium - Attacking Power Infrastructure under International Humanitarian Law, 20 October 2022, https://lieber.westpoint.edu/attacking-power-infrastructure-under-international-humanitarian-law/. Accessed 17 November 2024

Shue H, Wippman D (2002) Limiting Attacks on Dual-Use Facilities Performing Indispensable Civilian Functions. Cornell International Law Journal 35(3): 553–579

UN General Assembly (2024) Resolution 79/43 Artificial intelligence in the military domain and its implications for international peace and security, UN Doc. A/C.1/79/L.43

US DoD (2023) Political Declaration on Responsible Military Use of Artificial Intelligence and Autonomy, 1 November 2023, https://www.state.gov/political-declaration-on-responsible-military-use-of-artificial-intelligence-and-autonomy/. Accessed 21 November

Index

F. Capone, *Dual-use Objects under International Humanitarian Law: Towards a Paradigm Shift*, https://doi.org/10.1007/978-94-6265-679-6

Q

R

S

T

U

The manufacturer's authorised representative in the EU is Springer Nature Customer Service Centre GmbH, Europaplatz 3, 69115 Heidelberg, Germany. If you have any concerns regarding our products, please contact ProductSafety@springernature.com

Printed and bound by CPI Group (UK) Ltd, Croydon, CR0 4YY
30/09/2026
02225558-0008